THE REMOVAL OF THE CHOCTAW INDIANS

THE REMOVAL
OF THE
CHOCTAW
INDIANS

ARTHUR H. DeROSIER, JR.

THE UNIVERSITY OF TENNESSEE PRESS
KNOXVILLE

LIBRARY OF CONGRESS CATALOG CARD NUMBER 70–111044
STANDARD BOOK NUMBER 87049–113–X   12-17-71

TO MY WIFE, DELORES

FOREWORD

THE STORY of the removal of the Choctaw Nation from Mississippi lands to Indian Territory has heretofore received only a cursory treatment by historians—a somewhat curious fact when one considers that the removal represented an event of major importance in the history of the American Indian. The Choctaws, forming one of the largest Indian nations east of the Mississippi, were selected by the United States government as the first tribal population to be removed to the West under the treaties approved by John C. Calhoun in 1820 and Andrew Jackson in 1830. Indeed, the policy developed in relocating this population was one that the government would follow in all future Indian removals.

The Removal of the Choctaw Indians thus makes a special contribution in synthesizing here, for the first time in adequate detail, the tragic story that set this national pattern. Because it is a complex story as well, Arthur DeRosier also favors us by emphasizing the conflict of national, regional, and very personal interests involved, an understanding of which is so necessary to an appreciation of the Indian's milieu. But perhaps most revealing is the author's discussion and assessment of the major elements of his account, for, in tracing the genesis of removal, he has opened several provocative vistas on the general stream of American history.

The point is made convincingly, for instance, that the Choctaw Nation was not an ethnic fragment of small consequence but a powerful community which loomed large in lower Mississippi Valley diplomacy. Spain, France, Great Britain, and the United

States assiduously courted the Choctaw Nation on the premise that the power holding this populous tribe's fealty could expect to control the region. Choctaw leaders sensed this fact and developed a surprising perspicacity in diplomacy. This tradition of shrewd negotiation continued into the 1820s, constituting a significant obstruction to the accomplishment of United States goals in the Old Southwest.

The author illuminates the importance of Indian policy in United States government affairs before 1830. One must be impressed by the substantial amount of federal time, money, and effort that were applied in seeking solutions to the Indian problem (which, of course, consisted mainly of seeking ways to gain control of Indian lands).

The book provides a summary of the Indian policies of the early presidents, from Washington through Jackson. The author unmasks Thomas Jefferson through his penetrating examination of that president's Indian policy. Esteemed generally as an Indian humanitarian, Jefferson is exposed here as one no less determined than Andrew Jackson to sacrifice tribal interest to the accomplishment of national purpose. Some may even argue that the very genesis of the Indian removal program, so devastatingly successful in later times, will be found in the confidential note quoted here, written by Jefferson to Governor William C. C. Claiborne of Mississippi Territory.

The intense nationalism that followed the War of 1812 is seen with new vividness when viewed in the context of the Choctaw's plight. President Monroe's first message to Congress was a manifestation of that fierce spirit, rationalizing the liquidation of the Indian estate whenever it obstructed the American settler's advance: "for the earth was given to mankind to support the greatest number of which it is capable, and no tribe of people have a right to withhold the wants of others more than is necessary for their support and comfort." The author pictures the tide of settlers moving into Mississippi, and outnumbering the Indians five times over but living on one-third as much land. Coveting the Choctaw lands, they squatted there, daring the Indians to evict them, killed Choctaw livestock, and carried away Indian property with impunity. It is shown that the scattered voices of protest from other whites and from the Indians themselves were little heard as the nationalistic fervor mounted. Local enforcement officers and the courts averted their eyes from the Indians while Mississippi newspapers drummed up hate. One could almost foresee the future of the Choctaws.

Reemphasized, too, are the persistence—and creativity—of Secretary of War John C. Calhoun in achieving the national goal with reference to Indians. Calhoun, articulating Monroe's dictum, harassed Choctaw leaders with his rhetoric of removal. He stressed the advantages of moving west and warned the Indians that if they attempted to retain their eastern lands they would be at the mercy of the state. Failing to negotiate the removal treaty he wanted, he resorted to a "softening-up" process, inviting tribal leaders to Washington to be feted and more subtly pressured. He cultivated certain mixed-bloods, who were amenable to his wishes. And then, when he felt the time was propitious, he appointed the dynamic frontier hero, General Andrew Jackson, as one of the commissioners to negotiate a treaty "for the extinguishment of Indian title to lands within the state of Mississippi." Although Calhoun did not obtain all he asked in the resultant Treaty of Doak's Stand, the impact of his efforts in hammering out a national policy is incalculable.

Only with these perspectives and a knowledge of the interplay of strong personalities, both provided here by Mr. DeRosier, does one grasp the total Choctaw story. By the time that representatives of the confused and disillusioned Choctaws meet "amidst a carnival atmosphere," planned by government negotiators, to sign the historic Treaty of Dancing Rabbit Creek, the denouement is predictable. Indeed, to follow the gradual erosion of the morale and resistance of a once-dominant population, as pictured in this book, is in itself an educational experience. The story is recommended to all who wish to understand why the American Indian is such a tragic figure in our history.

ARRELL M. GIBSON
University of Oklahoma

Norman, Oklahoma
January, 1970

ACKNOWLEDGMENTS

In the development of any study that requires considerable research, travel, writing, and encouragement, a writer is indebted to more persons than he can acknowledge in writing. When visiting strange cities and libraries, he is assisted by numerous residents, library assistants, and passers-by. I would, however, like to acknowledge the assistance of many individuals who made this study possible.

I was fortunate enough to receive financial aid from the University of Southern Mississippi Research Council, the Research Planning Center at East Tennessee State University, and the Faculty Research Committee at the University of Oklahoma. Dr. Robert H. Wienefeld, a past chairman of the Department of History at the University of South Carolina, and the late Dr. W. H. Callcott, past dean of the Graduate School at the same institution, generously purchased research materials for me when I was a doctoral candidate.

During my travels to gather research materials, I was helped significantly by a number of persons and library staffs. I would especially like to acknowledge the aid of the staffs at the Library of Congress; the National Archives; the Duke University Library; the Southern Collection at the University of North Carolina; the South Caroliniana Library, University of South Carolina; the Alabama Department of Archives and History, Montgomery; the Department of Archives and History, Jackson, Mississippi; the University of Southern Mississippi Library; the State Library and Archives, Nashville, Tennessee; the Oklahoma State Historical Society, Oklahoma City; Manuscripts Division, Bizzell Library, University of Oklahoma; and the staff at the Sherrod Library, East Tennessee State University. I also am grateful to the late Robert Meriwether at the University of South Carolina and to Miss Charlotte Capers at the Mississippi Department of Archives and History.

I have been greatly helped by Dr. Sanford Newell, Dr. Lillian Kibler, Dr. J. Treadwell Davis, Dr. John E. Gonzales, Mrs. Josephine Soukup, and Mrs. Margie Theimer. I would especially like to acknowledge the help of a few individuals who contributed much of what is good in this manuscript and have earned my everlasting thanks: Dr. Robert D. Ochs, chairman of the Department of History, University of South Carolina, who guided me through the early research and writing; Dr. Arrell M. Gibson of the University of Oklahoma, a colleague with valuable suggestions; Mrs. Laura D. S. Harrell, research assistant, Department of Archives and History, Jackson, Mississippi, who gave much of her time to finding material for me; Mrs. Carolyn Wood, Mrs. Joan Oliver, and Mrs. Emma Lee Dyer, secretaries who typed and improved the manuscript; and Dr. Anne LeCroy of the East Tennessee State University English Department, who proofread the manuscript and offered valuable critical judgments and suggestions. Finally, I am deeply grateful to my wife for her help and sound judgment and to my children who often lost contact with their father during the writing of this volume.

ARTHUR H. DeRosier, Jr.

March, 1970
Johnson City, Tennessee

CONTENTS

ILLUSTRATIONS

MAPS

THE REMOVAL OF THE CHOCTAW INDIANS

.

CHAPTER ONE

A PROUD HERITAGE

On a cold February morning in 1832 the steamboat *Huron* weighed anchor in Vicksburg Harbor and slowly drifted out into the Mississippi River. This was no ordinary trip for the *Huron*. Its embarkation brought hundreds of onlookers to witness, with mixed emotions, an event of considerable historic importance—the removal of another draft of Choctaw Indians from Mississippi to Indian Territory.

Most of the spectators that morning were white settlers who, therefore, stood to benefit from Indian removal. Indeed, the majority clapped each other on the back and thanked God that in his infinite wisdom and justice he had finally recognized their plight and decreed, through President Jackson in Washington, that all eastern Indians were to be uprooted from their homes and moved west of the Mississippi River.[1] Whites on the frontier still thought of Indians as murdering savages, and they breathed a sigh of relief to see the departure of their long-time adversaries. Now, the settlers reasoned, they could plow their fields without carrying cumbersome rifles to ward off hostiles; they could sleep with their wooden windows open to let in the cool night breeze

[1] *Niles' Weekly Register* (Baltimore), February 25, 1832, p. 480.

3

without fearing a raid by renegade savages; and they could spend more of their time and energy in cultivating the land.

But while most people were joyous to see the *Huron* leave, some recognized the plight of the Indians, as noted by the editor of the *Vicksburg Daily Sentinel*:

> They are going away! With a visible reluctance which nothing has overcome but the stern necessity they feel impelling them, they have looked their last on the graves of their sires—the scenes of their youth, and have taken up their slow toilsome march with their household goods among them to their new homes in a strange land. They leave names to many of our rivers, towns, and counties, and so long as our State remains the Choctaws who once owned most of her soil will be remembered.[2]

Perhaps some of those standing on the bank wondered whether the removal was in accordance with the ideals expressed in the Declaration of Independence and the preamble to the Constitution of the United States. Did freedom of the individual include freedom to confiscate desired territory from its original owners? Were not forced treaties a violation of the sanctity of private property? These and other questions disturbed only a relatively small group of observers that morning—those who agreed with Roger Williams in his doctrine of brotherly love and considered it the only answer to the perplexing problem of coexistence with the Indian.[3]

As the steamboat moved slowly away from the wharf, the Choctaws pressed astern to watch their beloved Mississippi fade into the distance. What do people feel and think when they have been forced to leave ancestral homes to satisfy the desires of others? George W. Harkins, a Choctaw chief aboard the *Huron*,

[2] Franklin L. Riley, "Choctaw Land Claims," *Publications of the Mississippi Historical Society*, VIII (1904), 302.

[3] Williams, founder of Providence Plantation and the guiding spirit in the establishment of the Colony of Rhode Island, stoutly maintained the simple and just position that "the Indian was his brother equally with the Englishman." The Indian should not be thrust aside as a primitive beast, but rather accepted and cultivated as a full brother of God on earth. Vernon L. Parrington, *Main Currents in American Thought* (New York, 1930), I, 74.

asked himself this question; and as the ship moved from its mooring, he wrote an open letter to the American people explaining
his feelings. The letter, later published in *Niles' Weekly Register*,[4]
was divided into three main parts. It began as a diatribe against
the settlers for having so grossly wronged the Indians, although the chief held no grudge against the settlers because
of the unfortunate outcome of these past relations: "Much as the
State of Mississippi has wronged us, I cannot find in my heart any
other sentiment than an ardent wish for her prosperity and
happiness." This statement was followed by a moving plea to the
American people to help the Indian salvage what remained of his
deteriorating culture. The Choctaw chief continually emphasized
that the frontier settlers had won the confrontation—the Indian
was tired and beaten and wanted only mercy at the hands of the
victorious foe. In fact, Harkins felt that the only way for the
Indian to survive was to "form a government assimilated to that
of our white brethern [*sic*] ... as nearly as our conditions will permit." He was even willing that the Indian adopt white cultural
habits to prevent further destruction and to allow his people to
select the best elements of both cultures, thus developing an even
nobler race than that which existed before the coming of the white
man.

The third and most important part of the letter was a question
Harkins asked: Why and how did this tragedy happen to the
Choctaw Nation? To pose this question must have been his real
purpose in writing the open letter as the *Huron* moved his people
up the Mississippi River towards the Arkansas, for by so doing he
challenged future generations to look back on the entire removal
problem and to ask themselves the same question. Why?

The answer is still worth seeking. Chief Harkins might also
have asked why the Choctaw Nation was the first Indian tribe
to be removed to the trans-Mississippi West. He could have
claimed, rightly, that the Choctaws were not only highly civilized, but also one of the largest Indian nations residing east of

---

[4] February 25, 1832, p. 480.

the Mississippi River. He could have pointed to the peace-loving nature of the Choctaws and to their fine record in fighting alongside American soldiers in the Creek War of 1813. His nation was stable economically and politically, and it was settled to the land. In fact, an examination of the history and culture of the Choctaws fails to reveal any major provocation by these Indians, or moral justification by the United States, for what was to become one of the most tragic chapters in American history.

Linguistically, the Choctaws are of Muskhogean stock, with a culture not unlike that of other southern tribes of similar background. Although their origin and earliest history are matters of conjecture, tribal legends of the creation abound, and most of them center around the magnificent Choctaw mound, Nanih Waiya, the mother of all Choctaws.[5] A small number of tribesmen, for instance, support the legend that the original Choctaws were actually created within Nanih Waiya.[6] In the center of the mound the Great Spirit formed the first group of tribesmen who were allowed to crawl through a hole, or cave, in the mound into the light of day; but because these freshly made Choctaws were still wet and moist, the Great Spirit tacked them up on a rampart to dry and harden in the sun.[7]

The most widely accepted legend, however, taught that the ancestors of both the Choctaws and the Chickasaws[8] lived originally in Siouan country far to the northwest, under the leadership of two brothers, Chahta and Chikasa. In time, their population became so large that they found it difficult to exist in that

[5] This extremely large mound, in Winston County, Miss., represents one of the finest examples of Indian burial mounds in the United States today.

[6] Henry S. Halbert, "The Choctaw Creation Legend," *Publications of the Mississippi Historical Society*, IV (1901), 269–70.

[7] Halbert, "Nanih Waiya, The Sacred Mound of the Choctaws," *Publications of the Mississippi Historical Society*, II (1899), 229–30.

[8] The Chickasaw Indians made up the other prominent nation living in the State of Mississippi. The tribe, numbering only around 4,000, was very warlike and was located in the extreme northeastern section of the state. In many aspects the Chickasaws were quite different from the Choctaws, even though ethnologists believe they were probably of the same tribe at one time. By 1500 they were considered the fiercest Indian group in the Mississippi Valley and were feared by their fellow Indians as well as whites.

land. When the prophets of the tribe announced that far to the southeast was a land of fertile soil and abundant game, where the tribe could live in peace and prosperity forever, the entire population resolved to uproot itself and journey forth in search of the happy land. Chahta marched at their head bearing a pole which, at the conclusion of each day's journey, he planted erect in the earth in front of the camp. The next morning the pole would be found to be leaning one way or another; in that direction the tribesmen were to travel that day. One day when the tribe stopped on the west side of a creek and Chahta planted the pole before the camp as was his custom, a party under Chikasa crossed the creek and camped on its east side. Heavy rain began to fall that night, increasing in intensity by morning and continuing for several days, leaving the countryside drenched and muddy and the creek flooded and dangerous. Yet the pole, which had burrowed itself deeper into the muddy ground, stood straight and tall for all to see. It was proclaimed by Chahta that their long-sought land of Nanih Waiya had been found. Chikasa's party, in spite of the inclement weather, had proceeded on its way, not knowing that the promised land had been found. Many Choctaws maintained that this was how they and the Chickasaws became separate, though kindred, nations.[9]

Whatever the Choctaws' origin, once they arrived in the Mississippi area they developed into one of the largest and most advanced Indian nations east of the Mississippi River.[10] Contributing materially to the progress of the Choctaws was a democratic governmental system that divided the nation into three separate districts—the Northwestern, the Northeastern, and the Southern—each with a *mingo* (principal chief), elected by the men of the district, who served as the executive head.[11] Although

[9] Halbert, "Nanih Waiya," pp. 228–29.
[10] William McDonald, *Jacksonian Democracy 1829–1837*, Vol. XV of *The American Nation: A History*, ed. A. B. Hart (New York, 1906), 169–70. Barnard Shipp, *The Indians and Antiquities of America* (Philadelphia, 1897), p. 262.
[11] Dunbar Rowland, *History of Mississippi, The Heart of the South* (Chicago, 1925), I, 67. Allene DeShazo Smith, *Greenwood LeFlore and the Choctaw Indians of the Mississippi Valley* (Memphis, 1951), p. 141.

from time to time one of the *mingos*, notably Pushmataha and later Greenwood LeFlore, would gain sufficient power to influence the other two leaders, it is doubtful that the Choctaws ever had a single *mingo* who ruled the entire nation.[12] The position was not hereditary, but an illustrious ancestor was the greatest advantage an aspirant for office could possess.[13] Two other invaluable personal assets for a candidate were proved administrative ability and an enviable military record.[14] A person possessing any or all of these attributes could go far in Choctaw politics.

The *mingo* was responsible for the over-all government of his district. He was assisted by elected captains and subcaptains who ruled the several villages, or towns, and were responsible for implementing the *mingo*'s directives on the local level. Lastly, there were war chiefs, who represented the military arm of the district and were under the complete control of the *mingo*.[15] Herein lies one of the significant attributes of Choctaw government, the subordination of military to civilian authority.[16]

The source of greatness of the Choctaw political system was in the national council meeting. On a day appointed by the consent of all three *mingos*, the war chiefs, captains, and subcaptains assembled in the village square of the host *mingo*,[17] an area generally about sixty feet long and forty feet wide. On each side were two rows of posts about six feet high, the outer row chinked with mud, and the whole roofed over with straw or boards. The assembled delegates took their seats on two rows of wooden benches, covered with matting of woven cane or white bark, and smoked their pipes, slowly passing the pipes from one to another.[18]

---

[12] Angie Debo, *The Rise and Fall of the Choctaw Republic* (2nd ed.; Norman, 1961), p. 20.

[13] *Ibid.*

[14] Oliver LaFarge, *A Pictorial History of the American Indian* (New York, 1956), p. 29.

[15] John R. Swanton, *Source Material for the Social and Ceremonial Life of the Choctaw Indians* in *Bureau of American Ethnology, Bulletin 103* (Washington, D.C., 1931), p. 91.

[16] LaFarge, p. 29.

[17] Swanton, *Social and Ceremonial Life of the Choctaw*, pp. 95, 96.

[18] *Ibid.*, p. 96.

The precouncil ceremonies were elaborate and formal, indicative of the discipline and humility of the Choctaws. The host *mingo* lighted a fire atop the burial mound of the village. When the smoke rose in a straight line, he bent over the fire or looked skyward and, with his arms folded, prayed for at least thirty minutes. He then let his arms fall and turned successively east, north, west, and south, silently. If the *mingo* happened to have five issues to consider, he would hold up the appropriate number of fingers to the assembly, without a word, and then take his seat.[19]

The council meeting opened with a speech,[20] usually given by a salaried officer known as the *tichou mingo* ("servant of the chief"), who explained why the assembly had been called. The *tichou mingo*, the most powerful appointive officer in the local or tribal government, not only served as the official voice of his leader, but also arranged all ceremonies, feasts, and dances in his domain.[21] If the *tichou mingo* were an effective speaker, he could make a mediocre *mingo* or captain appear to be a great leader.

After the opening address had been concluded, any delegate could voice his opinion on the subject. Almost unlimited speaking time was allowed each delegate. After discussion and the peace pipe, the host *mingo* weighed the opinions and decisions of the council members and then gave his views of the conclusion. He spoke deliberately. At the end of each sentence, if what he said was approved, the *mingos* exclaimed *ma!* (yes) in a loud voice.[22] There was seldom any collusion between the *mingo* and the delegates. Elected officials, unlimited debate, civilian rule, and local self-government enabled the Choctaws to achieve an amazingly efficient and yet democratic political system.

As farmers the Choctaws had few peers.[23] After clearing the

---

[19] *Ibid.*, p. 101.

[20] *Ibid.*

[21] Swanton, "An Early Account of the Choctaw Indians," *Memoirs of the Anthropological Association*, V, No. 2 (1918), p. 54. Debo, *Choctaw Republic*, pp. 20–21.

[22] Swanton, *Social and Ceremonial Life of the Choctaw*, p. 97.

[23] Flora Warren Seymour, *The Five Civilized American Indian Tribes* in

land around their villages, by burning the underbrush and girdling the trees, they planted maize (their staple crop), beans, pumpkins, and melons.[24] William Bartram, the English botanist who visited the Gulf Coast of Mississippi in 1777, said they were the "most ingenious and industrious husbandmen, having large plantations, or country farms, where they employ much of their time in agricultural improvements, . . . by which means their territories are more generally cultivated, and better inhabited, than any other Indian republic that we know of."[25]

Many other students of Indian culture, from colonial times onward, have praised Choctaw agricultural activities.[26] John R. Swanton, of the Bureau of American Ethnology, wrote in 1931 that the Choctaws raised so much corn that they actually produced a surplus which they sold, for a substantial profit, to their neighbors.[27] Agricultural surpluses were not unheard of among Indian farmers, but the consistently large yields of Choctaw farmers drew continuing comment from outside observers. With ample food at their disposal, they were able to support a larger population than other tribes.[28] Additionally, seeking a diversified agricultural economy, the Choctaws did not sell all of their surplus corn, but instead used much of it in raising large herds of cattle.[29] Here again they achieved noteworthy success and an-

---

Little Blue Book No. 775, ed. by E. Haldeman-Julius (Girard, Kan., 1924), p. 11.

[24] Robert S. Cotterill, *The Southern Indians: The Story of the Civilized Tribes Before Removal* (Norman, 1954), p. 10.

[25] Mark Van Doren, ed., *The Travels of William Bartram* (New York, 1928), p. 404.

[26] In fact, I have never read an account of the American Indians that accuses the Choctaws of shoddy agricultural habits. They have been universally lauded in this field, and are always ranked very high, particularly in discussions of corn cultivation in America.

[27] Smith, p. 162. Swanton, *Social and Ceremonial Life of the Choctaw*, pp. 46–47.

[28] It is impossible to tell exactly how many persons belonged to any one tribe; the best estimates of the population of the Choctaws list their number at somewhere between 18,000 and 21,000 at the beginning of the nineteenth century.

[29] Swanton, *The Indian Tribes of North America* in *Bureau of American Ethnology, Bulletin 145* (Washington, D.C., 1952), p. 185.

nually produced stock enough to sell many head not only to other Indian nations but to white settlers as well.[30]

This agricultural success helped to stabilize the Choctaw Nation and to settle it in central and south Mississippi. The practice of tilling the soil and planting crops in the spring, and then reaping a harvest in the fall, instead of depending on hunting to supply their food, tended to root families to a specific location. Less time was available for hunting, fighting, and traveling the countryside in search of food. Their homes were permanent-type structures, log and stucco houses[31] grouped together near their farm land in concentrations so large that the early white explorers and settlers who made contact with the Choctaws spoke of the settlements as towns.[32] The settlements were normally located around the edge of the district as a protective barrier against potential enemies; inland, the district was sparsely settled and resembled extensive plantations with cabins or homes "a gunshot distance from each other."[33]

The Choctaw Indians were only moderately religious and little concerned with the fate of man outside the tribe.[34] Although circumstances forced them to deal with Spaniards, Frenchmen, and British as well as Americans and other tribesmen, they showed little real interest in diplomacy, much preferring to remain aloof and present an image of strength and prosperity to the outside world. The few excursions they made into the diplomatic arena were for such purposes as developing markets for their surplus commodities and requesting payment of overdue

[30] Cotterill, *Southern Indians,* p. 10.

[31] Debo, *Choctaw Republic,* pp. 10–13.

[32] LaFarge, p. 26.

[33] *Mississippi, A Guide to the Magnolia State* in *American Guide Series* (New York, 1938), p. 51.

[34] Swanton, *Social and Ceremonial Life of the Choctaw,* pp. 194–99. Horatio B. Cushman, *History of the Choctaw-Chickasaw and Natchez Indians* (Greenville, Tex., 1899), p. 201. Debo, *Choctaw Republic,* pp. 1-23. The whole first chapter of this volume indicates a lack of concern on the part of the Choctaws for their neighbors. Seymour Feiler, ed., *Jean-Bernard Bossu's Travels in the Interior of North America 1751–1762* (Norman, 1962), p. 166.

debts.[35] By the early 1800s, in fact, the Choctaws had become a commercial people with a narrow, isolationist outlook.[36]

When the Choctaws went to war, as in 1813, practical reasons probably governed their decision to fight, for they were not a warlike or belligerent nation.[37] Perhaps they reasoned that there was no point in wasting time killing others when there was profit to be made. However, they were magnificent warriors, especially on the defense, willing to die defending their land against aggressors.[38] The warrior's proudest boast was *"Choctaw siah"*—I am a Choctaw.[39] Even James Adair, who had no love for the Choctaws, grudgingly admitted that they both loved their land and would fight for it. He said, "except the intense love they bear to their native country and their utter contempt of any kind of danger in defence of it, I know no other virtue they are possessed of."[40] Even the women fought bravely, sometimes accompanying their husbands to battle, carrying ammunition and supplies and cheering their men on to greater efforts.[41]

In keeping with their desire for peace, Choctaws were slow to anger; but once enraged, their anger burned fiercely, and they fought with a skill that to many whites seemed almost supernatural.[42] Seldom careless or headstrong, they remained patient, cold, calculating, and brutal.[43] Nevertheless, unlike many tribes, the Choctaws never idealized war. One commentator summarized their love of peace as well as their expanding influence when he wrote that they "seem to have enjoyed the enviable position of being 'just folks,' . . . like the meek . . . they were in process of inheriting the earth by gradual extension of settlements because

[35] Swanton, *Social and Ceremonial Life of the Choctaw*, p. 95.

[36] Debo, *Choctaw Republic*, pp. 18, 23.

[37] Bossu views the Choctaws as a vicious, warlike tribe, but most other commentaries agree with the view of Angie Debo. Feiler, pp. 164–67. Debo, *Choctaw Republic*, p. 18.

[38] Debo, *Choctaw Republic*, p. 18.

[39] Cushman, p. 229.

[40] Samuel C. Williams, ed., *Adair's History of the American Indians* (Johnson City, Tenn., 1930), p. 305.

[41] Rowland, *Mississippi*, p. 65. Feiler, p. 164.

[42] Feiler, pp. 164, 166.

[43] Swanton, *Social and Ceremonial Life of the Choctaw*, pp. 162–69.

none of their neighbors could compete with them economically."[44]

These were the Choctaws, then, when they first met Europeans after 1500—a proud and powerful race, stable, democratic, and economically sound. Under such circumstances, it was to be no easy task for the descendants of these early European intruders to uproot the people of Chahta and force them to move west to a new land and a new life in 1831–33.

[44] *Ibid.*, p. 162.

CHAPTER TWO

CONFUSION OF POLICIES

Prior to the seventeenth century the Choctaws encountered Europeans on only one occasion: Hernando de Soto's famous three-year expedition to the southeastern part of the United States beginning in 1539. The expedition provided unfortunate circumstances under which the two races should meet, for de Soto's objective was gold, and his force ruthlessly plundered the Indian tribes. De Soto and his troops encountered the Choctaws near the present site of Mobile, Alabama, in October, 1540.[1] He demanded their treasures, but the Choctaws refused, and the ensuing battle was disastrous for both sides. For the confused Choctaws, it was a complete rout. De Soto's superior force had horses, which the Choctaws especially feared, as well as armor and lances; and his men literally overwhelmed the ill-equipped warriors. The Spanish chroniclers who accompanied de Soto recorded the battle as the most important encounter of the whole expedition, claiming a complete Spanish victory and about 3,000 Choctaws killed. Although the figure represents a gross exaggeration, the Choctaws probably did lose nearly 1,500 men.[2] Against the Choctaw loss, there were 22 Spanish soldiers killed and 148 wounded. De Soto,

[1] Debo, *Choctaw Republic*, p. 25.
[2] *Ibid.*, p. 26.

who had been slightly wounded himself, was forced to remain in camp for more than a month to allow his wounded men to recuperate.[3] The Choctaws did not quickly forget this encounter, which engendered a distrust of all whites that was still faintly evident a century and a half later when Choctaws once again met Europeans—this time the French, who were actively competing with other European powers for colonies in the New World.

Although the Portuguese and Spanish continued their explorations begun in the fifteenth and sixteenth centuries, they no longer dominated the colonial scene in the seventeenth century, when the Dutch, English, and French, who had earlier been preoccupied with domestic problems, entered the competition. The primary motive of all of the colonizers was economic. Mercantilism, the economic doctrine of the day, taught, among other things, that the nation with the most favorable balance of trade would control the destiny of Europe. The greatest country would be the one with access to superior amounts of colonial raw materials—materials that could be shipped to the mother country, transformed into finished products, and then resold in the colonies and on the continent at a substantial profit.

In their efforts to obtain colonies in North America, Europeans settled along the eastern seaboard from Newfoundland to Georgia; and by the end of the seventeenth century, the two major combatants, France and England, had evolved two distinctly different colonial policies.[4] The British, seeking permanent settlements for agricultural development, concentrated their efforts on areas in which a dense population of colonists could cultivate the soil. The French sought wide, sparsely settled areas where the fur trade could be developed with little competition.

In their expanding search for trapping lands, the French, after 1650, entered the Mississippi Valley, where they built trading posts and small settlements along the Gulf Coast, and, in 1718,

---

[3] *Ibid.*
[4] By the end of the Dutch Wars in 1678, Holland was eliminated as a competitor in North America.

established New Orleans. Other settlements were organized in what is now southern Mississippi, where they first came into contact with the Choctaws. At first the Indians were suspicious of their new neighbors because of their previous experiences with Spaniards. But by 1730 the French had won over many Indian tribes[5] through their capacity for adapting themselves to new surroundings and assimilating new ideas. The Choctaws, once they realized that the French had accepted them as equals, became close friends with their white neighbors. A mutual exchange of ideas on trapping, food, and survival techniques reinforced the growing friendship; and a number of intermarriages between the two races helped still further to cement friendly relations. Some of the children from these marriages later became important Choctaw figures.[6]

This harmonious relation between the French and the Choctaws lasted from 1700 to 1763, during which period the British and French, both in Europe and in the American colonies, carried on a lengthy struggle for supremacy that finally led to the Seven Years' War (1756–63) and the defeat of France. Subsequently, the Treaty of Paris removed all French control from the North American continent.

The abrupt loss of their French friends made the Choctaws anxious. What was to become of them at the hands of the British? Choctaws had supported the French during the many years of fighting; now that France's enemies had won, the Indians felt certain that they would be punished for their activities. Several councils were held in an effort to decide upon a course of action, and many impractical solutions were offered. Some tribesmen went so far as to suggest a full-scale war against the British colonists, while others recommended a plea for forgiveness. After lengthy discussions they decided to adopt a wait-and-see policy.

The British, realizing that control of the Choctaws would be

---

[5] Rowland, *Mississippi*, p. 65.

[6] One such marriage was between a young Choctaw girl from an important family and a French trapper named Louis LeFlore. Their son became the famous chief Greenwood LeFlore.

accompanied by major problems, decided that conciliation could best be achieved by continuing the French custom of offering annual gifts to the tribes of the area. Therefore, in November, 1763, the Choctaws and other Indian tribes assembled at Mobile at the request of the British; and to their amazement, they were presented gifts by their conquerors.[7] This custom was continued only until a treaty could be worked out with the Indians, however. Following negotiations with the Choctaws in Mobile, in March, 1765, the British governor, George Johnstone, made a treaty with them, defining the Indian nation's eastern and southern boundaries and emphatically forbidding encroachment by English settlers upon Choctaw land.[8]

It is possible that the British policy of confinement would have worked, had not the Creeks, lifetime enemies of the Choctaws, attacked the British camp at Mobile, murdering ten of its occupants and capturing several others. A bitter war ensued in which Governor Johnstone, reacting from fear of the Creeks, incited the Choctaws and other tribes to take up arms against their fellow Indians and to continue the hostilities intermittently for six long years. This war-mongering was unwise, for because of it the British came to be associated in the minds of the Choctaws with war and killing, whereas the French had been known for peace and friendship. Thus, the Choctaws were hardly surprised when, in 1775, the British colonists went to war against their own mother country. It seemed to the bewildered Indians that the British and Americans continually sought war, first with the Spanish and French, then with the Indians, and now even among themselves. The Choctaws, when they became involved at all, supported the rebellious colonists, with some of the warriors serving as scouts for Generals George Washington and Anthony Wayne.[9] But scouting was the extent of the tribe's participation

[7] Debo, *Choctaw Republic*, p. 30.

[8] Louis DeVorsey, Jr., *The Indian Boundary in the Southern Colonies, 1763–1775* (Chapel Hill, 1966), p. 210. Clarence C. Carter, "British Policy Towards the American Indians in the South, 1763-8," *The English Historical Review*, XXXIII (1918), 45.

[9] Debo, *Choctaw Republic*, p. 31.

17

in the conflict, for most of the Indians were indifferent.

After the Revolution, the new United States of America faced the same problem that had plagued the British in 1763: how to win the allegiance of the Indians. The question was a serious one for a young nation, and the United States immediately sought to resolve it. In 1785, only two years after the end of the conflict, the government sent Benjamin Hawkins of North Carolina, Andrew Pickens of South Carolina, and Joseph Martin of the Southwest Territory as commissioners to Hopewell, a small settlement on the Keowee River in South Carolina, to negotiate a treaty with several Indian nations, including the Choctaws. Thus, the first treaty between the United States government and the Choctaw Nation, the Treaty of Hopewell, was signed on January 6, 1786.[10] It contained eleven articles covering boundaries, commercial concessions, rights and duties, and details of Indian-American relations. Two of the articles deserve special mention because of their economic implications for the future. ARTICLE 9, for instance, provided:

> For the benefit and comfort of the Indians, and for the prevention of injuries or oppressions on the part of the citizens or Indians, the United States in Congress assembled shall have the sole and exclusive right of regulating the trade with the Indians, *and managing all their affairs in such manner as they think proper.*[11]

And ARTICLE 3 stated, "there is reserved for the use of the U.S., for the establishment of trading posts, three tracts of 6 miles square each within the general limits of the . . . described boundaries at such places as Congress may designate."[12]

This effort by the United States to settle the Indian problem of the Old Southwest was well timed, for the new nation was now faced with Spanish intrigue in that area. Spain had lost East

---

10 U.S. Congress, House of Representatives, "Indian Land Cessions in the United States," No. 736 in *Eighteenth Annual Report of the Bureau of American Ethnology to the Secretary of the Smithsonian Institution 1896–97*, 56th Cong., 1st sess. (Washington, D.C., 1899), II, 650.

11 *Ibid.*

12 *Ibid.*

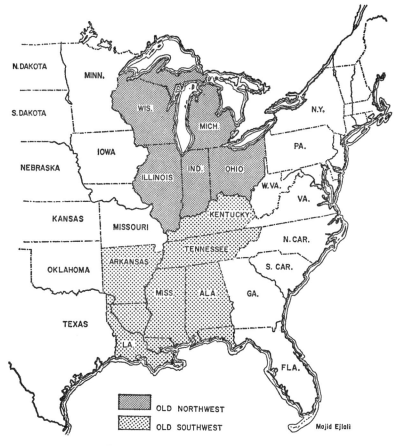

▓▓▓	OLD NORTHWEST
░░░	OLD SOUTHWEST

Majid Ejloli

Old Southwest and Old Northwest

and West Florida to England in 1763 in the French and Indian War but had regained the lost territory by the 1783 Peace of Paris as a reward for supporting the colonies—although reluctantly—against England in the American Revolution. Spain was no friend of democracy; on the contrary, she was eager to undertake any scheme to keep the southwestern frontier in turmoil.[13] One way to accomplish her aim was to arouse the Indians against the

[13] Winthrop Sargent to Timothy Pickering, November 1, 1799, Dunbar Rowland, ed., *The Mississippi Territorial Archives 1798–1803: Executive Journals of Governor Winthrop Sargent and Governor William Charles Cole Claiborne* (Nashville, 1905), I, 183.

United States and possibly start a war that would cripple the struggling new government in Philadelphia.

In the early 1790s, Spanish officials launched a program designed to win the allegiance of the Choctaws by capitalizing on both the Choctaws' affection for the French and the close Spanish-French alliance that existed at the time. If the Choctaws would now ally with Spain, they told the Indians, such action would induce the French to return to the area. To bolster their contention, the Spaniards even used Frenchmen as their negotiators. This strategy proved effective, and in 1791 the Spanish obtained from the Choctaws a tract of land near the mouth of the Yazoo River, at the site of a former English post, where they immediately started building a fort to defend their acquisition against other white settlers and to serve as a reminder of power to the Indians. When completed, the fort was named Nogales, and here the Spanish officials not only negotiated a treaty of friendship with the Choctaw, Chickasaw, Creek, and Cherokee nations,[14] but they also obtained another tract of land from the overawed Choctaws. On this most recently acquired land another military post, Fort Confederation, was erected to commemorate the friendship now existing between Choctaws and Spaniards.[15]

The deliberate campaign of the Spaniards to ingratiate themselves with the Indians alarmed the United States government; but because of other pressing problems, the government did no more than have Thomas Pinckney negotiate the Treaty of 1795 with Spain in an effort to hold the frontier by gaining revenue recessions. A few years later, however, the government was spurred into greater action when it received news of even more hostile plans being laid by the Spaniards and Indians.[16] Mississippi's Territorial[17] Governor Winthrop Sargent, in a letter dated November 7, 1799, informed Evan Jones, the American consul

14 Debo, *Choctaw Republic*, p. 33.
15 *Ibid.*
16 Winthrop Sargent to Timothy Pickering, November 1, 1799, Rowland, *Executive Journals*, I, 183.
17 The Mississippi Territory referred to here is the earlier one, and differs greatly from the Mississippi Territory after the Georgia land cession of 1802.

at the port of New Orleans, that the Spanish governor of Louisiana was preparing to hold a secret conference with tribal leaders in an effort to undermine their allegiance to the United States.[18]

Acting to meet the challenge, the Washington administration of President John Adams appointed a new and more knowledgeable Choctaw agent, Colonel John McKee,[19] who proved to be an excellent choice. Since 1792, McKee had served the governments of his home state of Virginia and his adopted state of Kentucky in negotiations with the Cherokee Indians.[20] In this capacity he had come to know the southern Indians as well as any white man; and his reputation for fairness, honesty, and success was well known to Secretary of State Timothy Pickering.

But honest dealings through reliable Indian agents unfortunately took time, and Governor Sargent desired immediate results. He decided to meet bribe with bribe. On November 9, 1799, he instructed McKee to offer money and presents to the leading "doubtful" Choctaw chiefs in an effort to neutralize Spanish influence,[21] and during the next six months the governor offered several similar suggestions. Sargent's policy for dealing with the Indians was simple. As stated in a report to Secretary of State Pickering, it was to "keep them in good humor, by a little bread, beef, and liquor, and some trifling presents, for which I request immediate provision, and such instructions as may be deemed proper . . . ."[22]

By June, 1800, the Spanish danger was all but eliminated.[23] Available records do not tell us exactly why the Spaniards were unable to upset the *status quo* in the Old Southwest. Perhaps a combination of circumstances—a reawakening of American interest in the area, Spanish military weakness in the territory, the

---

[18] Winthrop Sargent to Evan Jones, November 7, 1799, Rowland, *Executive Journals*, I, 187.

[19] Winthrop Sargent to Timothy Pickering, July 17, 1799, *ibid.*, p. 156.

[20] Dumas Malone, ed., *The Dictionary of American Biography* (New York, 1933), XII, 82.

[21] Winthrop Sargent to John McKee, November 9, 1799, Rowland, *Executive Journals*, I, 192.

[22] Winthrop Sargent to Timothy Pickering, August 20, 1798, *ibid.*, p. 32.

[23] Winthrop Sargent to Timothy Pickering, March 1, 1800, *ibid.*, p. 211.

Treaty of San Lorenzo, and the rising conflict with Napoleon—caused Spain to reconsider her policy and eventually to abandon it. Whatever the reasons, however, the territorial governor was able to report to the secretary of state on March 1, 1800, that the Spanish threat was virtually eliminated.

From the Choctaw point of view, the Spanish and American intrigues were minor problems during this post-Revolutionary War period. Much more important was the growing number of white settlers in Mississippi. The problem was a new one for the Indians, because the French trappers had not settled and cultivated the land; nor had the British, prior to 1775, colonized extensively in the Southwest except in the Natchez area. In fact, the British colonial government had been plagued with so many other grave problems that it deemed it necessary to issue the Proclamation of 1763, which prohibited any settlement west of the Appalachian Mountains.[24] But the Revolutionary War nullified that hated document, and settlers drifted into the Southwest in ever increasing numbers to settle on Choctaw lands. The influx raised many new questions, the gravest of which was a social one —could the two races exist harmoniously side by side?

It soon became evident that trouble lay ahead for the Choctaws. The newcomers accused the Indians of stealing, murdering, plundering, and other criminal acts. They also branded the Indians as lazy, slovenly, and as good-for-nothing drunkards.[25] Territorial Governor William C. C. Claiborne wrote in 1802, "the Choctaws who are at present in our Settlement, are (with a few exceptions) very worthless characters . . . ."[26] Fear of an Indian uprising persisted. The settlers demanded that a militia be

[24] Winthrop Sargent to Timothy Pickering, March 13, 1799, *ibid.*, p. 110. DeVorsey, pp. 27–47.

[25] W. C. C. Claiborne to James Madison, December 12, 1801, Rowland, *Executive Journals*, I, 350–51. W. C. C. Claiborne to Choctaw Indians, April 2, 1802, Dunbar Rowland, ed., *Official Letter Books of W. C. C. Claiborne 1801–1816* (Jackson, 1917), I, 67–68. James Wilkinson to W. C. C. Claiborne, May 10, 1803, Clarence E. Carter, ed., *The Territorial Papers of the United States* (Washington, D.C., 1937), V, 217.

[26] W. C. C. Claiborne to Henry Dearborn, April 8, 1802, Rowland, *Executive Journals*, I, 405.

organized to protect them, and General James Wilkinson set up a strong home guard.[27] By mid-1803 he confidently wrote Governor Claiborne that the militia of the Southwest was strong enough to handle any attack by the Indians.[28]

Meanwhile, the Choctaws were accumulating a list of grievances against the United States. They accused the settlers of stealing Indian land and property, killing any Indian who refused to move, and breaking every white law and treaty obligation then in effect.[29] Especially bitter was the Indians' condemnation of the settlers for selling whiskey in the nation. It was the quickest and easiest way to destroy the Choctaw culture, the Indian leaders pointed out, for it left the tribesmen easy prey for white treachery.[30] Although the Choctaws constantly exhorted the territorial governor to keep the white citizens in line, the governor did little more than issue an occasional proclamation or statement condemning recalcitrant whites. No concerted effort was ever made to end these abuses in Mississippi Territory.[31]

Despite their deteriorating relations with the settlers, the Choctaws still hoped for an equitable settlement, and especially so after the "Revolution of 1800" brought into power the great democrat, Thomas Jefferson. President Jefferson expressed a vital interest in the American Indian and said he hoped to adopt a policy that would eventually end the growing friction between the two races. Unfortunately, he seemed to be too busy with other presidential problems to transform this hope into reality.[32] Rather than implement his ideas by specific acts, Jefferson con-

[27] Rowland, *Mississippi*, I, 360.

[28] James Wilkinson to W. C. C. Claiborne, May 10, 1803, Carter, *Territorial Papers*, V, 217.

[29] W. C. C. Claiborne to John McKee, June 4, 1802, Rowland, *Executive Journals*, I, 450.

[30] Henry Dearborn to W. C. C. Claiborne, September 11, 1802, Rowland, *Official Letter Books*, I, 228–29.

[31] W. C. C. Claiborne to James Madison, December 12, 1801, Rowland, *Executive Journals*, I, 361.

[32] Adrienne Koch, *Jefferson and Madison the Great Collaboration* (New York, 1950). This volume shows clearly that Jefferson, upon assuming the presidency, forgot about the Indians until the problem was periodically forced upon him.

tented himself with lifelong philosophical musings on the need for a just policy towards the Indians.[33] Indians were not enfranchised, and it may have been that the always vote-conscious Jefferson, like many of his successors, never gave serious consideration to forcing his potential constituents to improve their behavior towards the Indians.

In many ways, Jefferson's ideas for handling the Indians were basically humane and far ahead of other contemporary pronouncements. From childhood he had been fascinated by the original occupants of America and had examined their governmental structure, habits, and languages, as evidenced in his famous *Notes on the State of Virginia* and in other writings.[34] Out of these studies he evolved many of his ideas he hoped to introduce during his tenure of office. He asserted, for instance, that the American Indian could no longer live a seminomadic life of hunting and fishing and should hasten the process of settling permanently in an agricultural region for the purpose of cultivating the land.[35] Indian men should farm and raise cattle, just as their white counterparts did, and the women should tend the home and rear the children. Civilizing influences on the Indians would equate the red man with the white, Jefferson said, "and let our settlements and theirs meet and blend together, to intermix, and become one people. Incorporating themselves with us as citizens of the United States, this is what the natural progress

[33] Thomas Jefferson to Alexander Von Humboldt, December 6, 1813, Saul K. Padover, *A Jefferson Profile as Revealed in his Letters* (New York, 1956), pp. 224–25.

[34] Thomas Jefferson to James Madison, January 30, 1787, Padover, pp. 45–46. Thomas Jefferson to John Adams, June 11, 1812, *ibid.*, pp. 205–206. Thomas Jefferson to William Dunbar, January 12, 1801, *ibid.*, p. 123. Thomas Jefferson, *Notes on the State of Virginia* (Chapel Hill, 1955), pp. 92–108.

[35] Thomas Jefferson to Benjamin Hawkins, February 18, 1803, Andrew A. Lipscomb and Albert E. Bergh, eds., *The Writings of Thomas Jefferson Memorial Edition Containing his Autobiography, Notes on Virginia, Parliamentary Manual, Official Papers, Messages and Addresses, and other Writings, Official and Private, now Collected and Published in their Entirety for the first time Including all of the Original Manuscripts, Deposited in the Department of State and Published in 1853 by order of the Joint Committee of Congress with Numerous Illustrations and A Comprehensive Analytical Index* (Washington, D.C., 1904), X, 362.

of things will, of course, bring on, and it will be better to promote than retard it."[36]

Jefferson proposed that, once the Indians were located on small farms, they should be introduced to an elementary educational system, with emphasis on the teaching of American law—this being the key subject in his program to change the Indian from a child of nature to an integral part of a white-dominated society.[37] Boys and girls would be taught to read and write. In addition, boys would receive instruction in the agricultural and mechanical trades, and girls would be taught spinning and weaving.[38]

Jefferson's ideas, as expressed in his public utterances, were commendable; they were also compatible with the Indian policy advocated by John C. Calhoun in 1818 while he was secretary of war. Here the parallel ends, however, because Jefferson, unlike Calhoun, failed to put his ideas into effect. He claimed later that the overwhelming domestic and foreign problems facing the young Republic during the first decade of the nineteenth century were responsible for his failure.[39] Spain stood ominously poised in the Old Southwest, while England, from her vantage point around the Great Lakes, stirred American-Indian controversy. His defense now seems weak, however. Even if these arguments were valid before the Napoleonic Wars in Europe and the Louisiana Purchase, they were not so thereafter.

Why then did Jefferson falter? The reason must be that he never actually intended to allow his wiser and more humane policies to prevail.[40] Evidence of this hypothesis is found in the letters he wrote to Indian agents and influential frontier leaders, advocating Indian agriculture strictly as a means of confining the Indians to a small plot of land so that the government could buy

[36] *Ibid.*, pp. 362–63.

[37] Thomas Jefferson to James Pemberton, June 21, 1808, *ibid.*, XII, 75.

[38] Thomas Jefferson to General Henry Dearborn, April 29, 1808, *ibid.*, p. 40.

[39] Max Beloff, *Thomas Jefferson and American Democracy* in *Teach Yourself History Library*, ed. by A. L. Rowse (London, 1948), p. 107.

[40] Thomas Jefferson to W. C. C. Claiborne, May 24, 1803, Lipscomb and Bergh, X, 391–92.

up the large surplus and sell it cheaply to frontier settlers.[41] His motives can also be interpreted from a letter he wrote to Andrew Jackson on February 16, 1803, in which he asserted that the basic reason for keeping agents among the Indians was to obtain their land. "Toward effecting this object, we consider leading the Indians to agriculture. . . . When they shall cultivate small spots of earth, and see how useless their extensive forests are, they will sell. . . ." Each Indian agent "shall be estimated by us in proportion to the benefits he can obtain for us," Jefferson said, and he ended his letter with the demand that his views "be pursued unremittingly."[42] During that same year Jefferson also wrote William Henry Harrison that he was not interested in the particular method used to secure large holdings of Indian lands, but rather that he was solely concerned with the end result.[43] The statement could easily be read as an invitation to practice fraud and intimidation.

Jefferson justified his militant position by stating that America needed a large portion of the lands between the Appalachian Mountains and the Mississippi River for purposes of defense.[44] In 1802 and 1803, he cited, in further support of his position, the impending Napoleonic invasion of Louisiana and the English and Spanish intrigues, which he said could be averted only by a strong white American population along the Mississippi and other rivers in the area.[45] To Governor W. C. C. Claiborne of Mississippi Territory, he wrote that the federal government must acquire all of the lands bordering the east side of the Mississippi River so that the United States could present "as strong a frontier on our western as we have on our eastern border."[46] These statements were made, ostensibly, for emergency needs; yet even when the emergency subsided, Jefferson did not alter his policy.

[41] Thomas Jefferson to Benjamin Hawkins, February 18, 1803, *ibid.*, p. 362.
[42] Thomas Jefferson to Andrew Jackson, February 16, 1803, *ibid.*, pp. 357–59.
[43] Thomas Jefferson to William Henry Harrison, February 27, 1803, *ibid.*, p. 373.
[44] Thomas Jefferson to W. C. C. Claiborne, May 24, 1803, *ibid.*, pp. 391–92.
[45] *Ibid.*, p. 392.
[46] *Ibid.*

Rather, he intensified it by adding a new idea: the Indians were to remove themselves to the new lands west of the river so as to leave whites in full possession of the Old Northwest and the Old Southwest.[47]

The demand for westward removal was President Jefferson's most significant and far-reaching innovation in American-Indian relations. Although it was seldom emphasized in treaty negotiations before the War of 1812, it was persuasively presented thereafter to the tribes east of the Mississippi River. On moral grounds, the motive for advocating westward removal was both good and bad. Under Calhoun's program, as established during his tenure as secretary of war (1817–25), it was a sound policy, because he considered the West a haven for the persecuted Indians of the East.[48] But Jefferson's ideas implied a human cattle drive, as white settlers pushed Indians before them. He maintained that the American Indians would be forced farther west as the white population advanced; ultimately, they would be driven to the Pacific coast and beyond! "When we shall be full on this side," Jefferson wrote, "we may lay off a range of States on the western bank [of the Mississippi River] from the head to the mouth, and so, range after range, advancing compactly as we multiply."[49]

An even more odious aspect of Jefferson's handling of Indian affairs was the means he employed to obtain Indian lands. He enlarged the government's Indian factories in the various nations[50] and encouraged the Indians to buy more and more goods

[47] Thomas Jefferson to M. DuPont DeNemours, November 1, 1803, Thomas Jefferson Randolph, ed., *Memoir, Correspondence, and Miscellanies, from the Papers of Thomas Jefferson* (Charlottesville, 1829), IV, 5–6.

[48] Richard K. Crallé, ed., *Reports and Public Letters of John C. Calhoun* (New York, 1888), V, 18–19.

[49] Thomas Jefferson to John Breckenridge, August 12, 1803, Randolph, III, 512.

[50] Ora Brooks Peake, *A History of the United States Indian Factory System 1795–1822* (Denver, 1954), p. 187. The factory system, as it was called, was earlier established to keep dishonest private traders from defrauding the Indians. Government-operated trading houses, or factories, were built on tribal lands, and goods were sold at fair prices. Even more important, private traders who desired to operate among the Indians had to be licensed by the government.

on credit. When the Indians' debts became so burdensome that they could not possibly pay the total bill, the Indian agents were instructed to reveal that the United States government would magnanimously liquidate the debts by accepting land cessions.[51] The policy worked well during Jefferson's administration. Writing to William Henry Harrison on February 27, 1803, the president said: "We shall push our trading houses, and be glad to see the good and influential individuals among them run in debt, because we observe that when these debts get beyond what the individual can pay they become willing to lop them off by a cession of lands."[52] Jefferson himself described the policy as bribery, and he had expounded it long before he won the presidency in 1800. In April of 1791, during the campaigns of Colonel Josiah Harmar against the Indians in Indiana and Ohio, he had advocated in a letter to James Monroe that, after the government successfully subdued the recalcitrant Indians, it should change its policy from "war to bribery."[53] At a later date, Jefferson had even stated that if this policy failed, he would propose a constitutional amendment which by force would move the Indians to the West.[54]

In defense of Jefferson it can be stated that he never suggested that the Indians be forced to surrender their lands without fair compensation. In fact, he often refused to accept treaties that were obviously fraudulent or offered the Indians ridiculously small payment for valuable lands.[55] However, because his instructions to the American commissioners did not demand honesty and justice in their dealings, his policy tended to sanction, if not increase, the fraudulent practices of the past.

The Choctaws felt the effects of Jefferson's Indian program

---

51 James D. Richardson, ed., *A Compilation of the Messages and Papers of the Presidents* (Washington, 1897), I, 422–23.

52 Thomas Jefferson to William Henry Harrison, February 27, 1803, Lipscomb and Bergh, X, 370.

53 Beloff, p. 141.

54 William Eustis to Silas Dinsmoor, April 20, 1811, Carter, *Territorial Papers*, VI, 192.

55 Thomas Jefferson to Henry Dearborn, September 2, 1807, Lipscomb and Bergh, XI, 354–55.

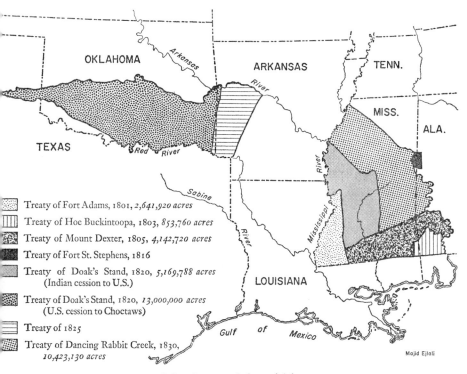

Treaty of Fort Adams, 1801, *2,641,920 acres*
Treaty of Hoe Buckintoopa, 1803, *853,760 acres*
Treaty of Mount Dexter, 1805, *4,142,720 acres*
Treaty of Fort St. Stephens, 1816
Treaty of Doak's Stand, 1820, *5,169,788 acres*
(Indian cession to U.S.)
Treaty of Doak's Stand, 1820, *13,000,000 acres*
(U.S. cession to Choctaws)
Treaty of 1825
Treaty of Dancing Rabbit Creek, 1830,
10,423,130 acres

Majid Ejlali

Land Cessions and Acquisitions

when, in December, 1801, the president sent General James Wilkinson, Benjamin Hawkins, and Andrew Pickens to Fort Adams, on the Mississippi River, to negotiate a treaty.[56] After two weeks of discussion, a formal treaty was signed on December 17, 1801. The signing was obviously an attempt on the part of the Choctaws to appease the government, for the treaty ceded to the United States 2,641,920 acres of valuable land from the mouth of the Yazoo River south to the thirty-first parallel. It further gave the United States the privilege of laying out and opening a wagon road through the Choctaw Nation to facilitate transportation from east to west.[57]

To the Choctaws, the Treaty of Fort Adams was a generous

[56] Cushman, p. 102.
[57] U.S. Congress, House of Representatives, "Indian Land Cessions," II, 650.

concession on their part that should have satisfied the United States government for many years thereafter. Less than six months later, however, General Wilkinson was instructed to return to the Choctaw Nation and arrange a new treaty.[58] In this instance, a new treaty was needed because no recognizable boundary line existed to define the northern and eastern limits of the Choctaws' land. Even so, the Choctaws were unwilling to negotiate again with the government. Governor Claiborne tried to persuade the Indians to reopen the talks, telling them that he was powerless to punish whites who settled on Choctaw lands when he did not know where the boundary line was located.[59] All that the United States wanted, he said, was to establish the line that Great Britain had negotiated with the Choctaws in 1765 but never identified because other problems had taken precedence. Finally the Indians agreed to negotiate, and there ensued three and one-half months of extensive talks with U.S. officials before the Treaty of Fort Confederation was concluded on October 17, 1802.[60] This treaty called for a complete delineation of the Choctaw Nation in accordance with the British treaty of 1765. When the survey was completed in 1803, the United States took possession of a small area of Choctaw territory in what is presently Jefferson County on the Mississippi River.[61]

The Choctaw chiefs signed the Treaty of Fort Confederation with great reluctance, and they made it abundantly clear that they would not entertain any further treaty proposals. In less than one year, however, demand for more Choctaw land arose from the frontier settlers. Citizens of the Old Southwest were still disturbed because of the past Spanish problem, and the government was eager to pacify them. Jefferson therefore had his territorial agents suggest a treaty cession to cancel the Choctaw debts

---

[58] Henry Dearborn to James Wilkinson, June 2, 1802, Carter, *Territorial Papers*, V, 153.
[59] Henry Dearborn to W. C. C. Claiborne, June 7, 1802, Rowland, *Executive Journals*, I, 476.
[60] *House Doc. No. 736*, p. 662.
[61] Rowland, *Executive Journals*, I, 476–78.

to the British supply firm of Panton, Leslie and Company.[62] General Wilkinson, again given the task of convincing the Choctaws that a cession of land for the debt was an equitable procedure, met a number of Choctaw chiefs in the Indian Village of Hoe Buckintoopa in August, 1803. At first the leaders refused to discuss the issue. But when Wilkinson presented them with the overdue bills for immediate payment, the Choctaws reconsidered and on August 31, 1803, signed the Treaty of Hoe Buckintoopa. Thus, still more Choctaw land—853,760 acres of land lying above Mobile in the southern Mississippi Territory—had now been ceded to the United States government.[63]

Although the white settlers of the Southwest were elated by these three successive treaties with the Choctaws that had been negotiated for their benefit, their appetite for land was seemingly insatiable. Thus far the treaties represented minor agreements ceding scattered areas of land to the settlers, who now pressured the government for thousands of acres that could be converted into cotton plantations. To satisfy these demands the government began building additional trading houses in the nation to encourage more and larger debts among the Indians. By 1805, the firm of Panton, Leslie and Company claimed debts of $46,000 against the Choctaws.[64] Presenting its bill for payment in May, 1805, the company found, as was expected, that the Choctaws were unable to meet their obligations. The following month the government sent General James Robertson of Tennessee and Indian Agent Silas Dinsmoor of New Hampshire to begin preliminary negotiations with the Choctaws at Fort St. Stephens on the Tombigbee River.[65] The Indians were furious; at first they refused to see the commissioners, but they soon realized the hopelessness of their stand and consented to meet the government representatives at Mount Dexter (near present Macon in Noxubee County) in November to arrange a treaty.

[62] Henry Dearborn to James Wilkinson, April 16, 1803, Carter, *Territorial Papers*, V, 213.
[63] *House Doc. No. 736*, p. 664.
[64] Rowland, *Mississippi*, I, 408.
[65] Cushman, p. 108.

The talks began on November 6 and continued until November 16, when the Treaty of Mount Dexter was signed.[66] During the week and a half of negotiations, conferences were held every day, many of them marked by bitter arguments. On numerous occasions the Choctaws threatened to leave, but they stayed on, perhaps realizing that delay would aggravate the problem rather than solve it.[67] Finally, in great disgust, the Indians capitulated and consented to a settlement. In return for 4,142,720 acres of fertile land located in south central Mississippi Territory,[68] the Choctaws received $50,500 in cash, $48,000 of which was to be paid to Panton, Leslie and Company, plus an annuity of $3,000.[69] By this treaty alone the government had more Choctaw land than it had gained from all the previous agreements combined. The treaty accomplished the purpose behind Jefferson's policy of allowing the Indians to bankrupt themselves out of all their territory. Ironically, Jefferson disapproved of the 1805 treaty, for he felt that the small sum offered the Indians for such an enormous amount of good farm land was unfair, and he refused to send the treaty to the Senate for ratification.[70] Two years later, however, the United States and Spain were on the verge of war over the possession of Florida, and the government needed to mollify the southwestern settlers. Jefferson therefore sent the old treaty to the Senate, although reluctantly, where it was ratified on January 15, 1808.[71]

Spain and the Indians were having their own boundary problems during the first decade of the nineteenth century while the United States government was negotiating for land cessions from the Choctaws. Until the French betrayed Spanish confidence in 1803 by selling the Louisiana Territory to the United States, the Spanish government in East and West Florida had been lenient

[66] John McKee, "Diary 1804-1805," November 5-November 16, 1805, p. 39, MSS. Southern Collection, University of North Carolina.
[67] Ibid.
[68] Cotterill, Southern Indians, p. 149.
[69] Ibid.
[70] Robert S. Cotterill, "A Chapter of Panton, Leslie and Company," Journal of Southern History, X (February-November, 1944), 287.
[71] Ibid., p. 289.

in regard to the boundary separating its possessions from those of the United States.[72] But after the Louisiana Purchase, Spain decided to keep firm control of its remaining territory and, consequently, began patrolling the boundary to keep out intruders. This strict border control put the Spaniards into direct conflict with the Choctaws, who had little regard for any international boundaries. Like other American Indians, they found it difficult to embrace the idea of individual ownership of land, whether by nations or families. To them, all land belonged to the Great Spirit, who had placed it on earth for all people to use jointly rather than individually. Thus, the Choctaws who lived near the thirty-first parallel, which delimited the Spanish domain, often crossed the border into Spanish territory and were arrested for trespassing. In this instance, the United States acted wisely toward their transgression. It protected the Indians against the Spaniards, and the result was a greater Choctaw dependence on, and respect for, the federal government.[73]

Whether the Choctaws would ally themselves with the United States was another matter. They paid all their debts, ceded land on different occasions, and never fought against the United States; but would they actively support the United States in a war against a powerful European nation—or, even more significantly, in a war against some other Indian nation? In the latter case, Choctaw support of the federal government would actually increase the hold of the United States over the Indians. It seemed more likely, therefore, that the Indians would follow the aggressive policy urged by the Shawnee chief Tecumseh and his brother, the Prophet. These two powerful leaders traveled through the South in 1811 encouraging all the tribes to unite and refuse to cede any more land to the whites, and, if that failed, to destroy the whites before the Indians were completely uprooted and banished across the Mississippi. The settlers in the Old Southwest

[72] W. C. C. Claiborne to Governor Vinzente Folch, March 7, 1804, Rowland, *Official Letter Books*, II, 19–20.

[73] David Holmes to Governor Vinzente Folch of West Florida, September 4, 1810, Carter, *Territorial Papers*, VI, 104–105.

followed the progress of Tecumseh's exhortations with a fear bordering on panic as war with Great Britain began in the summer of 1812.[74] Mississippi Territory settlers were especially fearful because their militia was now without arms and ammunition.[75] Established earlier by Governor Claiborne, the militia had been allowed to deteriorate to the point where it would have been almost impossible to field an effective fighting unit. All that the territorial government could do was to threaten the Choctaws with reprisals if they intervened in the war with the British. Governor Claiborne told the Choctaw warriors that ". . . this quarrel does not concern the red man. —Let them therefore remain quiet and join neither side . . . or the U.S. will have to punish them by burning their fields and homes."[76]

The Choctaws paid scant attention to Claiborne's threats. Nevertheless, they did not seriously contemplate then, or at any time, joining forces with Britain or Tecumseh against the United States. The leading Choctaw chief during the period, and until his death in 1825, was Pushmataha, one of the great Indian leaders of all time. Pushmataha listened to the arguments as they were presented by Tecumseh, the British, and the United States; then he issued a statement calling on the Choctaws to support the United States. The question before the American Indian was not one of past injustices, Pushmataha said, but of future relations. The statement was a brilliant one, concluding with the words, "Reflect . . . on the great uncertainty of war with the American people. . . . Be not deceived with illusive hopes. . . . Listen to the voice of prudence, ere you rashly act. But do as you may. . . . I shall join our friends, the Americans, in this war."[77]

Largely through the efforts of Pushmataha and another great Choctaw chief, Mushulatubbee, the Choctaw warriors initially

---

[74] John McKee to John Pitchlynn, June 10, 1812, Andrew Jackson MSS, Library of Congress, Washington, D.C.

[75] David Holmes to James Wilkinson, July 22, 1812, Carter, *Territorial Papers*, VI, 299.

[76] W. C. C. Claiborne to Chiefs, Headmen, and Warriors of the Choctaw Nation, August, 1812, Rowland, *Official Letter Books*, VI, 154.

[77] Cushman, pp. 315–18.

remained apart from the conflict, but their allegiance to the U.S. was soon to be tested.[78] In August of 1813, a force of Creeks, aroused by the angry, militant words and the apparent logic of Tecumseh and his brother, attacked Fort Mims in Alabama, massacred its citizens, and precipitated the Creek War which soon engulfed the whole Old Southwest. Agent John McKee, fearing that many of the Choctaws might join the Creeks, proposed that the government urge "by liberal rewards" a neutral policy.[79] The new territorial governor, David Holmes, was more optimistic, however, believing that "at present they could be engaged to act on the side of the United States."[80]

The Choctaws were, in fact, incensed by the Creek War. They felt that the Creek "primitives" had betrayed other southern tribes by turning the fury of the whites against all Indians. To the relief of white settlers in Mississippi, Pushmataha offered the military power of the Choctaw Nation to the United States government.[81] John McKee was jubilant and forwarded the good news to General Ferdinand Claiborne, who was organizing a force of Mississippians to march against the Creeks. On November 9, 1813, General Claiborne entered the Choctaw Nation with his troops and was warmly received.[82] For a full week he and Pushmataha worked out the military details for a campaign against the Creeks. Available arms and ammunition would determine the number of Choctaws to be included in the army; and as supplies were received from the East, the military forces would be increased. General Claiborne's forces then headed east, crossing the Alabama River on November 17. A Natchez newspaper carried a letter from the General that stated, in part: "I was flanked on the march by a select detachment of volunteers

---

[78] John McKee to Colonel John Coffee, October 15, 1813, Andrew Jackson MSS.

[79] John McKee to John Pitchlynn, September 20, 1813, *ibid.*

[80] David Holmes to John Armstrong, August 3, 1813, Carter, *Territorial Papers*, VI, 391.

[81] Ferdinand L. Claiborne talk with Pushmataha, November 9, 1813, Indian Miscellaneous 17....–1901, MSS, Library of Congress, Washington, D.C.

[82] *Ibid.*

and militia, under Captains Kennedy, Batis & Lieut. Osborne, and by the Choctaws under Pushmataha."[83]

About seven hundred Choctaws fought with Claiborne in Alabama during the winter months of December and January. All were ill-fed and ill-clothed and only about fifty were armed with effective weapons.[84] Yet despite these handicaps, Pushmataha led his warriors to two decisive victories over the Creeks on the Black Warrior River. The bravery of the Choctaw warriors was notable, surpassing the expectations of John McKee, who reported as much to General Andrew Jackson.[85] The Indians returned to their homes, taking with them the heartfelt thanks of the citizens.

But the Choctaw warriors were destined to remain at home only a few months. In August, General Jackson, impressed by their excellent record, asked them to join his army against the British. Although they had not received "a cent of reward" for their previous services, the three districts of the Choctaw Nation voted overwhelmingly to join the general at Mobile.[86] From that point a thousand Choctaw warriors raced with Jackson to New Orleans to participate in one of the great battles in American military history. The Choctaws again distinguished themselves, as Pushmataha—now a brigadier general—led a successful flanking movement against the seasoned British soldiers.[87] Jackson had high praise for the Choctaw warriors who fought with him at New Orleans; he thanked them officially in the name of of the United States government. Praise for the Choctaws also came from the territorial legislature of Mississippi, which passed a resolution citing the Choctaw effort and rewarding each warrior with presents.[88] Exuberant and proud, the Choctaws felt they had proved to the white citizens of the area that they were

[83] *Mississippi Republican* (Natchez), December 15, 1813.
[84] John McKee to Andrew Jackson, January 6, 1814, Andrew Jackson MSS.
[85] John McKee to Andrew Jackson, January 26, 1814, *ibid.*
[86] John McKee to Andrew Jackson, September 9, 13, 1814, *ibid.*
[87] Pushmataha received a commission as brigadier general from the United States government.
[88] John G. Long, ed., "Resolution from State Capital, Mississippi," *Chronicles of Oklahoma*, VI, No. 4 (December, 1928), pp. 481–82.

a brave and sensible people wanting only friendship with their neighbors. They now dared to hope that the long period of bickering and land-grabbing was over and that the two races could at last live side by side as friends.

For two years it seemed that the Choctaws' hope had been realized. They continued to receive approving notice from the government and were treated well by the white settlers. Even on October 24, 1816, when the Choctaws signed another treaty made necessary by boundary difficulties arising from the Creek War, the treaty negotiations were more like a friendly banquet than a meeting of opposing forces.[89] The Choctaw chiefs joined the United States commissioners at Fort St. Stephens, reminisced about the war effort, and exchanged greetings and vows of good will.[90] By this treaty the United States acquired a small grant of land east of the Tombigbee River in exchange for $6,000 annually for twenty years and merchandise up to the sum of $10,000. The Choctaws also were promised that they would always be the friend of America and that never again would the United States allow them to be mistreated.[91] The sincerity of the statement cannot be doubted, but history proved it to be more of a pious hope than a declaration of fact. In 1817, the year Mississippi was admitted to the Union, a surge of nationalism was destined to shatter any hope for coexistence on the frontier.

[89] William Crawford to David Meriwether, June 4, 1816, Carter, *Territorial Papers*, VI, 691.

[90] George S. Gaines, "Reminiscences of Early Times in the Mississippi Territory" (unpublished typewritten copy in Mississippi Department of Archives and History, Jackson, 1843), p. 5.

[91] Walter Lowrie and Walter S. Franklin, eds., *American State Papers: Documents, Legislative and Executive, of the Congress of the United States, from the first session of the Fourteenth to the second session of the Nineteenth Congress, inclusive: Commencing December 4, 1815, and ending March 3, 1827* (Washington, D.C., 1834), VI, 95.

CHAPTER THREE

CALHOUN'S POLICY OF
MODERATION

The administration of James Madison ended in March, 1817, and James Monroe assumed the presidency of the United States. The simple transfer of power from one president to another in reality symbolized the emergence of America on the world scene as a full-fledged nation. The bitter fighting and defeats of the War of 1812 and the *status quo* Treaty of Ghent were soon forgotten in favor of the glory of Lake Erie, the Thames, and New Orleans. Assuredly, Americans were God's chosen people, many reasoned, for they had emerged from certain defeat to ultimate victory. America embarked upon a period of intense nationalism which completely dominated Monroe's administration. Such events as the acquistion of Florida, the Seminole War, the Missouri Compromise, and the Monroe Doctrine reflected an unprecedented period of national pride and growth which spread into every phase of American life. The changing attitudes of the period affected even the handling of the Indian problem and coincided with the emergence of a new policy. Indeed, of all the national issues faced by the American people between 1817–37, only slavery and nullification were more important than the new Indian policy.

The architect of the new policy was John C. Calhoun of South

Carolina. On October 10, 1817, President Monroe offered the young Carolinian the position of secretary of war in his cabinet. Calhoun was advised by his friends not to accept the appointment because the War Department was regarded as a political graveyard; Henry Clay, Isaac Shelby, and William Lowndes had already turned down the position.[1] He was warned that "he would lose his reputation in taking charge of a department, especially one in a state of such disorder and confusion as the War Department. . . ."[2] Calhoun ignored the advice, accepted the appointment, and informed Monroe that he would take immediate charge of the department. Far from agreeing that the office, because of the low esteem in which it was held, would hurt his political career, he reasoned that any order he might bring out of chaos would be that much more to his credit. Perhaps, if his reorganization could make the War Department as efficient and powerful as certain other federal agencies, he could become popular enough to be considered for high elective office.

Calhoun immediately embarked upon a program of reform. His self-confidence and ability soon made him a great favorite of the president.[3] Even Secretary of State John Quincy Adams admired Calhoun, confiding in his *Diary* shortly after the appointment that "Calhoun thinks for himself, independently of all the rest, with sound judgment, quick discrimination, and keen observation."[4] Three years later, Adams was still impressed: "Calhoun is a man of fair and candid mind, of honorable principles, of clear and quick understanding, of cool self-possession, of enlarged philosophical views, and of ardent patriotism."[5] Monroe and Adams were justified in their high esteem of the

[1] William E. Dodd, *Statesmen of the Old South, or From Radicalism to Conservative Revolt* (New York, 1936), pp. 54–55.

[2] *Life of John C. Calhoun. Presenting a Condensed History of Political Events from 1811 to 1843* (autobiographical pamphlet) (New York, 1843), p. 109.

[3] Margaret L. Coit, *John C. Calhoun, American Portrait* (Boston, 1950), p. 126.

[4] Allan Nevins, ed., *The Diary of John Quincy Adams 1794–1845, American Diplomacy, and Political, Social and Intellectual Life, from Washington to Polk* (New York, 1951), p. 191.

[5] *Ibid.*, p. 265.

young Carolinian for, despite the fact that his later career became one of the most controversial in American history, Calhoun was an outstanding secretary of war. He completely reorganized every function of the War Department, from the structure of the army to the handling of the Indians, and when he resigned in 1825 was hailed by many as the "Father of the War Department."[6]

Calhoun gained that title partly because of his handling of the Indian problem,[7] which involved replacing the government's aimless, drifting, inept, and patchwork program that had been in effect since 1783 with a new one having the necessary qualities to be lasting. The secretary of war studied the Indian problem carefully before he offered a solution. Equally cautious, President Monroe pleaded ignorance and left the problem solely in Calhoun's hands, although he did hint that it was time for the United States "to act with kindness and liberality" towards the original occupants of North America. The president also indicated that the Indians should also be taught the advantages of civilization.[8] Monroe's first annual message to Congress, on December 2, 1817, included Calhoun's plan on the future policy:

> ... It is our duty to make new efforts for the preservation, improvement, and civilization of the native inhabitants. The hunter state can exist only in the vast uncultivated desert. It yields to the more dense and compact form and greater force of civilized population; and of right it ought to yield, for the earth was given to mankind to support the greatest number of which it is capable, and no tribe of people have a right to withhold from the wants of others more than is necessary for their own support and comfort.[9]

Stated more plainly, the president was advocating two basic principles: (1) that the United States preserve and civilize the

---

[6] Thomas L. McKenney to Andrew Jackson, April 23, 1829, Records of the Office of Indian Affairs, Letters Sent, MSS, War Department, National Archives, p. 417.

[7] *Niles' Register*, March 27, 1824.

[8] Richardson, I, 578.

[9] *Ibid.*, p. 585.

Indians, and (2) that the United States not allow the Indians to control more land than they could cultivate. Now it became Calhoun's task to coordinate these two principles into one humane policy that would work to the advantage of both the settlers and the Indians.

Calhoun studied the situation for another year before finally completing the policy and presenting it to the House of Representatives in a special War Department report on December 8, 1818.[10] In introducing the report, the war secretary noted that the Indians east of the Mississippi River had become less warlike during the past hundred years after contact with the white man.[11] They were now an object of commiseration, not of terror, for their power had diminished as more and more Europeans settled in the United States. He argued that it was time to modernize American policy towards the Indians to meet the needs of the day.[12]

In the report, Calhoun suggested three basic changes that would completely alter the aimless policy of the past: stop considering Indian tribes as legal nations, seek to save Indians from extinction, and inculcate among the tribes the concept of ownership of land.[13] The first changes would correct the traditional fallacy of regarding the separate tribes as independent nations. Calhoun considered this attitude to be the major stumbling block to any permanent accord with the Indians: "they neither are . . . nor ought to be considered nations." Indians should be subject to the same controls exercised by the government over all other people living within its national borders. "By a proper combination of force and persuasion, of punishments and rewards, they ought to be brought within the pales of law and civilization,"

[10] John C. Calhoun to United States House of Representatives, December 8, 1818, Crallé, V, 18–19.

[11] *Ibid.*

[12] Thomas L. McKenney, *Memoirs, Official and Personal; with Sketches of Travels among the Northern and Southern Indians; Embracing a War Excursion and Descriptions of Scenes along the Western Borders* (New York, 1846), I, 34.

[13] John C. Calhoun to United States House of Representatives, December 8, 1818, Crallé, V, 18–19.

he wrote. If they were to be allowed to decide their own fate, they would soon be overwhelmed by the growing population before recognizing the wisdom of a new governmental policy which offered protection and security.[14] It would then be too late to reconsider, and the Indians would be swept away by advancing hordes of whites.

Turning to his second recommendation, Calhoun outlined the means by which he proposed to save the Indian from extinction.[15] He would first replace the Indian "manners" and "customs" with the Constitution and the laws of the United States. Then, beginning with the tribes that were most advanced in civilization, he would reduce their settlements to a reasonable size and move them west of the Mississippi River, with the understanding that the United States would make no further demands of their land.

To bring about the third basic change—that of teaching the Indians the concept of land-ownership—each Indian would be given a certain number of acres, and the aggregate of these tracts would then represent the tribal limits in land. In time, Calhoun suggested, this process would fix the idea of land-ownership in the Indian's mind.

Much of Calhoun's program depended upon education, and the secretary proposed to meet that by establishing educational facilities for the Choctaws. The United States would provide all tribes with annuities that would contain ample funds for schools. Attendance at these schools would be compulsory for all Indian children.[16] Eventually, Calhoun hoped, the quality of instruction would be equal to that provided for whites in certain sections of the country. In the beginning, however, until such time as the tribes showed an aptitude for the liberal arts, a system of vocational education would be instituted.[17] The first schools would

[14] Report to the House on the System of Trade, December 8, 1818, *Records of the War Department*, III, 4.

[15] John C. Calhoun to United States House of Representatives, December 8, 1818, Crallé, V, 18–19.

[16] *Mississippi State Gazette* (Natchez), March 27, 1819.

[17] Circular from Baptist Society for Propogating the Gospel Among the Heathen to Thomas L. McKenney (undated, around 1820), John McKee MSS, Library of Congress.

42

teach very little "reading, writing, and arithmetic"; rather they would concentrate on teaching agricultural techniques, home-making, Christianity, and citizenship.[18]

The secretary did not believe in forcing the Indians to accept his policy. Thus, in the last section of his report, he proposed an alternative solution: "Those who might not choose to submit ought to be permitted to remain on their present lands," he said. "When they are sufficiently advanced in civilization they would be permitted to participate in such civil and political rights as the ... states ... might safely extend to them."[19] Calhoun warned that if the Indians retained their present lands much longer they would be at the mercy of the states and would eventually be forced to abandon their Indian culture and conform to the laws of those states. He concluded by advising them against remaining in Mississippi; they were urged to move west of the Mississippi River where they could develop as a people, unhampered by white interference.

Repeatedly, Calhoun emphasized that force would never be used to carry out his program, but he was apprehensive about the fate of the Indians if his plan were not adopted. "It is only by causing our opinion of their interest to prevail," he wrote, "that they can be civilized and saved from extinction."[20] In his opinion, there was no middle ground; either the Indians would adopt the program or they would be doomed. Despite Calhoun's careful preparation, the proposals were almost completely ignored by Congress following his speech of late 1818, but they did serve him as a guide during his tenure in the War Department.[21]

The secretary discharged numerous undesirable Indian agents and replaced them with men of higher character who could be

[18] This type of school was later adopted by Richard H. Pratt in establishing Carlisle Academy in Pennsylvania, and Booker T. Washington in establishing Tuskegee Institute in Alabama.

[19] John C. Calhoun to United States House of Representatives, December 8, 1818, Crallé, V, 19.

[20] *Ibid.*

[21] Schools were opened in the Choctaw Nation during Calhoun's years as secretary of war (1817–25), but they were sponsored by missionary societies, not by the federal government. *Southern Galaxy* (Natchez), March 11, 1830.

accepted by the Indians as friends.[22] Also, he proposed that all relations with the Indians be handled through a superintendent of Indian affairs,[23] responsible to the secretary of war.[24] Those who wanted to trade with the Indians could do so only after buying a license from the superintendent at an annual cost ranging from one hundred to five hundred dollars, depending upon the amount of trade undertaken. A license violation would call for a severe penalty. The sale of alcoholic beverages would be strictly forbidden. Trading houses, as well as individuals, would need the license and would also be required to keep books showing the prices of goods bought and sold. Furthermore, the books would be subject to inspection by an authorized agent. The licenses were costly for those days, but they were meant to be, for Calhoun's intention was to restrict the Indian trade to a select few who could be carefully watched and controlled by the government.[25]

A major decision facing the secretary of war was whether to encourage removal of the Indians first and educate them later, or to start the education process immediately. He decided to undertake both programs simultaneously. While suggesting removal he would also encourage missionary efforts to educate and civilize the Indians. This should present no difficulty because missionaries were already active in tribal areas, especially among the Choctaws.[26] Although other religious groups endeavored to convert the Choctaws, the Presbyterians eventually became the most numerous, the most popular with Choctaws, and the most successful.

In 1818, the year of Calhoun's report to Congress, the Ameri-

[22] *Mississippi State Gazette,* April 16, 1818.

[23] This position was established in 1824 with the appointment of a close friend, Thomas L. McKenney, as the first superintendent. McKenney was an excellent choice.

[24] John C. Calhoun to United States House of Representatives, December 8, 1818, Crallé, V, 14–15.

[25] *Ibid. Mississippi State Gazette,* April 16, 1818.

[26] Arthur H. DeRosier, Jr., "Pioneers with Conflicting Ideals: Christianity and Slavery in the Choctaw Nation," *The Journal of Mississippi History,* XXI, No. 3 (July, 1959), pp. 174–84.

can Board of Commissioners for Foreign Missions of the Presbyterian and Congregational churches sent to the nation two New England missionaries, Cyrus Kingsbury and Cyrus Byington, along with their families and helpers. Under the leadership of Kingsbury, this hardy band of Christians built Eliot Mission School on the Yalobusha River about thirty miles above its junction with the Yazoo River.[27] At first the Choctaws resented the uninvited intruders, but when they saw that the missionaries wanted to teach and serve, as well as convert, they joined in and helped build Eliot School, which opened its doors to Choctaw children in 1819.[28] Calhoun and Agent John McKee, pleased with the missionaries' efforts, generously supported the project.[29]

The main difficulty that faced the missionaries was lack of adequate funds. Since the Presbyterian Church did not have the resources to pay for such costly undertakings among all of the Indian tribes, its efforts seemed doomed to failure unless some outside support could be procured. Fortunately, both the government of the United States and the Indians came to the support of the missionaries. On February 19, 1819, the Congress in Washington passed an act appropriating ten thousand dollars a year for education among the several Indian tribes.[30] Also, Pushmataha had suggested that the Choctaws set aside from their annuity two thousand dollars a year from each of the three districts for the education of Indian children.[31] His suggestion was enthusiastically accepted in all three districts. Calhoun praised the Choctaws for their support, which he took as proof that his policy was working.

By early 1820, Eliot School was flourishing. The Reverend Kingsbury reported to Secretary Calhoun that he had fifty-four excellent students and applications from many more.[32] The Choc-

---

[27] *Panopolist, and Missionary Herald* (Boston), XVI (1819), 389.

[28] *Ibid.*, p. 509.

[29] Gaines, "Reminiscences," p. 10.

[30] *Niles' Register*, March 13, 1819, p. 59. McKenney, *Memoirs*, I, 34–35.

[31] Resolution in Pushmataha's district, March 21, 1820, Office of Indian Trade, Record Copies Letters Sent, MSS, Bureau of Indian Affairs, National Archives.

[32] *Missionary Herald* (Boston), XVI (1820), 80–81. Cyrus Kingsbury to Pushmataha, April 20, 1820, John McKee MSS.

taw chiefs often reminded the missionaries that many schools were needed to educate more and more children. On one occasion they wrote, "Brothers, we wish to repeat to all our white friends everywhere, that we are very thankful for all your favors, . . . our nation is open for more missionaries and our hearts are ready to receive them."[33]

As Indian education progressed, Calhoun pursued his policy of removal. He did not envision the removal of all eastern Indian tribes at the same time. Instead, he preferred to begin with a large tribe that was known for its high level of economic, social, and political development. The successful removal of such a tribe would be prestigious and would force other Indian groups to consider their own removal to the West. No Indian nation could meet these requirements better than the Choctaws of Mississippi.

In May of 1818, Calhoun decided to launch the first effort to obtain Choctaw lands under his new policy. He appointed three commissioners—Choctaw Agent John McKee, Mississippi State Senator Daniel Burnet, and General William Carroll—to negotiate with the Choctaws[34] for an east-west strip of land in southern Mississippi "to increase the security of the Southwestern section of our union."[35] The negotiators were instructed to be polite and courteous to the chiefs at all times, never to demand anything, but rather to suggest certain possibilities to the Indians.[36] If the Choctaws refused a cession in southern Mississippi, or anywhere else, the negotiators were to thank them for their time and retire from the nation.[37] The commissioners were also informed that they could use up to $53,000 for expenses, and another

33 *Missionary Herald*, XVI (1820), 370.

34 John C. Calhoun to James Monroe, April 16, 1818, Letters to the President of the United States, War Department, MSS, National Archives. Daniel Burnet to David Holmes, June 23, 1818, Governor's Documents (Series E), Letters Received, MSS, Mississippi Department of Archives and History, Jackson, Mississippi.

35 John C. Calhoun to John McKee and Daniel Burnet, May 2, 1818, Andrew Jackson MSS, Library of Congress.

36 John C. Calhoun to John McKee, May 2, 1818, Indian Affairs, Letters Sent, War Department, MSS, National Archives.

37 Thomas L. McKenney to Daniel Burnet, date burned, John McKee MSS.

$4,500 for incidentals, such as presents for the chiefs, secretaries, and interpreters. The wording of the instructions indicated that Calhoun was unsure of himself and still feeling his way. He gave no specific instructions, but stated, "the time or place of holding the treaty, and the terms to be offered, are left to your judgment & discretion. . . ."[38] Such inexplicit guidance was not characteristic of Calhoun, a man who usually took a positive stand and demanded compliance from his subordinates. But his Indian policy was still in a formative stage in mid-1818, and he had to learn how the Choctaws would react to a suggestion that they move west of the Mississippi River.[39]

The three American commissioners met with the Choctaw chiefs in the nation during October, 1818. As soon as the Indians learned that the secretary of war desired their removal west, they broke off the discussions and voted unanimously against a cession.[40] The Choctaws were so positive in their stand that the commissioners decided to abandon the negotiations and leave the nation. McKee advised Calhoun that the opposition "originated entirely with the halfbreeds and whitemen residing in the country. . . ."[41] He further stated that, after talking to some of the influential chiefs, the commission decided to postpone negotiations for cession. He suggested at least one year.

Calhoun was neither surprised nor embittered by this outcome, for he had considered the plan premature before negotiations began and, therefore, likely to fail. Even so, he had proceeded with the project in order to test the Choctaw's resolution regarding removal. The money appropriated for the negotiations was simply transferred to a fund to pay off Indian annuities for 1818.[42] Calhoun informed the Choctaws that the government

[38] John C. Calhoun to John McKee and Daniel Burnet, May 2, 1818, Andrew Jackson MSS.

[39] *Ibid.*

[40] John McKee to John C. Calhoun, October 27, 1818, Letters Received by Secretary of War 1801–1860, War Department, MSS, National Archives.

[41] *Ibid.* McKee's statement was a gross exaggeration to cover up the failure of the negotiations.

[42] Andrew Jackson to John C. Calhoun, November 30, 1818, Andrew Jackson MSS.

accepted their decision, but hoped that they would soon reconsider and recognize the advantages of moving west before they
were overwhelmed by white settlers. He even went so far as to
invite the chiefs to visit him in Washington as the guests of the
United States government.[43]

The white people of Mississippi, not at all pleased with the
outcome of the negotiations, urged a "get-tough" policy by the
federal government.[44] Congress reacted to the pressure by appointing Representative George Poindexter, spokesman for Mississippi, to head a congressional committee that would study the
possibilities of resettling the Choctaw Indians on new lands west
of the Mississippi River in a peaceful but persistent removal
effort.[45]

As a Mississippi politician who desired Indian lands for his
constituents, Poindexter proved a poor choice for the committee
chairmanship. The committee conducted no formal hearings on
the failure of the 1818 Choctaw removal effort. Rather, Poindexter spent his time trying to convince his colleagues in Congress of the need for a more direct approach to Indian removal.
In an address before the House of Representatives on December
1, 1818, Poindexter said that, for some years, the Choctaws had
been making annual hunting expeditions west of the river because of the scarcity of game in Mississippi. He deplored the
practice, not because it was in direct violation of the Treaty of
Hopewell, but because it prolonged the Choctaw residence in
Mississippi. "So long as the Choctaw tribe of Indians are permitted to live and hunt on the lands of the United States west
of the Mississippi," Congressman Poindexter said, "they will
never cede to the United States any part of the valuable country
which they occupy by treaty East of said river."[46]

---

43 John C. Calhoun to John McKee, October 30, 1818, Indian Affairs, Letters
Sent, War Department, MSS, National Archives.

44 David Holmes to William Crawford, October 9, 1818, Executive Journal
Govs. Holmes, Poindexter, Leake, Brandon, 1817–27, MSS, Mississippi Department of Archives and History, Jackson, Mississippi.

45 Lowrie and Franklin, VI, 180.

46 *Ibid.*, p. 181.

Secretary Calhoun preferred to wait at least a year before again undertaking treaty negotiations with the Choctaws, but the negative reaction to his failure in Mississippi in 1818 forced him to try again, reluctantly, in February, 1819.[47] Many westerners, including Andrew Jackson, were more hopeful than the war secretary, however, informing him that the Choctaws were ready to listen to reasonable terms. James Pitchlynn, a mixed-blood son of an American interpreter, wrote to Jackson on March 18, 1819: "I have got several families of the Choctaws who are willing to move west of the Mississippi, and I believe, if there was a treaty held in the nation, there would be one-third or a half of the nation would move in the fall."[48]

Such encouraging letters as the one from Pitchlynn to Jackson failed to convince Calhoun that removal was possible, but to satisfy public opinion he appointed John McKee, Andrew Jackson, and Daniel Burnet as commissioners of the United States government to treat with the Choctaws. His reluctance to negotiate at that particular time was indicated in his instructions to Jackson: "It is the wish of the government that a treaty should not be held, unless there is a strong probability of success, of which you will judge. . . ."[49] This hesitant approach angered Jackson, who disliked asking the Indians to do anything, preferring instead to tell them to negotiate—or else![50] Jackson quickly wrote to McKee to suggest a means of ignoring Calhoun's obsequious instructions.[51] The Choctaws should be assembled and informed of the consequences that might result from the passage of a bill for immediate Indian removal, such as one currently being sponsored by Congressman Poindexter, if they refused to negotiate. Jackson would tell them that if they did not move west soon, Arkansas Territory would fill up with settlers and

[47] John C. Calhoun to John McKee, February 24, 1819, Military Affairs 1800–61, Letters Sent, War Department, MSS, National Archives.
[48] Lowrie and Franklin, VI, 229.
[49] John C. Calhoun to Andrew Jackson, March 29, 1819, Andrew Jackson MSS.
[50] Andrew Jackson to A. J. Donelson, February 5, 1818, Andrew J. Donelson MSS, Library of Congress.
[51] Andrew Jackson to John McKee, April 22, 1819, Andrew Jackson MSS.

they would be completely surrounded by white men.[52] And should this occur the Choctaws would "become extinct and lost."[53] In other words, time was running out, and the Indians had to choose now between extinction and survival. He claimed that his policy would save the Indians, whereas Calhoun's would lead to their extermination. And he ended the letter by ridiculing Calhoun for his refusal to force the Choctaws to move.

Andrew Jackson has always been remembered for his frankness, a characteristic abundantly evident in his relations with Calhoun and the Choctaw Indians. Jackson often made decisions not only without seeking Calhoun's advice but also without following it when it had been given to him. For example, when he learned from James Pitchlynn that a number of Choctaws were willing to move west, he took it upon himself to determine the compensations that would be paid to those who emigrated. He told Pitchlynn in a letter that the United States would give the Choctaws an area of land in the West equal to what they had in Mississippi, a fair compensation for improvements, ". . . a gun, a blanket, & a trap—or . . . a kettle," and that the United States would furnish them with provisions until they could harvest a crop.[54] Such promises that Jackson made on his own volition forced Calhoun into the untenable position of fulfilling them or else repudiating them and reprimanding the popular frontier general. The former choice was by far the easier.

In August of 1819, Jackson, McKee, and Burnet met with the Choctaw chiefs on the Yazoo River and presented their arguments for removal. For three days Jackson lectured, threatened, and cajoled the Indians—but to no avail.[55] On August 12, Pushmataha arose and, speaking for the entire nation, answered his former comrade in arms. His voice was loud and firm. In a few

[52] John Jamison to John C. Calhoun, June 16, 1819, Indian Affairs, Letters Sent, War Department, MSS, National Archives.

[53] Andrew Jackson to John McKee, April 22, 1819, Andrew Jackson MSS.

[54] Andrew Jackson and James Pitchlynn to John C. Calhoun, December 31, 1818, Letters Received by the Secretary of War 1801–1860, War Department, MSS, National Archives.

[55] Andrew Jackson to John McKee, August 4, 1819, Andrew Jackson MSS.

short sentences he eloquently summed up the aspirations of the American Indians. "This day we have made up our minds deliberately to answer our great father's talk," he said. "Children even after they have grown to be men, ought to regard the advice of their father. . . . I am sorry I cannot comply with the request of my father. . . . We wish to remain here, . . . and do not wish to be transplanted into another soil."[56]

Those Choctaws who had "straggled" to Arkansas Territory were renegades, Pushmataha said, and he begged the president to use the army to force them to return to the nation so that they could be handled by Indian law. Furthermore, he added, the land offered for Indian occupancy west of the Mississippi River was very poor; the government was trying to cheat the Indian by asking him to exchange good land in Mississippi for an equal amount of poor western land. When Jackson protested, Pushmataha shouted: "I am well acquainted with the country contemplated for us. I have often had my feet sorely bruised there by the roughness of its surface."[57] At the conclusion of Pushmataha's ultimatum, the Indians broke camp and returned to their homes.

Jackson was extremely annoyed by the failure of his commission to negotiate a treaty. He had been so certain of success that he had anticipated it in letters to friends in the East, with the result that *Niles' Register* reported that he would obtain a sizeable cession of land.[58] As an aftermath of failure of the talks, the hero of New Orleans wrote a scathing letter to Calhoun, including a diatribe against John McKee because the Indian agent liked the Choctaws and would "use no influence which he believed to be inconsistent with the interest of the [Choctaw] Nation."[59] Further, Jackson condemned the entire Indian policy, asserting that "Policy alone introduced the measure of treating with our own *subjects* . . . and this policy was correct so long as the arm of

[56] Lowrie and Franklin, VI, 230.
[57] *Ibid.*
[58] *Niles' Register*, August 14, 1819, p. 416.
[59] Andrew Jackson to John C. Calhoun, August 25, 1819, Andrew Jackson MSS.

government was insufficient . . . it is high time the legislature should control the Indian tribes."[60] The vicious implications of the letter foreshadowed what the future would hold for the Indians once the quick-tempered western general won a prominent place in the government.

The Choctaws' reaction to the negotiations of 1819 included not merely their refusal of the removal offer, but a rekindling of anger over broken promises in the past. Three years before, they had been assured that they would never again be called upon to cede land to the United States. Yet, in that short span of time the government had twice repudiated its solemn word. The Choctaws did not believe Jackson's prediction that they would perish if they remained in Mississippi, for they trusted Calhoun and believed in his policy of moderation and education. But they wondered whether Calhoun could hold out against the predominant western sentiment. The chiefs desired to visit Washington and meet the secretary of war in person,[61] but lacking the money necessary to finance the trip, decided to trust the secretary of war and hope he would prevail against their opponents.[62]

Even though Calhoun had been reasonably certain that the commission would not be successful in securing a treaty, he was noticeably upset by Jackson's attack on his policy. His position of moderation had created a number of bitter enemies: Jackson, the State of Mississippi, and possibly some of the Choctaws themselves. Calhoun knew, as 1820 approached, that a third failure might prove fatal, not only to his career, but to the American Indians as well.

[60] *Ibid.*
[61] John McKee to John C. Calhoun, August 13, 1819, Indian Affairs, Letters Sent, War Department, MSS, National Archives.
[62] Lowrie and Franklin, VI, 230.

CHAPTER FOUR

THE TREATY OF DOAK'S STAND

Calhoun's early efforts in the War Department had earned the plaudits of President Monroe and his fellow cabinet members. He had modernized the army, removed incompetent subordinates, and introduced a new filing system. In Indian affairs, however, the secretary had not been quite so successful. He had instituted a moderate, long-term policy aimed at the eventual—and voluntary—removal of the Indians through education, treaties, and the promise of a reasonable payment for Indian lands; but he had failed to consider the desires of the frontier settlers. To these settlers, all Indians should be removed at once. By refusing to support their views, Calhoun placed his entire political future in jeopardy. The two efforts to negotiate a treaty with the Choctaws in 1818 and 1819 had accomplished nothing, except that his position had become less tenable with each failure. He could successfully carry out his policy only if he obtained the necessary time to educate both the Indians and the frontiersmen to its advantages. If he failed, the American Indians would probably be exterminated by war or at least be so degraded that their eventual extinction would be inevitable.

Time was the war secretary's most urgent need. He tried to gain a temporary postponement of further removal efforts, but to do so he needed the support of the populous and conservative East against the more militant West. Unfortunately such support for his policy was not forthcoming. Easterners were more interested in tariff and banking than in Indians. Many of them looked upon the Indian as a sort of animal to be pitied momentarily, as at side shows, and then forgotten.[1] Also, both the northeasterners and the southeasterners were eager to win the support of the growing West, and they would not allow so trivial a thing as Calhoun's policy of moderation towards the Indians to alienate the West.

The advocates of removal in Mississippi violently opposed Calhoun's delaying tactics. On January 5, 1820, George Poindexter, in an address to the Mississippi legislature, proposed that the United States government purchase the Choctaw lands "for a small consideration."[2] The *Mississippi State Gazette* reported that the governor, the legislature, and the people of Mississippi were grossly "annoyed" with the Indian problem and suggested that the Choctaws be removed from the lands "which they hold to the great detriment of this state. . . ."[3]

Early in January, 1820, Calhoun was again bombarded by letters from Mississippians urging that the time was ripe to conclude a removal treaty with the Choctaws. There was pressure even from certain factions within the Indian nation. For example, James Pitchlynn told President Monroe that Head Chief Red Foot and the senior captains of the Six Towns district "requested me to send this talk to you that we think it injustice that a part of our Nation should reside on the United States lands, . . . it is the wish of this part of the Choctaw Nation to cede their lands to you for lands west of the Mississippi. . . ."[4] He claimed that

[1] William Ficklin to Henry Schoolcraft, March 16, 1820, Henry Schoolcraft MSS, Library of Congress.

[2] George Poindexter to Mississippi Senate and House of Representatives, January 5, 1820, Executive Journal of Govs. Holmes, Poindexter, Leake, Brandon, 1817–27, MSS.

[3] *Mississippi State Gazette*, January 8, 1820.

[4] James Pitchlynn to James Monroe, January 29, 1820, Letters Received by the Secretary of War 1801–1860, MSS.

54

the Choctaws would accept a treaty if the federal government would offer fair compensation for improvements.

The most outspoken and persistent advocate of western removal was Andrew Jackson, who continually criticized the War Department's policy towards the Indians and especially Calhoun's encouragement of missionary activities.[5] Jackson harked back to 1819, claiming that he could have obtained a favorable treaty easily if the missionaries and the Indian agent in the nation had not influenced the Choctaws to stay in Mississippi.[6] He told Calhoun that if all of the white men were driven out of the Choctaw Nation, and if he were given unlimited authority, he would immediately negotiate a treaty favorable to the United States.[7]

Calhoun realized that he could not successfully oppose the seemingly unanimous western sentiment for immediate removal. He procrastinated as long as possible, hoping that the removal sentiment would die out. But by May, realizing that the frontier feeling was not diminishing but actually growing stronger, he adopted a course of action so dangerous that it might destroy everything he had strived to accomplish for the past three years. He would authorize another treaty effort in Mississippi and appoint Andrew Jackson one of the chief negotiators with apparently unlimited power. Actually, the secretary would manage Jackson from Washington by the expedient of controlling the money and supplies appropriated for the treaty effort. He would unequivocally demand that the negotiators treat the Indians fairly and honestly. And if all else failed, he would simply refuse to accept any treaty that was not honestly negotiated with the Choctaws.[8] Calhoun realized that he had to face both ways simultaneously, leading Jackson and the westerners to believe that he was supporting their views by allowing the negotiations to proceed, and leading the Choctaws to believe that he was maintaining

[5] Andrew Jackson to John C. Calhoun, February 28, 1820, Andrew Jackson MSS.
[6] Andrew Jackson to John McKee, July 21, 1820, John McKee MSS.
[7] Andrew Jackson to John C. Calhoun, February 28, 1820, Andrew Jackson MSS.
[8] John C. Calhoun to John McKee, May 2, 1820, John McKee MSS.

his policy of moderation. When the proposed treaty was concluded, he hoped, both he and Jackson would be heroes—to Indians and whites alike. If not, he feared, moderation in Indian affairs would be replaced by militant nationalism.

On May 16, a letter from Mississippi Representative Christopher Rankin told Jackson that he and General Thomas Hinds of Mississippi had been appointed commissioners to treat with the Choctaw Indians. Rankin also said that Jackson's appointment was a great victory for Mississippi and the West since the hero of New Orleans was a westerner himself and knew how to handle belligerent Indians.[9] On May 24, the War Department officially notified Jackson of his appointment in a stiff, formal letter that made clear Calhoun's reluctance to turn to the westerner.[10] Not once did the secretary congratulate the frontier general on his appointment or indicate a personal interest in the proceedings. He simply stated: "The President is very desirous to employ you upon this duty, and it will afford him great satisfaction if it should be agreeable to you to accept the appointment. I . . . request the favor of an early answer."[11]

Included in the letter were Calhoun's general instructions to the negotiators. Congress had appropriated twenty thousand dollars to defray the expenses of holding a treaty "for the extinguishment of Indian title to lands within the state of Mississippi." All of the money was put at their disposal, but the secretary requested an itemized account of all expenditures for his files.[12] He informed the commissioners that they had "full powers to exercise . . . [their] own judgment and discretion as to the time, place, and manner of commencing and conducting the negotiations. . . ." Further, Calhoun demanded that he be kept informed of every new development in the negotiations so that he could

[9] Christopher Rankin to Andrew Jackson, May 16, 1820, Andrew Jackson MSS.
[10] John C. Calhoun to Andrew Jackson, May 24, 1820, *ibid.*
[11] *Ibid.*
[12] *Ibid.*

56

ascertain whether the Indians were being treated fairly by the representatives of the federal government.[13]

Jackson received the letter on June 18 and answered it the next day, expressing surprise that he was again chosen to negotiate with the Choctaws. He complained that such an undertaking was a tremendous burden for him at that particular time, and continued, "I had determined never to have anything to do again in Indian treaties; but finding that the President of the U. States is desirous that I should engage in this duty, . . . had determined me . . . to accept the appointment."[14]

In this letter and subsequent ones, Jackson claimed that his greatest desire was to help the Choctaws; he congratulated the secretary of war on the excellent job he was doing to educate and to civilize the Indians.[15] He said, however, that in order to make this policy successful, it would be necessary to concentrate all Choctaws in one central location many miles away from the white frontier settlers.[16] "The pride of a real Indian is in the strength of his nation, and that is the chord I mean to touch, to obtain the object in view,"[17] Jackson wrote. He continually emphasized that he would not force the Indians to remove; instead, he would convince them by diplomatic means that they must move west.[18] This new attitude of moderation expressed in Jackson's letters both pleased and baffled Calhoun. He wondered why Jackson had changed his position—what he hoped to gain. The secretary of war must also have wondered whether the term "diplomacy" meant the same thing on the rough western frontier that it did in the District of Columbia.

The reasons for Jackson's abrupt change in attitude can perhaps be traced to changes in his position. Now that he had been

13 *Ibid.*
14 Andrew Jackson to John C. Calhoun, June 19, 1820, *ibid.*
15 *Niles' Register,* April 20, 1820, p. 155.
16 Lowrie and Franklin, VI, 230.
17 Andrew Jackson to John C. Calhoun, June 19, 1820, Andrew Jackson MSS.
18 "Unpublished Letters from Andrew Jackson," *Southern Historical Association Publications,* II, No. 1 (January, 1898), p. 13.

given a free hand in negotiating with the Choctaws, he had no need to continue his criticism of the War Department. Also, and more to the point, as the actual representative of the War Department he would be, to the Indians, a symbol of the government's current humanitarian policy. If he dishonored this symbol he would discredit his government in the eyes of the Indians and himself in the eyes of his fellow citizens.[19] Jackson's correspondence indicated his belief that Calhoun was trying to trap him into making this grave mistake. Therefore, by graciously accepting the War Department's policy, he refused to accept the bait.

When the pivotal treaty negotiations of 1820 started, Calhoun, although far from enthusiastic in his support of Jackson as chief negotiator, realized that the choice of a lesser western personality would have created discontent on the frontier. Jackson, on his part, held in abeyance—at least temporarily—his impatience with Calhoun's approach and directives. It is likely that this mutual distrust partially accounted for the success of the treaty negotiations.

After pondering Jackson's suggestion that the Choctaws be offered specific western lands, Calhoun finally decided to accept it. He told Jackson that the exact lands the Choctaws would receive in return for their eastern lands could not be designated. The war secretary was not at all familiar with the region west of the Mississippi River.[20] However, Calhoun did know something about the recent Quapaw cession lands. On August 24, 1818, the Quapaws ceded to the United States most of what is today Arkansas south of the Arkansas River and southern Oklahoma. The following year, Major William Bradford, the commanding officer at Fort Smith, drew the eastern boundary of the Quapaw cession, indicating that all settlers must move east of a line drawn between the sources of the Kiamichi and the Poteau rivers.[21]

[19] John C. Calhoun to Andrew Jackson, July 20, 1820, Andrew Jackson MSS.
[20] John C. Calhoun to Thomas Hinds and Andrew Jackson, July 12, 1820, ibid.
[21] Francis Paul Prucha, *American Indian Policy in the Formative Years: The Indian Trade and Intercourse Acts 1790–1834* (Cambridge, Mass., 1962), p. 171.

Because this vast land now was available to the government, Calhoun authorized the commissioners to offer the Choctaws a portion of the Quapaw cession, "to be located on it anywhere you may judge proper";[22] but the farther south and west the better.[23] Jackson thanked Calhoun and promised him a fair treaty.

During the summer of 1820, Jackson and Hinds diligently applied themselves to resolving the many details of a treaty negotiation. Representatives of the Choctaw Nation reluctantly agreed, mainly out of respect for their old comrade-in-arms, Andrew Jackson, to meet the United States commissioners on the first Monday in October.[24] The Choctaws made no effort, however, to disguise their lack of interest in any proposition the United States government might offer. This attitude angered Jackson and led him to alter somewhat the moderate position he had accepted two months earlier. He warned the Choctaws that they would destroy their nation if they refused to listen to reason, and he made it plain that he intended to save them from themselves whether they liked it or not.[25] One way he saw of accomplishing his aim was to bribe the chiefs, but Congress had authorized only twenty thousand dollars for the negotiations—hardly enough to cover the treaty expenses, leaving little or nothing for bribery.[26] It seemed to Jackson that even Congress was determined to thwart his efforts, but this conviction merely increased his determination to succeed.

Despite the Choctaws' reluctance to negotiate, the government's position was far from hopeless. In the first place, Pitchlynn did have a nucleus of Choctaws who favored removal.[27] Second, Jackson did have the twenty thousand dollars, and he

22 John C. Calhoun to Thomas Hinds and Andrew Jackson, July 12, 1820, Andrew Jackson MSS.

23 John C. Calhoun to Andrew Jackson, July 20, 1820, *ibid.*

24 Andrew Jackson and Thomas Hinds to John C. Calhoun, August 9, 1820, Letters Received by the Secretary of War 1801–1860, MSS.

25 "Unpublished Letters from Andrew Jackson," pp. 15–16.

26 Andrew Jackson to John C. Calhoun, August 2, 1820, Andrew Jackson MSS. Andrew Jackson to John C. Calhoun, August 2, 1820, Indian Affairs, MSS.

27 James Pitchlynn to James Monroe, January 29, 1820, Letters Received by the Secretary of War 1801–1860, MSS.

proceeded to spend it liberally on a twenty-day supply of beef, corn, liquor, and other provisions, hoping that a three-week frontier picnic would soften the Choctaws' hearts and dull their senses while he tried to purchase their lands.[28] He realized that such action was a form of bribery, but considered it a legal form that Calhoun would, albeit grudgingly, accept. The government's position was strengthened also by the fact that many of the Choctaw chiefs were beginning to consider the land exchange as a definite possibility, despite their strong statements to the contrary. John McKee wrote to Jackson in August:

> The day before yesterday I had a conference with Puckshu-nubbee on the subject of the treaty,—He will meet the commissioners on the most friendly terms, but will not consent to sell or exchange a foot of land, and resisted to the end in this declaration adding that it would not be necessary to make such preparations for the occasion for he would order all his people to take their provisions with them, in order that the government should not be burdened with unnecessary expenses. All this however is from policy, to throw from his shoulders on the leading captains, the responsibility of making the sale or exchange which he feels will come.[29]

Jackson, in a letter to Calhoun during the same month, reported that Red Foot "wishes to see me or hear the talk of his father the President, and he does not wish to sell any lands, but has no objection to exchange for land on the west of the Mississippi. This increases a belief that we may secure a part or maybe getting the whole territory."[30] By midsummer, Calhoun was convinced that the two years of education in the missionary schools of Mississippi were beginning to teach the Choctaws the value of moving west to avoid future contact with white people.[31]

[28] "Unpublished Letters from Andrew Jackson," p. 15.

[29] John McKee to Andrew Jackson, August (burned), 1820, John McKee MSS.

[30] Andrew Jackson to John C. Calhoun, August 10, 1820, Letters Received by the Secretary of War 1801–1860, MSS.

[31] *Mississippi State Gazette*, April 22, 1820. U.S. Congress, House of Representatives. "Letter from the Secretary of War, Transmitting Pursuant to a Resolution of the House of Representatives of the 6th July inst. a Report of

Once Jackson saw signs of weakening in the Choctaw ranks he reverted to his old tactics of trying to overawe the Indians. He asked the War Department to increase the military strength of the army in the Old Southwest to protect American citizens from, as he called them, the barbarous redskins.[32] Jackson's close friend and spokesman in the Senate, Thomas Hart Benton, advocated the same policy from Washington, demanding that "the tribes must be abandoned."[33] To Jackson, the best thing that could happen to the Choctaws was "to be removed by me for they are standing in the way of progress."[34] As the time for the negotiations approached, he told Calhoun, "It appears to me that it is high time to do away with the farce of treating with Indian tribes . . . the large mass of the . . . Indians are ripe for emigration. . . ."[35]

While the commissioners were trying to frighten the Choctaws into submission, they were also completing their plans for the forthcoming negotiations. Jackson sent agents to locate the most desirable site; and after reading their reports, he chose Doak's Stand, a flat, grassy area on the Natchez road that was easily accessible from any point in the Choctaw Nation.[36] He and Hinds also made agreements with William Eastin and Major William B. Lewis, close personal friends of Jackson's, to supply rations for the Choctaws. Each Indian was to receive a daily ration of one and one-half pounds of beef, one pint of corn, and salt—plus free access to liquor. For each ration, Eastin and Lewis were to receive a commission of nine cents.[37] Local merchants

---

the Progress which has been made in the Civilization of the Indian Tribes and the sums which have been Expended on that Object," No. 46 in *House Documents*, Vol. XXXIII, 16th Cong., 1st sess. (Washington, D.C., 1820), pp. 1–2.

[32] Andrew Jackson to John C. Calhoun, August 11, 1820, Andrew Jackson MSS.

[33] Thomas Hart Benton to John McKee (date burned), 1820, John McKee MSS.

[34] Andrew Jackson to John McKee, August 24, 1820, *ibid*.

[35] Andrew Jackson to John C. Calhoun, September 2, 1820, Andrew Jackson MSS.

[36] "Unpublished Letters from Andrew Jackson," p. 15.

[37] Lowrie and Franklin, VI, 233.

got the contracts for tents, liquors, and other necessary supplies.[38]

Finally, after all the preparations had been made, Jackson left Nashville for the Choctaw Nation on September 14.[39] He arrived at Doak's Stand on September 28, two days before General Hinds arrived with seventeen Mississippi militiamen to be used as a police force for the large and unwieldy gathering.[40]

By October 2, the Indians were straggling into the treaty site; and on the following day the two principal chiefs, Pushmataha and Puckshunubbee, arrived with about eighty tribesmen. Most of the Indians drew their rations, but Puckshunubbee's men refused because, feeling sure that they would not accept Jackson's treaty proposals, they did not want to accept the president's hospitality under false pretenses.[41] When asked why they distrusted their old friend from Tennessee, they replied that David Folsom, Cyrus Kingsbury, and other white friends had told them that the commissioners were there to cheat them out of their heritage. Angered by this statement, Jackson addressed the Indians on October 3, scolding them for their distrust. He told them that he would wait only three more days for the remainder of the Choctaws to assemble, and if a majority of the tribesmen were not present then, he would cancel the negotiations. If the negotiations failed, he said, the blame would fall upon their white advisors who were lying to the Choctaws in order to continue cheating and robbing them of their possessions. Do not fear the bad whites, he advised, "for the arm of your father the President is strong, and will protect the poor Indian from the threats of the white man and half-breed, who are growing rich by their labor, and by living on the main roads through the country."[42] Jackson concluded his talk with an important concession, calculated to appeal to the Choctaw sense of pride. The United States government would exchange with the Choctaws a large parcel of

[38] John McKee to Andrew Jackson (date burned), 1820, John McKee MSS.
[39] Andrew Jackson to John C. Calhoun, September 15, 1820, Andrew Jackson MSS.
[40] Lowrie and Franklin, VI, 234.
[41] Ibid.
[42] Ibid.

land in the West for a small part of their nation in Mississippi. If they accepted this exchange, the Choctaws could either stay in Mississippi on the remainder of their lands or move to their new Indian lands. The decision mattered little to Jackson, he implied, for he was interested only in their happiness and continued prosperity.[43]

During the next few days, as more Indians continued to arrive at the treaty grounds, the chiefs and captains freely discussed Jackson's October 3 address, both among themselves and in consultation with their white friends. Mushulatubbee and Pushmataha considered the offer quite fair and acceptable, but the assent of these two chiefs was not enough.[44] Jackson knew, from the start, that there was a white missionary among the Choctaws who could defeat his goal simply by counseling against it. This person was the Presbyterian leader Cyrus Kingsbury, who had become a potent influence in the nation since his arrival in 1818. He had continually advised against removal; but on October 5, after the commissioners had explained to him the views of Calhoun and the president, he gave his approval of treaty talks.[45] This approval was crucial, for with Kingsbury on their side, the commissioners felt that some sort of treaty at Doak's Stand was as good as guaranteed.

Much of the tension gripping the treaty grounds was now relieved, for the Indians felt that they were making agreements with Calhoun, who had their welfare in mind, and not with the western settlers, who merely wanted to uproot them. A friendly atmosphere, complete with ball games, wrestling, races, and drinking, replaced the old feeling of distrust.[46] Even Puckshunubbee, who had been the most uncompromising of all the chiefs, now agreed that discussions might continue as planned by the white negotiators.[47]

On October 10, the formal negotiations were opened by Jack-

---

43 *Ibid.*
44 Andrew Jackson to John McKee, October 10, 1820, John McKee MSS.
45 *The Missionary Herald,* XVII (1821), p. 208.
46 Lowrie and Franklin, VI, 235.
47 *Ibid.*

son's speech to more than five hundred Choctaws. Welcoming them to the treaty ground, he congratulated them on their willingness to join with the United States government in an effort to save themselves from the evils that had befallen most of the American tribes. He continued:

> It is stated to your father the President that a large proportion of his Choctaw children are in distressed condition, and require his friendly assistance. They live upon poor land, and are not willing to cultivate it. The game is destroyed, and many of them are often reduced to almost starvation. A few are to be found in Alabama, Louisiana, and Mississippi. A number are scattered over the country from Tennessee to New Orleans. Many have become beggars and drunkards, and are dying in wretchedness and want. Humanity requires that something be done for them.[48]

Jackson then explained why it was important for the Indians to heed his proposals. As the nineteenth century progressed, he said, more and more white settlers were moving to the Old Southwest and demanding Indian lands from the government. Already there were five white settlers to every Indian in Mississippi, and yet the settlers were living on one-third as much land as the Indians held.[49] The demands of the whites could no longer be ignored by the president. Thus, in the interest of peace, President Monroe had decided to treat with the Indians before it was too late, before frontier pressures had swept away the aborigines. As outlined by the speaker, the president's proposition was simple: exchange some of the Choctaws' eastern lands for a larger tract in the West. Jackson then concluded by pleading with the Choctaws: "As children of the same family, we entreat you to do justice to one another. Let everyone act and judge for himself. Those who may want to stay here, let them do so. If they wish to remove beyond the Mississippi, let them go."[50]

When Jackson finished speaking, the leading Choctaws retired

---

[48] *Ibid.* This statement was not true, but the same theme was usually presented to all Indians as a general course of treaty procedure.

[49] *Ibid.*, p. 236.

[50] *Ibid.*, p. 237.

to their council house to ponder upon his remarks and debate on the proper course of action. For two days the Americans marked time while the Choctaws discussed the entire removal dilemma.[51] Finally, on October 13, when he considered the moment propitious, Jackson submitted to the council his government's proposition for a treaty, which he felt was unusually generous. The Choctaws would cede:

> ... a slip of land ... beginning on the Choctaw boundary, east of Pearl river, at a point due south of the White Oak spring on the Old Indian path; thence, north a direct line, to strike the Mississippi one mile below the Black Creek, to the lake into which it flows; thence, a direct line, to strike the Mississippi one mile below the mouth of the Arkansas river; thence, down the Mississippi river, to our boundary, and round and along the same to the beginning.[52]

For this relatively useless land the United States would give the Choctaws all of the magnificent farm and hunting lands from the Arkansas River south to the Red River, and west to the headwaters of the Arkansas River. As will be seen in a later chapter, none of the Indian or white negotiators knew exactly what lands were being exchanged, a fact which would cause many headaches for the U.S. government in the not too distant future. However, despite these uncertainties, the Choctaws were ceding approximately one-third of their remaining Mississippi lands— over 5,000,000 acres—for up to 13,000,000 acres in Arkansas and the future Indian Territory. Jackson also stipulated that each man who emigrated west would receive a blanket, kettle, rifle, gun, bullet molds and wipers, ammunition, and corn enough to last each family one year. Schools, stores, blacksmith shops, and agents would be provided as in Mississippi.[53]

By the following day, Jackson was quite certain that the Choctaws would accept his recommendations and conclude a treaty.

[51] *Ibid.*, pp. 237–38.
[52] *Ibid.*, p. 238. The land ceded by the United States in the West was almost three times larger than the Mississippi land received from the Indians.
[53] *Ibid.*

However, many of the chiefs, led by Jackson's old comrade-in-arms Pushmataha, seriously doubted the wisdom of accepting the "bargain" offered them by the United States.[54] Pushmataha accused Jackson of trying to deceive the Choctaws with his glowing account of the western lands:

> It is indeed a very extensive land, but a vast amount of it is exceedingly poor and sterile, tractless, sandy deserts, nude of vegetation of any kind. As to tall trees, there is no timber anywhere except on the bottom lands, and it is low and boukey [sic] even there. The grass is everywhere very short, and for the game it is not plenty, except buffalo and deer. . . . The bottoms of the rivers are generally good soil, but liable to inundation during the spring season, and in summers the rivers and the creeks dry up and become so salty that the water is awful to use. . . .[55]

For three days longer the Choctaw chiefs and captains debated Jackson's recommendations. The majority opposed further negotiations and would have voted to return to their homes had Pushmataha not stood in their way.[56] Although he knew that the lands offered for exchange in the West were not as good for farming as the tribe's Mississippi lands, even though they were three times larger, this great chief was a realist. He knew that Jackson was not exaggerating the threat that was posed by the growing white multitude in Mississippi. It was better to be humiliated, he reasoned, than exterminated. Therefore, Pushmataha submerged his own desires and persuaded the unwilling chiefs to reconsider.[57]

In the end, however, it was Jackson who persuaded the Choctaws to sign the treaty. He did it by losing his temper, finally, over their opposition. On October 17, for the first time during

---

[54] John Hersey to Thomas L. McKenney, October 30, 1820, Office of Indian Trade, Record Copies, Letters Sent (1816–1820), MSS, Bureau of Indian Affairs, National Archives.

[55] *Ibid.* It is interesting to note that Jackson's assessment of the lands in present-day southeastern Oklahoma was more correct than Pushmataha's. It is not a sandy, windy, and useless area, but a well-watered, heavily timbered section of America.

[56] Rowland, *Mississippi*, I, 100.

[57] John Hersey to Thomas L. McKenney, October 30, 1820, Office of Indian Trade, MSS.

the negotiations, he threatened them with the loss of American friendship:[58] "If the Choctaw children of your father the President will adopt the measures here recommended, they will be happy; if they should not," he warned, "they may be lost forever." And he continued angrily, "This is the last attempt, we repeat it, that will be made to treat on this side of the Mississippi...." If they wanted to sign the treaty, he concluded, they must do so the next day; otherwise the commissioners would return to Washington and report failure. Jackson's threats alarmed the Choctaws, and they reluctantly decided to comply with his wishes. The Treaty of Doak's Stand was signed on October 18, 1820.[59]

In Mississippi, overjoyed citizens celebrated as they had not done since their state was admitted to the Union in 1817.[60] Andrew Jackson and Thomas Hinds were praised not only in Mississippi but throughout the Old Southwest. Mississippi Governor George Poindexter heartily thanked the commissioners for their work and prophesied that the treaty "offered the basis of a final extinguishment of Indian title east of the Mississippi, at no distant day."[61] The *Port Gibson Correspondent* congratulated the commissioners and said the five million acres acquired from the Choctaws, which Jackson had called "that useless little slip of land," was "as fine as any in the United States, ... exhibiting at once the most pleasing variety of hill and dale, prairie and grove, and furnishing a variety of soil, and a salubrity of air, not surpassed by any other region...."[62] The *Mississippi Republican* proclaimed the Treaty of Doak's Stand as Jackson's greatest accomplishment since the Battle of New Orleans.[63]

A joint resolution of the Mississippi Senate and House of Rep-

[58] Lowrie and Franklin, VI, 239–40.
[59] *Ibid.*, p. 241. See app. A for full text of treaty.
[60] *Mississippi Republican*, October 31, 1820.
[61] George Poindexter to Andrew Jackson, October 25, 1820, Andrew Jackson MSS.
[62] *Port Gibson Correspondent* (Port Gibson, Miss.), October 28, 1820.
[63] *Mississippi Republican*, October 31, 1820.

resentatives thanked and praised the negotiators,[64] and President Monroe and Secretary Calhoun also offered congratulations.[65] A short time later, Mississippi named its new capital, located in the heart of the territory ceded in 1820, after Andrew Jackson, and the county in which it is located after Thomas Hinds.[66]

The Treaty of Doak's Stand, the first significant achievement of Calhoun's policy of moderation, was accepted by most Americans as advantageous to both Indians and whites. The treaty had given to the Choctaws a vast tract of land of undetermined value in the western part of Arkansas Territory and the eastern part of Indian country,[67] and it had transferred to the United States a valuable tract of land in Mississippi where thousands of white settlers might develop the black delta lands of the lower Yazoo River into large, productive plantations. Surely, it was thought, all true southerners would rejoice at the opening of this vast acreage of virgin soil to the cotton culture that was fast forcing the southern part of the United States into a unique mold.[68] Most southerners cheered when the Treaty of Doak's Stand was ratified by the Senate on January 19, 1821.[69]

Concerning the Choctaw view of the Treaty of Doak's Stand, Jackson wrote on October 18 that "notwithstanding the opposition heretofore made to the treaty, they, at this time seem to be almost universally satisfied."[70] But Jackson's statement was far from true. Dejected and sullen, the Choctaws made their way back to their Mississippi homes, feeling that they had been betrayed; the government had sold them out to satisfy settlers in the Old Southwest.[71] Nor did they take much comfort from the

---

[64] *Mississippi State Gazette*, July 7, 1821. George Poindexter annual Message to legislature of Mississippi, November 7, 1821, Executive Journal Govs. Holmes, Poindexter, Leake, Brandon, 1817–27, MSS.

[65] Richardson, I, 648–49.

[66] *Port Gibson Correspondent*, December 7, 1821.

[67] *Arkansas Gazette* (Little Rock), January 20, 1821.

[68] John Spencer Bassett, ed., *Correspondence of Andrew Jackson* (Washington, D.C., 1928), III, 33.

[69] David Holmes to Andrew Jackson, January 29, 1821, Andrew Jackson MSS.

[70] Lowrie and Franklin, VI, 241.

[71] John Hersey to Thomas L. McKenney, October 30, 1820, Office of Indian Trade, MSS.

solemn promises of Hinds and Jackson that no more Indian land would be exchanged; they had heard such promises before. The only reassuring part of the treaty was ARTICLE 15, which pledged perpetual peace and harmony between Choctaws and white men. But the Indians wondered whether these were sincere pledges that the government intended to keep—or more empty words. History answered their question grimly: the Treaty of Doak's Stand, "the first treaty embodying steps toward removal west and the actual assignment of lands in the Indian Territory,"[72] foreshadowed the removal and degradation of all Indians.

[72] G. E. E. Linquist, "Indian Treaty Making," *Chronicles of Oklahoma*, XXVI, No. 4 (Winter, 1948–49), p. 445.

CHAPTER FIVE

ELATION AND DISAPPOINTMENT

The understandable elation of the settlers in Mississippi over their acquisition of five million acres was not shared by those across the border in Arkansas Territory. Emotions there reached the other extreme. For what the representatives of the Monroe government had done was simply to give the Indians land that was already occupied by white settlers. The enraged citizens of the territory made their feelings known through the *Arkansas Gazette*,[1] startling many Mississippi editors with their vehemence. As early as October 7, 1820, while the treaty negotiations were still in the early stages, the *Gazette* spoke out:

It is no doubt good policy in the states to get rid of all the Indians within their limits as soon as possible; and in doing so, they care very little where they send them, provided they get them out of the limits of their state. The practice heretofore, has been to remove those poor deluded wretches into the weakest and most remote Territories. This we consider the worst policy our government can pursue with the Indians, as the Territories into which they are sent are generally thinly populated, and consequently not able to resist the aggressions of a fierce and savage enemy, whose resentment has already been raised to the

1 This newspaper was—and still is—one of the best in the South.

highest pitch, and who, probably, in making the exchange, cal-
culates on glutting his vengeance on a weak and defenceless
people, for unjuries [*sic*] which he has sustained in his native
country.[2]

On November 25, the editor of the *Mississippi Gazette* answered the tirades against Calhoun and Jackson that appeared
repeatedly in the Arkansas newspaper. He asserted that the Choctaw Indians were civilized and well mannered, and advised the
citizens of Arkansas Territory that they had nothing to fear
from the gentle Choctaws.[3] He also stated that Mississippi had a
right to force its Indians to Arkansas Territory because Mississippi was already a state and hence much more important, at the
present time, than the Arkansas Territory. Arkansas should accept the Indian burden until it attained statehood; then the citizens could force the Indian further west into another territory.
The editor concluded: "In the course of time, the territory of
Arkansas, will also claim a state of independence, the Indians
must then be removed from her soil—and she will set but little
importance upon the arguments now volunteered for her, against
the treaty which may effect it."[4]

During the same month, the Arkansas territorial government
launched an all-out effort to prevent the treaty from clearing the
United States Senate. This difficult task was placed in the hands
of James Woodson Bates, the congressional delegate from Arkansas Territory and a man of great ability and indefatigable
energy. Bates pleaded his cause with such fervor and eloquence
that many congressmen began to question the justice of the
treaty. He succeeded in postponing consideration of the treaty
and used the time in a frantic effort to win more votes for his
cause. On November 28 he wrote to Calhoun pleading for a re-
consideration because the land ceded in Arkansas Territory contained five of the most populous counties and about one third

[2] *Arkansas Gazette*, October 7, 1820.
[3] *Mississippi State Gazette*, November 25, 1820.
[4] *Ibid*.

71

of its population.[5] With typical frontier bluntness, Bates ridiculed the government's Indian policy:

I acknowledge myself decisively and *inconcilatly* [*sic*] *hostile to the policy of pushing Indians to the frontier*—both as to its wisdom and its humanity; but . . . it has received the eulogy of scientific philanthropists, in their closets, who learn the savage character from the unerring medium of the *books*: and the system has been adopted by the federal government. . . .[6]

While Bates was trying to win votes in Washington, the *Arkansas Gazette* was ridiculing the government not only for giving the Indians three times the amount of land it had received in return, but also for pledging them guns, household utensils, blacksmithing equipment, food for a full year, and annuities.[7] Worse than the cession of the land itself, stated the *Gazette*, was the fact that the government would force three thousand white settlers in Arkansas to uproot their homes merely to pacify other white residents of Mississippi. This treatment was unfair, and the Congress of the United States should rise in indignation and defeat such a preposterous treaty.[8] In every weekly issue from November, 1820, to February, 1821, the *Gazette* published an editorial accusing the government of trying to make Arkansas into another "Botany Bay"[9] and of "destroying the peace and happiness of a large portion of our citizens."[10] On January 13, six days before the U.S. Senate ratified the treaty, the newspaper's vitriolic comment was, "never, since the union of these states, has there been a treaty concluded with any Indian Nation so disadvantageous to the United States, or so injurious to any section of country, as this will be to the Territory of Arkansas."[11]

[5] James W. Bates to John C. Calhoun, November 28, 1820, Carter, *Territorial Papers*, XIX, 238.
[6] James W. Bates to John C. Calhoun, November 28, 1820, Letters Received by the Secretary of War 1801–1860, MSS.
[7] *Arkansas Gazette*, January 6, 1821.
[8] *Ibid.*, January 13, 1821.
[9] *Ibid.*, December 16, 1820.
[10] *Ibid.*, November 25, 1820.
[11] *Ibid.*, January 13, 1821.

In contrast to the claims made in the *Gazette*'s losing battle, most prominent newspapers and magazines supported the treaty. The *Port Gibson Correspondent*, in an open letter to the *Gazette*, said that the Choctaws were a highly civilized race of Indians, historically friendly to the United States and its citizens.[12] The *Gazette* retorted that if the Choctaws were such an asset, why did Mississippi want to get rid of them? The editor of the *Niles' Register*, also defending the treaty, wrote on March 17, "if a territory containing so large a white population has been transferred by the United States, it is doubtless, because settlement upon it were unauthorized. . . . We sincerely pity the poor people . . . but they cannot complain of it. . . ."[13] The *National Intelligencer* not only praised the treaty but warned Arkansas that it was only the first of many treaties that would eventually move all eastern Indians west of the Mississippi River.[14]

Once the treaty was ratified the Arkansas people were forced to accept it, but most of them did so grudgingly and despondently, and the *Gazette* wrote, "all are discouraged and disheartened."[15] Mainly, the people were "exasperated against the commissioners . . . for they cared much less for their fellow-citizens than they did for the ruthless savages, to whom they have been so liberal at the expense of hundreds of ruined families."[16] Many inhabitants of the Arkansas Territory threatened to emigrate to Texas, and several exploring parties set out for Texas in 1821 to discuss the possibilities with the Mexican government.[17] Only a few settlers actually carried out the threat, however. Most of them elected to remain on their lands to see whether the federal government was really going to enforce the treaty.

Calhoun, seemingly oblivious to the many protests, prepared to carry out the terms of the treaty. On January 26, he informed

---

12 *Ibid.*, March 10, 1821. The *Correspondent*'s letter was reprinted in the *Gazette*.
13 *Niles' Register*, March 17, 1821, p. 34.
14 Reprinted in the *Port Gibson Correspondent*, January 27, 1821.
15 Article reprinted in the *Mississippi State Gazette*, April 14, 1821.
16 *Ibid.*
17 *Arkansas Gazette*, January 24, 1821.

Agent McKee that a United States surveyor, Colonel Thomas Freeman, had been appointed to survey the new Choctaw boundary in Mississippi.[18] Calhoun also appointed another surveyor, Henry Downs, to run an altered boundary line in Arkansas Territory, instructing him to survey the actual boundary set up by the treaty, but also to run another line (an unofficial one) that would give the Choctaws the same amount of land without upsetting the *status quo* of the whites.[19] News of this alternate plan pleased the territorial governor of Arkansas, and he wrote to the *Arkansas Gazette*, "I am happy to have it in my power to say to the good people of Arkansas, . . . that they will not be disturbed in their possessions . . . for a new arrangement will be made . . . so as to put the Indians west of the white settlements.[20]

Calhoun appointed Edmund Folsom, a long-time resident in the Choctaw Nation, to guide the Indians west, and told him to try to settle them as far away from the white people as possible in order that a future alteration of the existing line could be made without further dislocation of the inhabitants.[21]

Then Calhoun took other steps necessary to convert the removal requirements of the treaty into action. A total of $65,000 was appropriated for supplies, and Thomas L. McKenney, superintendent of Indian Trade, was instructed to send five hundred blankets, kettles, and rifles, and one thousand pounds of rifle powder and lead to Natchez, Mississippi. These goods, plus corn and meat, were to be issued only to those Choctaws who would move to the new territory.[22]

Calhoun seized every opportunity to economize and urged frugality in almost every letter he wrote about the removal. When many of the items sent to Natchez were not used because few Indians had chosen to move west, Calhoun told the new

[18] John C. Calhoun to John McKee, January 26, 1821, Indian Affairs, MSS.
[19] John C. Calhoun to Henry Downs, March 27, 1821, *ibid.*
[20] *Arkansas Gazette*, June 30, 1821.
[21] Lowrie and Franklin, VI, 394.
[22] *Ibid.*, pp. 393–94.

Choctaw agent, William Ward,[23] that "you will endeavor to get them off in payment of the annuity, or in any other way *that may present* itself and which you think advantageous to the U. States."[24] Despite Calhoun's best efforts, however, the removal policy proved costly. One of the ships, carrying more than half of the goods consigned to Natchez, never reached its destination—presumably the victim of pirates or of a storm at sea.[25] After an initial outburst of temper, the frugal secretary replaced the lost goods and redoubled his efforts toward thrift.

Throughout 1821, the war secretary's efforts to move the Choctaws west were unsuccessful. He tried to impress upon them that they were allowed only twelve months, after the signing of the treaty, in which to receive payment for their Mississippi land.[26] When they were indifferent to this warning, he promised to build a road through the nation to facilitate their exodus[27] and even offered to increase the rations that each emigrating Choctaw would receive.[28] The efforts were futile, however; and by November, Calhoun admitted, "From the latest accounts from the Choctaw Nation there is great reason to believe that very few, if any of that Nation are inclined at present to emigrate west of the Mississippi."[29] Even the Indian agent, William Ward, was of little help to Calhoun. He opposed the running of an unofficial line because, if the fact became known to the Indians, they would hesitate to leave the state. He wanted all tribesmen on the land ceded in 1820 to leave Mississippi now. The Choctaws, Ward argued, were already little disposed to move; and if they were further angered by rumors that an unofficial line was being

23 Calhoun informed Ward of his appointment on March 1, 1821, upon the resignation of John McKee.

24 John C. Calhoun to William Ward, May 19, 1821, Indian Affairs, MSS.

25 Thomas L. McKenney to John C. Calhoun, October 9, 1821, Letters Received by Secretary of War 1801–1860, MSS.

26 John C. Calhoun to William Ward, July 16, 1821, Indian Affairs, MSS.

27 Christopher Rankin to John C. Calhoun, June 11, 1821, Letters Received by Secretary of War 1801–1860, MSS.

28 Thomas L. McKenney to John C. Calhoun, September 5 and 19, 1821, *ibid.*

29 John C. Calhoun to Thomas L. McKenney, November 11, 1821, Carter, *Territorial Papers*, XIX, 354.

drawn—one that would cost them part of their newly acquired Arkansas lands—no tribesman would emigrate, for he would fear that the remainder of their new lands would be lost in short order.

Edmund Folsom, who had been appointed in April to remove the Choctaws to their new home, was also admitting a temporary failure by November, complaining that the Choctaws simply would not leave Mississippi. For this, he blamed the whites and those of mixed blood in the nation for the predicament, noting that they continually lectured the Indians on their rights and privileges under the terms of the treaty. Folsom pleaded with the secretary for more funds with which to combat this influence, and in return he promised a full-scale removal by late 1822.[30] Calhoun refused the request but retaliated against the Choctaws by instructing Ward not to deliver any presents to the chiefs until they agreed to move west.[31] This action prompted a Mississippi newspaper to imply that Calhoun was trying to "pay off" the Choctaws if they would leave the state.[32]

Throughout 1822, Calhoun continued to urge the Choctaws to move, but privately he was glad of their refusal as long as the matter of a possible boundary alteration was unresolved. In February he discussed the boundary line with James Bates and promised that the War Department would do everything in its power to rectify the existing situation that placed white citizens of Arkansas within the new Choctaw land. At first Bates was dubious of Calhoun's intention to carry out this promise, which he suspected might be just so much political talk aimed at pacifying the Arkansas citizens. He wrote to the *Gazette* asserting that Calhoun could not be trusted, "for I fear they [Calhoun's promises] are like pleasant dreams—calculated to amuse and tantalize the mind, but never to be realized."[33] But by June, after several conferences with Calhoun, Bates had become convinced that the secretary was sincerely interested in the welfare of Ar-

---

[30] Lowrie and Franklin, VI, 395.
[31] John C. Calhoun to William Ward, March 5, 1822, Indian Affairs, MSS.
[32] *Port Gibson Correspondent*, July 19, 1822.
[33] *Arkansas Gazette*, March 5, 1822.

kansas Territory. He then wrote that Calhoun "manifested a spirit of liberality," and he urged the citizens of Arkansas Territory to support the government's policy.[34]

By mid-1822, Calhoun began to question the wisdom of his own policy. Until then, he had agreed with those in Mississippi who said that the Indians should be moved west first and the boundary line be renegotiated later to meet the prevailing western conditions. But Calhoun had now convinced himself that the boundary line should be permanently fixed before the Choctaws emigrated.[35] This change in position incensed the people of Mississippi, and Governor Walter Leake accused the secretary of war of accepting a bribe from Arkansas Territory to destroy the Treaty of Doak's Stand.[36] The accusation was untrue, for Calhoun was endeavoring to hasten, not hinder, the removal of the Choctaws.

By January of 1823, Calhoun had convinced the president and Congress that the boundary line in Arkansas had to be renegotiated to avoid hardships for both Indians and whites.[37] Congress appropriated funds for negotiations aimed at altering the 1820 treaty with respect to the boundary and suggested that Calhoun appoint commissioners to meet with the Choctaw chiefs later in the year.[38] Pleased by this action, the secretary of war decided that he would appoint General Thomas Hinds of Mississippi and William Woodward of Arkansas Territory for the purpose. They could be sent to the Choctaw Nation in the late fall to convince the chiefs of the wisdom of relinquishing part of their newly acquired Arkansas land in exchange for certain considerations.[39]

[34] *Ibid.*, June 4, 1822.
[35] John C. Calhoun to Senator Henry Johnson, February 15, 1823, Indian Affairs, MSS.
[36] *Port Gibson Correspondent*, July 19, 1822. Leake to legislature of Mississippi, June 24, 1822, Executive Journal of Govs. Holmes, Poindexter, Leake, Brandon, 1817–27, MSS, Mississippi Department of Archives and History.
[37] The House of Representatives to President James Monroe and John C. Calhoun, January 28, 1823, Letters Received by Secretary of War 1801–1860, MSS.
[38] *Niles' Register*, March 8, 1823.
[39] *Arkansas Gazette*, March 2, 1823.

The idea of tampering with the treaty angered the Mississippians anew. It had been signed and ratified, and, instead of being altered, it should be forced upon both the Choctaws and the people of Arkansas Territory.[40] William Ward assured Calhoun that the Choctaws positively refused to meet any commissioners, especially Thomas Hinds. "I am requested by some of the chiefs," Ward wrote, "to ask the President . . . if it would be agreeable that they should visit the City of Washington to hold a talk with the President about the land beyond the Mississippi in preference to make a treaty with any commissioners that might be sent."[41]

Calhoun refused the Choctaws' request and ignored William Ward's warning; for, as he informed President Monroe, "another year should not pass away, without concentrating the Indians on, the place proposed for their permanent home."[42] But he also admitted, as did Jackson and Hinds, that "little is known of the country, which has been fixed on for the Indians," and that an immediate correction of the error would save the treaty and prevent hardships.[43]

In October, Calhoun sent letters of appointment and instructions to Hinds and Woodward. The commissioners were requested to meet the Choctaws in December at the Choctaw Agency in Mississippi. The letters were routed through Choctaw agent Ward, who seized the opportunity to sabotage the discussions by destroying the letter addressed to Hinds.[44] When Woodward arrived in the nation in early December, he was, first of all, astonished to learn that Hinds would not be present, and then angry when he discovered the reason for Hinds's absence. He made an unauthorized search for the lost instructions and found that Ward had "wilfully and deliberately suppressed highly im-

[40] William Ward to John C. Calhoun, August 12, 1823, Letters Received by Secretary of War 1801–1860, MSS.
[41] Ibid.
[42] John C. Calhoun to James Monroe, October 29, 1823, James Monroe MSS, Library of Congress.
[43] Ibid.
[44] William Woodward to John C. Calhoun, December 11, 1823, Letters Received by Secretary of War 1801–1860, MSS.

portant papers."[45] But to Woodward's chagrin, General Hinds came to the defense of William Ward. Ward, when asked by Hinds why he had not forwarded the letter, replied, "I understand from many sources, that you would not accept, and have so informed the secretary of war!"[46] Hinds agreed that he would have refused the appointment and congratulated Ward on his efficiency after which he left the nation and returned home, leaving the furious Woodward to return to Little Rock empty handed.[47]

Woodward's report of the debacle sent Calhoun into a towering rage, but he realized that if he made a public issue of the episode he would be ridiculed in Washington. Hence, he not only played down the incident, but also, reversing his previous decision, invited the Choctaw chiefs to come to Washington in June of 1824 to talk directly with him and the president. Calhoun did not relish the prospect of entertaining seven Indian leaders in Washington, but it seemed the best way of preventing the people in Arkansas Territory from making an issue out of Ward's insubordination. In his report to the president, Calhoun closed the issue of the proposed negotiations of 1823 by simply stating, "The communication for General Hinds, (who was directed to make the principal arrangements for the treaty) it appears never reached him, owning to some failure of the mails, or other cause unknown to this department."[48]

Calhoun went to great lengths to ensure the success of the forthcoming meeting in Washington. He obtained two thousand dollars from Congress[49] to pay for a modest but adequate reception for the chiefs. The stipend included a whiskey allowance of three dollars a day for each commissioner; however, it proved grossly inadequate (to the amazement of Washington society),

[45] *Arkansas Gazette,* January 7, 1824.
[46] *Ibid.*
[47] William Woodward to John C. Calhoun, December 11, 1823, Letters Received by Secretary of War 1801–1860, MSS.
[48] John C. Calhoun to James Monroe, February 13, 1824, Letters to the President of the United States, MSS.
[49] John C. Calhoun to Henry W. Conway, May 22, 1824, Records of the Office of Indian Affairs, Letters Sent 1824–1833, MSS, War Department, National Archives.

for each Indian averaged $8.21 a day for whiskey over a period of three months.[50] Calhoun consented to a Choctaw request to increase the delegation from seven to twelve. This enabled Pushmataha to appoint all four of the chiefs and subchiefs in each of the three districts, and thereby avoid slighting certain leaders in favor of others.[51]

The entire experience of the meeting turned out to be frustrating and exasperating for Calhoun, despite his careful preparations. It even started inauspiciously: negotiations had been scheduled to begin on June 15; but, with typical disregard for the white man's concept of time, the Choctaws did not even leave their nation until September 23,[52] and they did not arrive in Washington until November 1.[53]

At the first session of the meeting, the secretary of war offered to settle the boundary question by removing the few Choctaws who had already settled on the Arkansas lands to an enlarged area farther west in the Indian Territory.[54] Once the Indians moved west of the white settlers, he said, they could permanently establish their new nation. Rather unrealistically, Calhoun promised that the white man would leave the entire West as far as Mexico open to the Indians.[55] His request for a further cession of land in Mississippi was emphatically refused. He then softened his request by asking for only a small area near Monroe County, Mississippi, to enable that section of the state to set up a judicial district; but the Choctaws flatly refused this request, too. They

[50] Thomas L. McKenney to Choctaw Chiefs, June 17, 1825, *ibid*.

[51] John C. Calhoun to William Ward, June 30, 1824, *ibid*.

[52] William Ward to John C. Calhoun, September 23, 1824, Choctaw Agency 1824–1833, Letters Received, MSS, Records of Bureau of Indian Affairs, National Archives. John C. Calhoun to William Ward, June 24, 1824, Records of the Office of Indian Affairs, MSS. Actually, Indians did not disregard punctuality; they had a completely different concept of time. Setting a definite date to do something did not make sense to Indians because of their linguistic view of time.

[53] Thomas L. McKenney to Cyrus Kingsbury, November 5, 1824, Records of the Office of Indian Affairs, MSS.

[54] Lowrie and Franklin, VI, 551.

[55] Land west of Arkansas Territory was considered by many to be unfit for white habitation. John C. Calhoun to Choctaw Delegation, November 9, 1824, Records of the Office of Indian Affairs, MSS.

PUSHMATAHA

MUSHULATUBBEE, principal chief
COURTESY SMITHSONIAN INSTITUTION

CHIEF GREENWOOD LEFLORE
MISSISSIPPI DEPARTMENT OF ARCHIVES AND HISTORY

CYRUS KINGSBURY, Presbyterian missionary
COURTESY THE PRESBYTERIAN HISTORICAL SOCIETY

JOHN MCKEE, Indian agent
ALABAMA DEPARTMENT OF ARCHIVES AND HISTORY

would cede no more land east of the Mississippi River.[56] They did show interest in the settlement of the Arkansas boundary question.[57] Throughout his talks with the Indians, the secretary of war was courteous and thoughtful. He refrained from demanding compliance with any of his proposals, but rather allowed all suggestions to be debated in order that compromises could be made.

When Calhoun recognized the Choctaws' determination to remain in Mississippi, he turned his full attention to the western boundary. He explained that nothing short of a complete removal from Mississippi would satisfy the government. In return for complying with this wish, the tribe would be given five thousand dollars in cash immediately upon completing its removal and six thousand dollars annually for ten years, with at least three thousand of the latter sum earmarked for education.[58] The Choctaw delegation was insulted by the offer, considering it a mere pittance, and abruptly terminated the negotiations by making preparations to return to Mississippi.[59] Frantically, Calhoun made many informal offers to induce them to remain and conclude the negotiations. On one of these trials, he suggested to the chiefs that they present to the War Department a list of demands that might lead to effecting a compromise. This was exactly what the shrewd chiefs had expected, and they were ready with a list of demands so long and exacting that it overwhelmed the unsuspecting secretary. They demanded complete compliance with the treaty of 1820, which allowed any or all Choctaws to live on the tribe's remaining Mississippi land, thirty thousand dollars' worth of presents over a two-year period, nine thousand dollars a year for twenty years to support an institution for higher education among the Mississippi Choctaws, a like amount to educate their children in colleges, and three thousand dollars a year for twenty years for the education of the Choctaws beyond the Mississippi River.[60] On one point at least—education—the Choctaws' interest

[56] John C. Calhoun to Thomas H. Williams, November 15, 1824, *ibid.*
[57] Lowrie and Franklin, VI, 551.
[58] *Ibid.*
[59] David Folsom to John C. Calhoun, November 20, 1824, John McKee MSS.
[60] Lowrie and Franklin, VI, 552.

and that of the Calhoun program were in accord. As stated by the Choctaw delegation:

> The price we ask may be more than has been usually given for value. We wish our children educated. . . . We feel our ignorance, and we begin to see the benefits of education. We are, therefore, anxious that our rising generation should acquire a knowledge of literature and the arts, and learn to travel in those paths which have conducted your people, by regular generations to their present summit of wealth and greatness.[61]

The Choctaw terms were debated for several weeks until finally, on January 20, both sides accepted a compromise and the Treaty of 1825 was signed. The treaty included the following provisions: (1) a six-thousand-dollar per year perpetual annuity to be sold to the government for a lump sum settlement or continued permanently any time after twenty years, (2) an additional six thousand dollars a year for sixteen years as promised in the Treaty of Doak's Stand, (3) government waiver of all claims to back debts owed by the Choctaws, (4) government compensation to all Choctaws who fought in the War of 1812,[62] and (5) Choctaw evacuation of most Arkansas lands after the completion of a careful survey.[63] It was obvious from the terms that the Indians had become skillful negotiators and, furthermore, that Calhoun was willing to compromise to obtain an equitable settlement.[64]

The Treaty of 1825 was a favorable one for the Choctaw Indians, but it had been marred by the tragic death of their great chief, Pushmataha. He died in Washington on December 24, 1824, before the treaty was signed, of croup that he contracted during the negotiations. Until his death at age sixty, Pushmataha had been in complete control of his faculties and had led all of the Choctaw negotiations.

Because of his many services to the United States, including

61 *Ibid.*
62 *Ibid.*, pp. 553–54.
63 *House Document No. 736*, p. 708.
64 John McKee to Pushmataha, November 11, 1824, John McKee MSS.

his military leadership in the War of 1812, Pushmataha was given a mile-long military funeral and was buried alongside of other American heroes in the nation's capital. Andrew Jackson called Pushmataha "the greatest and bravest Indian I ever knew. He was wise in counsel, eloquent in an extraordinary degree, and on all occasions and under all circumstances the white man's friend."[65] John Randolph referred to him as "one of nature's nobility, a man who would have adorned any society." And at his funeral Randolph said, "He lies quietly by the side of our statesmen and high magistrates in the region, for there is one such—where the red man and the white man are on a level."[66]

Pushmataha died during a moment of great triumph for the Choctaws. His passing, and the resignation of John Calhoun two months later, deprived the exponents of enlightened moderation of their two most eloquent spokesmen. Both had striven for the same goals: the well-being of the Indians and the peaceful integration of the Indian into the new way of life that had developed in the West with the coming of the white man. They had hoped to achieve their goals through a process of education that would teach tolerance, understanding, and moderation to both whites and Indians; and the Treaty of 1825 now stood as eloquent testimony to their achievement.

The Indians' appreciation of the Calhoun policy was summarized in a letter they presented to Congress before they left Washington in February:

> The voice of the President, the sentiments of philanthropy which seem to pervade the people, the schools and religious institutions which have been established among us—all give us the consoling assurance that we are not doomed to extinction. . . . The theory of your government is justice and good faith to all men. You will not submit to injury from one party because it is powerful, nor will you oppress another because it is weak. Im-

---

[65] Rowland, *Mississippi*, I, 551.

[66] George S. Gaines, "Dancing Rabbit Creek Treaty," *Historical and Patriotic Series of Alabama State Department of Archives and History*, No. 10 (1928), p. 20.

pressed with that persuasion, we are confident that our rights will be respected.[67]

With his policy finally succeeding, after eight years, John C. Calhoun resigned from the War Department at the end of February, 1825. Commenting on Calhoun's handling of Indian affairs, Charles Wiltse observed that "If Calhoun's Indian policies were less successful than his efforts in behalf of the Army, it was not because they were less sound but rather that they were too advanced for the time."[68]

[67] Lowrie and Franklin, VI, 559.
[68] Charles M. Wiltse, *John C. Calhoun Nationalist, 1782–1828* (Indianapolis, New York, 1944), I, 298.

CHAPTER SIX

PATIENCE AND MODERATION CONTINUED

In March, 1825, the line of Virginia presidents came to an end when John Quincy Adams of Massachusetts replaced James Monroe as president of the United States. There was to be little change in basic policies, however; for Adams, as well as his vice-president, John C. Calhoun, had been members of President Monroe's cabinet. Many of Monroe's policies, initiated and developed by these two men, were thus destined to be maintained during the next four years.

The new president appointed James Barbour of Virginia as secretary of war. Barbour retained, and even expanded, "Calhoun moderation" in Indian affairs; but the leading exponent of this policy was Thomas L. McKenney, head of the recently established Bureau of Indian Affairs. McKenney was a life-long friend of Calhoun, and had served as superintendent of Indian trade from 1817 until 1822, at which time Congress had abolished the office. Two years later, when Calhoun had organized the Bureau of Indian Affairs to supervise and control all matters pertaining to the Indians, he had named McKenney, one of the few Indian experts in the country, as its head. For the seven years that McKenney retained the position, he continually urged moderation in Indian affairs.

The newly adopted Treaty of 1825 required the government to run a boundary line to delimit the Choctaw Nation in Arkansas Territory, and also to remove from Mississippi those Choctaws who wanted to emigrate west. In the inaugural month of March, the War Department approached the first of these problems by appointing James S. Conway of Arkansas, in association with the St. Louis, Missouri, surveying company of Sullivan and Brown,[1] to set the boundary line. The following month, the surveyors began the arduous and costly task of running the line through the wilderness.

In Arkansas Territory, a lack of satisfaction with the 1825 treaty was already evident. Although the terms called for a return to the settlers of most of the land that they had lost by the Treaty of Doak's Stand in 1820, they could not expect total recovery. Until the surveyors completed the new line, they could only guess at how much land the Choctaws would retain. The *Arkansas Gazette*, anticipating that no more than half of the land would be returned to Arkansas,[2] started another campaign against the federal government, complaining that "our fellow citizens have as little cause to be satisfied with the new Treaty, as they had with the old one. . . . We lose by it, almost the whole of the County of Miller, and a considerable portion of the County of Crawford, together with about three thousand of our inhabitants. . . ."[3]

To mitigate local feeling against the United States government, Henry W. Conway, the new territorial governor, requested that Secretary of War Barbour allow all of the people in the territory to retain their lands until January, 1826, which would give ample time for harvesting to those who would have to abandon their lands as a result of the new treaty.[4] Barbour replied that he was not authorized to suspend the treaty. He inti-

---

[1] Henry W. Conway to Bureau of Indian Affairs, March 2, 1825, Office of Indian Affairs, Registers of Letters Received 1824-30, MSS, Records of the War Department, National Archives.

[2] *Arkansas Gazette*, March 15, 1825.

[3] *Ibid.*, March 8, 1825.

[4] *Ibid.*, April 19, 1825.

mated, however, that it would take a year to run the line, and that no one really would be forced to move during the interim.[5]

Shortly after the survey got underway in April, 1825, the *Gazette* began to temper its claim of a few weeks earlier. By May 10, it reported that the Arkansas loss would not amount to half of the original land; nevertheless, the Choctaws would still retain a tract of Arkansas land 60 miles wide and 125 miles long from the Arkansas River to the Red River. But when the survey was completed on December 7, the newspaper acknowledged that the actual situation was even less onerous for the settlers. They had lost very little land to the Choctaws.[6] The new western boundary ran from 100 paces east of Fort Smith south to the Red River.[7] Although not fully satisfied with the new boundary, the people of Arkansas Territory did admit that the final settlement was more acceptable than they had anticipated when the survey began.[8]

At about the time the survey was begun, the Bureau of Indian Affairs started working towards the task of moving the Choctaw emigrants to their new homes.[9] Bureau Chief McKenney appointed William McClellan of Mississippi as the Choctaw agent in the West and charged him with the responsibility of convincing the Choctaws that the federal government was concerned about their fate and would assist them in the removal.[10]

McClellan's first job was to clear the designated Arkansas land of settlers to make room for the expected Choctaw influx.[11] Starting in May, he spent two months persuading the settlers to evacuate their homes. "I found them very much scattered," he wrote. "They expressed great willingness; and stated that they

[5] *Ibid.*

[6] *Ibid.*, December 20, 1825.

[7] Arrell M. Gibson, *Oklahoma; A History of Five Centuries* (Norman, 1965), p. 85.

[8] *Arkansas Gazette*, December 20, 1825.

[9] William McClellan to James Barbour, April 15, 1825, Choctaw Emigration 1826–1833, Letters Received, MSS, Records of the Bureau of Indian Affairs, National Archives.

[10] William McClellan to James Barbour, October 25, 1825, *ibid.*

[11] *Savannah Republican*, November 23, 1825.

would set out in two moons, for other lands."[12] With this situation apparently well in hand, he returned to Mississippi to begin the laborious task of moving hundreds of Indians through many miles of woods and swamps to their new land. The Choctaws, however, refused to emigrate. Despite McClellan's glowing accounts of the new territory,[13] the Indians chose to stay where they were. They had hunted frequently on the Arkansas land, and they regarded it as vastly inferior to their Mississippi holdings. Moreover, many white commentators agreed with them in their estimate of the western lands. John R. Boyles, a merchant from Fayetteville, Tennessee, had traveled throughout the western country in April, 1825, and he described the land in a letter to his daughter as generally "poor and swampy. . . . Not much game except squirrels which are in very great plenty."[14]

The Choctaws' refusal to leave Mississippi did not seem to surprise or upset Secretary of War Barbour. To the contrary, he was eager to postpone the Choctaw emigration because the Arkansas people were already pressing him to negotiate again with the Indians for the return of all lands that had been held by the territory prior to the Treaty of Doak's Stand.[15] Thus, early in 1826, Barbour decided to suspend all removal efforts for at least one year. He authorized the new territorial governor, Frank Izard, to open discussions with the Choctaws in an effort to negotiate a new boundary line that would allow all Arkansas citizens to remain on their own lands.[16] He also instructed McKenney to write to the Mississippi Choctaw agent, William Ward, and explain the wishes of the government in the matter. Ward was authorized to bring the Choctaw chiefs back to Washington as soon as possible so that a new treaty could be nego-

---

[12] William McClellan to James Barbour, October 25, 1825, Choctaw Emigration 1826–1833, MSS.

[13] William McClellan to Thomas L. McKenney, November 12, 1825, *ibid.*

[14] John R. Boyles to Daughter, April 25, 1825, Eliza H. (Ball) Gordon Boyles MSS., Duke University Library.

[15] Thomas L. McKenney to William Ward, January 16, 1826, Records of the Office of Indian Affairs, MSS.

[16] R. M. Johnson to James Barbour, January 6, 1826, Choctaw Agency 1824–1833, Letters Received, MSS., Bureau of Indian Affairs, National Archives.

tiated before Congress adjourned in the fall.[17] The time was propitious for a new Choctaw treaty, according to Senator Richard M. Johnson of Kentucky, who advised Barbour, "I am sure . . . that from the anxious desire those people manifest to increase their literary fund and from the influence of Col. Ward, there is much more than an equal chance for the Choctaws to accept the offer. . . ."[18]

McKenney was hoping earnestly to settle the land problem created by the Treaty of 1820—finally and in favor of Arkansas.[19] A new agreement that would once again alter the western boundary of Arkansas Territory would make such a settlement possible. Thus, he attempted zealously to bring the Choctaw chiefs to Washington. He urged agent Ward to *"press"* for a new treaty, and to convince the chiefs that this was "the last time that the United States wants some of their land."[20] He even called on the missionaries to help, promising that if they did he would not forget their patriotism when they were in need of extra supplies or funds.[21] It was bribery, but McKenney naïvely believed that the Choctaws would benefit from such a cession. They would then be free of white dissension and could develop peacefully without outside interference. McKenney drew the line at any more overt form of bribery, however; and when John Pitchlynn, Jr., offered to exert his influence for the government cause "provided my interest can be promoted thereby,"[22] McKenney not only declined his offer but scolded him for lack of principle.

[17] Henry W. Conway to James Barbour, January 14, 1826, *ibid.*

[18] R. M. Johnson to James Barbour, January 14, 1826, *ibid.*

[19] To effect this end, bureau chief McKenney wanted to negotiate a new treaty that would locate the line somewhere near the original Arkansas boundary created on March 2, 1819. The act of that date listed Arkansas's boundaries as that part of the Territory of Missouri north of Louisiana and "south of a line beginning on the Mississippi River, at thirty six degrees North Latitude running thence West to the river St. Francois, thence up the same to thirty-six degrees thirty minutes north latitude, and thence west, to the western territorial boundary line. . . ." Carter, *Territorial Papers,* XIX, 44–45.

[20] Thomas L. McKenney to William Ward, January 16, 1826, Records of the Office of Indian Affairs, MSS.

[21] Thomas L. McKenney to William Ward, January 7, 1826, *ibid.*

[22] John Pitchlynn, Jr., to James Barbour, February 26, 1826, Choctaw Emigration 1826–1833, MSS.

Regardless of the motives of the War Department, the Choctaw chiefs refused even to discuss the possibility of a new treaty. On March 16 two of them, Mushulatubbee and Robert Cole, made their refusal emphatic;[23] and two days later seven Choctaw chiefs informed Secretary Barbour that "We, having heard a proposition for a further cession of land beyond the river Mississippi, have come to a resolution *that we will sell no more land on any terms.*"[24]

Disappointed by his failure, McKenney discovered that several factors were contributing to the Choctaws' recalcitrance. The nation was being ravaged by smallpox, carried by a party of warriors who had visited New Orleans,[25] and by April more than four hundred Choctaw men, women, and children had died of the dread disease. Also, ever since Pushmataha's death, a lack of leadership had been causing the chiefs to war among themselves—a condition that led a mixed-blood chief, J. L. McDonald, to warn McKenney that, unless a new and powerful leader came forward to weld the Choctaws into a harmonious nation, they were doomed to extinction.[26] Swayed by these circumstances, McKenney wrote to the chiefs on May 9 assuring them that the United States would never try to take advantage of its Choctaw friends. "I tell you," he said, "you will never be pushed off your land. If you go, it will be by your own consent, and free will."[27]

Congress, however, did not share this sympathy. On May 20 it passed an act "to enable the President of the United States to hold a treaty with the Choctaw and Chickasaw nations."[28] The

[23] William Ward to Thomas L. McKenney, March 16, 1826, Choctaw Agency 1824–1833, MSS.

[24] Lowrie and Franklin, VI, 704.

[25] *Savannah Georgian*, April 28, 1826.

[26] J. L. McDonald to Thomas L. McKenney, April 27, 1826, Choctaw Agency 1824–1833, MSS.

[27] Thomas L. McKenney to David Folsom, May 9, 1826, Records of the Office of Indian Affairs, MSS.

[28] *Savannah Georgian*, July 8, 1826. The word *enable* is quite misleading. They really meant *force*, as many congressmen were in a mood to do something direct about the lingering Choctaw removal problem. They wanted to complete the distasteful task as quickly as possible, since most believed that sooner or later all Choctaws—and all other Indians—had to be relocated west of white settlements.

bill allowed the federal government to send commissioners to meet with the Choctaws and purchase more land in Mississippi. During the debate on the bill, one of its proponents, Mississippi Senator Thomas B. Reed, had advanced some of the arguments then being used to urge its passage. Mississippi and the Choctaw Nation, he said, could not exist side by side with entirely different codes of law. Mississippi criminals and debtors were escaping justice by fleeing to the nation and living out the rest of their lives among the Indians. The tribe, he felt, should not be allowed "to convert their country into an asylum for vagabond debtors."[29] He doubted that the Choctaws could be civilized by the dregs of white society any more than by kind thoughts from Washington. Consequently, the Choctaws should either surrender their lands to Mississippi and become citizens of that state, or leave the state for the West.[30]

News of this congressional act aroused disgust and anger among the Choctaws. Repeatedly, they said, the United States had promised that no further cession would be demanded of them, and each time the promise had been quickly broken. Determined now to be prepared for the commissioners, the Choctaws held several councils during the summer of 1826 to work out a united policy. But these councils lacked effectiveness because repeated defeat was beginning to erode some of the former spirit of resistance, especially among the older chiefs. They admitted they were tired of fighting the whites and were willing to listen to offers.[31] Former agent John McKee, noting this change of heart, told Barbour that he had observed among the older Choctaws a certain fatalism with regard to migration, although the overwhelming opinion of the nation was still against further concessions to the white man.[32]

29 *State Journal* (Jackson, Mississippi), May 3, 1826.

30 *Ibid.*

31 William Ward to James Barbour, August 9, 1826, Choctaw Agency 1824–1833, MSS.

32 John McKee to James Barbour, September 13, 1826, Choctaw Emigration 1826–1833, MSS. At this time McKee was serving in Congress as a representative from the Tuscaloosa district of Alabama.

Fearing that the weary old chiefs might be tempted to sell out their nation, the tribe deposed Mushulatubbee and Robert Cole of the Northwestern District and elected David Folsom and Greenwood LeFlore in their place.[33] Both of the new chiefs were of mixed blood and were much opposed to any further cession of land.

While these councils were taking place, the federal government was developing its own strategy. William Clark of Missouri, Thomas Hinds of Mississippi, and John Coffee of Alabama and Tennessee were appointed as United States commissioners. All three favored Andrew Jackson's policy:[34] that of removing all Indians then living east of the Mississippi River, using force if necessary. News of the replacement of the old chiefs by younger, more militant ones was a disappointing blow to the commissioners, for they felt sure that their mission could end only in failure.[35] Nevertheless, they decided to bully the Choctaws and make impossible demands, hoping that the Indians would realize what might happen to them in the future. As Jackson wrote General Coffee, "you might get the whole territory or none...."[36]

The commissioners met with the Indian representatives in the fall of 1826, during the period November 6 to 19, near Wilson in the Choctaw Nation. The new chiefs, declining to bring to the conference the rank and file, who might succumb to bribery and corruption, entrusted their interests to a committee of thirteen, all of whom they considered relatively unsusceptible to temptation.[37] The commissioners offered one million dollars for the Choctaw Mississippi territory, transportation to the West, and reservations in Mississippi for those who elected to remain there under state jurisdiction. To this offer the committee of thir-

---

[33] Lowrie and Franklin, VI, 708.

[34] Especially John Coffee, who had been a business partner and close friend of Andrew Jackson since they served together in the War of 1812.

[35] John C. Calhoun to Andrew Jackson, October 11, 1826, Andrew Jackson MSS.

[36] Andrew Jackson to John Coffee, August 20, 1826, Bassett, IV, 310.

[37] Lowrie and Franklin, VI, 709.

teen gave a firm, and almost unanimous, no, commenting that if they could not trust a guarantee of their present territory, they could not have faith in a guarantee of other lands.[38] They also refused to cede a small tract in the Tombigbee River area that the commissioners had been instructed to get if their larger demands were refused.[39] The commissioners, after expressing their displeasure at the absence of the Choctaw rank and file and at the obstinacy of the committee of thirteen, departed.

To the citizens of Mississippi, the Choctaws' refusal to accept this offer was an outrage. Some citizens demanded that the government drive the aborigines out of the state; others urged another treaty effort, with Andrew Jackson as the chief negotiator;[40] but the majority called for a reexamination of the government's method of handling the Indian problem. Congressman William Haile of Mississippi suggested that the missionaries be instructed to teach the expediency of removal in their schools and churches.[41] He also called a meeting of representatives of all southern states to discuss the Indian problem and develop a unified policy. At this meeting representatives from North Carolina, Georgia, Florida, Tennessee, Alabama, and Mississippi adopted a report (drafted by Senators Reed of Mississippi and Thomas W. Cobb of Georgia) that called for total Indian removal. Although the representatives did not formally prescribe a means of carrying out this objective, they did suggest that state laws abolishing Indian nations would be quite effective as a final resort, if the Indians could not be induced to move west by any other means.[42]

Although Thomas McKenney was again disappointed at the failure of this treaty effort, he still entertained hopes for the future. Agent Ward had told him in a letter that he sensed "something like a spirit (with many of the half-breeds as well as In-

[38] *Ibid.*, p. 713.
[39] *Ibid.*, p. 715.
[40] *Natchez Gazette*, February 8, 1827.
[41] *Niles' Register*, January 6, 1827, p. 317.
[42] *Savannah Georgian*, April 4, 1827.

dians) to move this fall beyond the Mississippi." Ward contended
that the Choctaws were uncertain:

> in regard to those very possessions in Arkansas, to which they
> have been invited to remove. These Indians have been met by
> propositions for a cession of their lands on both sides of the
> Mississippi. They are filled with uncertainty! But do no more
> than express "surprise" and resolve not to sell. And it is not nat-
> ural for them on witnessing propositions for the purchase of their
> country both East and West of the Mississippi, that they should
> remain stationary until they can be satisfied that one is prepared
> for them which they will not be asked to sell.[43]

McKenney felt that the reason for the two failures was the
American "mode of approaching them."[44] He suggested that the
United States approach all Indian tribes a little more intelligently,
perhaps by holding a series of councils in the Old Northwest and
the Old Southwest to explain to the tribes the advantages of complete removal. "Furthermore," he said, "send men of character
and fidelity to advise and help them and not scoundrels. Send
presents. In other words, win their confidence."[45] To convince
the Choctaws of the wisdom of evacuating their Mississippi lands,
McKenney decided to visit the nation and negotiate a removal
treaty, if at all possible. In fact, while he was in the South, Mc-
Kenney felt that it would be a good idea to visit the other major
tribes and consul with them all. Possibly he might negotiate a
whole series of treaties which would remove the tribes westward
and eliminate for all time the friction between Indians and
whites.[46]

During the early months of 1827, McKenney made all necessary preparations for a long trek throughout the Old Southwest.
Leaving Washington in July, he spent four and one-half months
traveling through the Cherokee, Creek, and Chickasaw nations

[43] Thomas L. McKenney to James Barbour, January 4, 1827, Carter, *Territorial Papers*, XX, 355.
[44] Thomas L. McKenney to James Barbour, December 27, 1826, Records of the Office of Indian Affairs, MSS.
[45] *Ibid.*
[46] *Ibid.*

preaching peace and moderation. On October 15 he entered the Choctaw Nation, where he was warmly received and treated to a magnificent banquet followed by dances and tribal ceremonies. The enthusiastic reception led him to believe that he would have little trouble negotiating with the Choctaws. That night he wrote to the secretary of war, "I think I shall succeed."[47]

But during the next two days in the council meetings, it became evident that the chiefs and warriors still held the same conservative views on removal that they had expressed the preceding year. McKenney described the predicament the Choctaws would face in Mississippi if that state happened to pass a law abolishing the nation. The only way to save their noble heritage, he urged, was to move away from their aggressive neighbors immediately.[48] Without even a preliminary discussion of McKenney's recommendation, the chiefs promptly answered, "We are thankful for your advice—but more than sorry, that we have been unanimous in declining to accept it."[49] McKenney's reply, a paternalistic one reminiscent of Calhoun's policy, was, "I cannot but feel troubled for you. . . . Let my voice keep sounding in your ears . . . and if you get into trouble send me word and if I can, I will help you. . . . I am the red man's friend, and shall always be so."[50]

Again the head of Indian affairs refused to be disheartened by his failure to negotiate a new treaty. He remained with the Choctaws for three more days, trying to learn why they were so violently opposed to saving themselves from extinction. At last he hit upon what he thought was the answer. He wrote to Barbour that the chiefs were aware of the hopeless position of the Choctaws in Mississippi, but that they were afraid they would be killed if they should advocate removal against the wishes of the nation. McKenney concluded, "from all I can gather . . . nothing but the recent changes in chiefs, or rather their pledges to the

[47] Thomas L. McKenney to James Barbour, October 15, 1827, Choctaw Agency 1824–1833, MSS.
[48] McKenney, *Memoirs*, I, 183.
[49] *Ibid.*, p. 338.
[50] *Ibid.*, p. 339.

nation, kept the council from adopting openly, and fully, and cheerfully, and *unanimously*, the proposition submitted. . . ."[51]

Although McKenney failed to obtain a treaty on this trip, his meeting with the Choctaws did produce two important results. One was that the Indians agreed to go on an expedition to investigate their new western lands and then report their findings to the entire nation.[52] If they were satisfied with the lands, McKenney hoped, they might reconsider their decision to stay in Mississippi. Secondly, McKenney's trip had decreased Indian resentment against the white man.[53] The Indians apparently liked the bureau chief as a person; and his efforts at just dealings convinced the tribe, at least to some extent, that the government was not completely controlled by militant westerners making unreasonable demands.

Once back in Washington, McKenney took steps to organize the Choctaw expedition to the West, despite the disapproval of certain southern and southwestern congressmen who were tired of being criticized by their electorate each time the government failed to negotiate a new Indian treaty. To end such criticism, these statesmen decided to force the issue by enacting a Choctaw removal bill.[54] On May 22, 1828, after five months of bitter debate, the House passed the bill by a close ten-vote margin; but it was defeated in the Senate.[55]

Even while congressional debates on the removal bill were still in progress, McKenney completed plans for the Choctaw western expedition. He chose as leader the twenty-eight-year-old chief, Greenwood LeFlore,[56] wisely foreseeing that this mixed-blood leader would some day be the successor to Pushmataha.

---

[51] *Ibid.*, p. 337.
[52] Thomas L. McKenney to James Barbour, November 28, 1827, Records of the Office of Indian Affairs, MSS.
[53] *Niles' Register*, December 29, 1827, p. 274.
[54] *Ibid.*, January 19, 1828, p. 339.
[55] *Ibid.*, May 31, 1828, p. 226.
[56] McKenney felt that it would eventually be easier to make a deal with a person who was a mixed-blood than with a full-blooded Indian. William Ward to Peter Porter, October 11, 1828, Choctaw Agency 1824–1833, MSS.

SECRETARY OF WAR JOHN C. CALHOUN
COURTESY NATIONAL PORTRAIT GALLERY, SMITHSONIAN INSTITUTION, WASHINGTON, D.C.

SUPERINTENDENT THOMAS L. MCKENNEY
P. S. DUVAL, LITHOGRAPHER, PHILADELPHIA

GENERAL THOMAS HINDS
MISSISSIPPI DEPARTMENT OF ARCHIVES AND HISTORY

SECRETARY OF WAR JOHN EATON
FROM KENNETH MCKELLAR, **TENNESSEE SENATORS AS SEEN BY ONE OF THEIR SUCCESSORS**

JOHN COFFEE
ALABAMA DEPARTMENT OF ARCHIVES AND HISTORY

He wrote to LeFlore informing him of his appointment and, feeding the young Indian's ego, expressed the thought that LeFlore might possibly become the greatest Choctaw leader of all time. "You should keep your eye on the time when your term of office expires," the bureau chief wrote, "and like Moses and Aaron rise up and point your people to a goodly land. . . . I expect to live to see you . . . great . . . . You have the power to be so."[57] In his correspondence with the Choctaw leader, McKenney never lost an opportunity to preach removal. On one occasion he made this eloquent plea: "I wish you could get into my heart and see all that's there: and into my eyes and see what I see. I tell you, you have before you and your children happiness and prosperity on the one hand, and on the other misery and destruction!"[58]

Meanwhile, a congressional bill to secure an appropriation for the Choctaw expedition[59] was introduced on April 17 and passed on May 24, 1828.[60] McKenney was eager for the expedition to start as soon as the appropriation was obtained; but countless delays, caused mainly by the inability of the government to collect the necessary supplies, caused a postponement until the middle of August.[61] At that time, the expedition set out for Memphis, Tennessee, where it then boarded a steamboat for St. Louis. At St. Louis the party picked up the bulk of its supplies at Jefferson Barracks and then traveled overland on horseback towards the Choctaw western territory.[62]

The expedition arrived in the Kiamichi area late in September. McKenney had described the lands in such glowing terms that LeFlore expected to find a Utopia where the Indians could once

[57] Thomas L. McKenney to Greenwood LeFlore, January 15, 1828, Records of the Office of Indian Affairs, MSS.

[58] Thomas L. McKenney to Greenwood LeFlore, February 15, 1828, *ibid.*

[59] *Niles' Register*, April 26, 1828, p. 144.

[60] *Savannah Georgian*, May 26, 1828.

[61] Thomas L. McKenney to William Ward, June 10, 1828, Records of the Office of Indian Affairs, MSS.

[62] Benjamin Johnson to Thomas L. McKenney, September 30, 1828, Choctaw Emigration 1826–1833, MSS.

again develop a mighty nation. He had written that he was going "to explore the new promised land which said land flows with milk and honey."[63] Instead, he found a mountainous country with soil vastly inferior to that in the Choctaws' Mississippi home.[64] Throughout October and November the exploring party toured the new land from one end to the other. They found that the western part lacked two vital resources, water and wood, both of which were abundant in Mississippi. As LeFlore led his warriors through their new land, he wondered which fate would be worse: emigration to this alien country, or extinction in Mississippi. For himself, he decided that if the bulk of his nation were forced to emigrate west, he would somehow find a way to remain in Mississippi.[65] The exploring party, having completed its task, arrived back in Mississippi in December.

Their arrival marked the end of an era in Indian relations, for while the exploring party was in the West, Andrew Jackson had been elected president of the United States. The event signaled the end of the moderate Indian policy as followed by John C. Calhoun and Thomas L. McKenney.

Over a twelve-year period, Calhoun's policy had countenanced bribery, threats, insulting language, and propaganda; but it had never used, or threatened to use, military force. The Choctaws were allowed to decide for themselves whether they would migrate. They had never been forced to sign a treaty. Nor had those who lived on ceded land been forced to emigrate west rather than move to other Mississippi lands. During the entire period, in fact, no more than fifty Choctaws emigrated.[66] Most estimates suggest fifteen, and one as few as eight.[67] Now, the

[63] Greenwood LeFlore to Thomas L. McKenney, May 3, 1828, Choctaw Agency 1824–1833, MSS.

[64] Thomas L. McKenney to William McClellan, November 25, 1828, Records of the Office of Indian Affairs, MSS.

[65] Greenwood LeFlore to David Folsom, November 23, 1828, Choctaw Agency 1824–1833, MSS.

[66] S. S. Hamilton to John Eaton, December 16, 1830, Records of the Office of Indian Affairs, MSS.

[67] William L. McClellan to Peter Porter, September 28, 1828, Carter, *Territorial Papers*, XX, 753.

wishful thinking of this period of "moderation" was coming to an end. Indian policy under President Jackson would shift to a more militant one demanding immediate removal, and by whatever means necessary.

CHAPTER SEVEN

THE END DRAWS NEAR

The West regarded Andrew Jackson's election in 1828 as assurance that a solution for the Indian land problem would be provided. A westerner was now in office—one who sympathized with his part of the country and understood the need for Indian displacement. "Old Hickory" would undoubtedly discontinue John Calhoun's Indian policy and introduce a new one that would force all eastern tribes to emigrate west without further delay. A policy of action would finally end the twelve-year stalemate.

Mississippi, especially, rejoiced at Jackson's election. With its estimated population of 23,400 Indians, it had almost as many Indians as all states of the North combined.[1] If the Indians could be relocated, Mississippi—because of its superior cotton lands—could become one of the greatest and richest states in the country. So eager was the government of Mississippi to change the existing Indian policy that it attempted to eliminate the Choctaw and Chickasaw nations even before Jackson was inaugurated. On February 4, 1829, the Mississippi House of Representatives passed an act "to extend legal process into that part of the state now occupied by the Chickasaw and Choctaw tribes of Indians."[2]

[1] *Niles' Register*, April 25, 1827, p. 132.
[2] A. Hutchinson, ed., *Code of Mississippi being an Analytical Compilation of*

The law simply enlarged all of the counties bordering on the Indian nations, thereby bringing the Indian lands within the jurisdiction of the state government.

To the disappointment of Mississippi, however, no immediate change was made in national policy regarding the Indians. Jackson, in his first inaugural address, amazed his extremist friends by simply stating: "It will be my sincere and constant desire to observe toward the Indian tribes within our limits a just and liberal policy, and to give . . . humane and considerable attention to their rights and their wants. . . ."[3]

Jackson further disturbed his western friends by allowing the leading spokesman of moderation, Thomas L. McKenney, to stay in office as head of the Bureau of Indian Affairs.[4] McKenney was retained, however, because of his comprehensive knowledge of American Indians—not because of his convictions. To counterbalance McKenney's moderate views, Jackson appointed as the new secretary of war handsome John Eaton,[5] a fellow-Tennessean and an extremist in Indian affairs. McKenney, seemingly oblivious of the change in administrations, continued to follow his policy of moderation. On February 17, 1829, he instructed Major Edward W. DuVal, the Indian agent at Little Rock, Arkansas Territory, "to allow no white person to enter and settle on Indian Lands, within your Agency, who shall not, on entering, present to you approved testimonials of his good character for industry, honesty, and sobriety; not then without the consent of the Indians."[6] McKenney also instructed DuVal to continue to check those who were allowed to enter the Indian lands to see that they did not become "lazy, dishonest, or intemperate" and thereby set a bad example for the Indians.

Even so, no one in the War Department or the Choctaw Na-

---

the *Public and General Statutes of the Territory and State, with Tabular References to the Local and Private Acts, from 1789 to 1848* (Jackson, 1848), p. 135.

[3] Richardson, II, 1001.

[4] *Arkansas Gazette*, May 6, 1829.

[5] Margaret L. O'Neill Eaton, "Autobiography" (original handwritten manuscript at Library of Congress, dictated in 1873), p. 30.

[6] *Arkansas Gazette*, August 26, 1829.

tion expected McKenney's Indian policy to be continued indefinitely. Once Jackson completed other pressing matters, he would surely inaugurate his own policy, even though it might deviate only slightly from existing policy. On the other hand, however, he might well call for the immediate removal of all Indians. One popular assumption was that the president would advise the Indians either to move west or to become citizens of the various states they then occupied.[7] Many felt that such clearly stated alternatives would force the Choctaw tribesmen to reconsider their negative stand. They might possibly migrate voluntarily to the tribe's western lands, to Texas, or to other trans-Mississippi areas. One enthusiastic citizen reporting a preposterous rumor advised Jackson that: "Should the U. States obtain a retrocession of the Province of Texas from the Mexican Republic, the Choctaw Indians will petition *en masse* for a tract of land on the head waters of the Brassos River."[8]

Finally, on July 30, 1829, the War Department made known in private communiques its new Indian policy. Secretary Eaton informed Chief Folsom that the Indians could not survive if they continued to live in an area surrounded by civilized whites, for the states were eager to extend their laws to include all Indians—an action that would have disastrous results on tribal culture. The communique suggested that Jackson, who was later accused of being a nationalist by historians and laymen alike, was willing to pursue a states' rights course if it would advance a desired nationalistic goal. Eaton told Folsom that the individual states had controlling influence over their internal problems, and that the federal government was powerless to interfere in the states' affairs, even to protect persons who might be injured by the administration of these affairs. It appeared, then, that the only way the Choctaws could avoid a confrontation with the State of Mississippi was by ending their foolish obstinacy and moving to the

[7] John Bond to Richard M. Johnson, July 6, 1829, Choctaw Emigration 1826–1833, MSS.
[8] T. Child to Andrew Jackson, July 11, 1829, *ibid.*

trans-Mississippi west.[9] At about this same time, Eaton also wrote to William Ward to tell him that all whites who spoke out against the new policy would be excluded from the Choctaw Nation under McKenney's "directive of earlier that year."[10]

The Choctaws read Eaton's communique and discussed the implications for their future. Their discussions were heated and reactions mixed. The old leaders, such as Mushulatubbee, who had fought the legalism and the logic of the white man in days long past and who had resisted removal on many previous occasions, were tired and worn out and willing to discuss a "fair" solution.[11] But the youth of the nation, led by David Folsom and Greenwood LeFlore, were still adamant; they proposed to hold fast to their Mississippi homeland even if it meant eventual extinction.[12] In the summer of 1829, the voice of youth was by far the stronger of the two in the Choctaw Nation, but a desire for a moderate compromise was growing. Thus, early in October the Choctaw chiefs, captains, and warriors met in a general council to decide upon a course of action.[13] In spite of their noise and fury, the young leaders were unable to command the majority they needed. The older generation quietly resumed command of the situation and refused to pass a resolution denouncing the new U.S. Indian policy. Folsom pushed through the council a resolution requesting the War Department to send another Choctaw exploring party to the West to reexamine carefully the Choctaw lands for four months.[14] If he could not win now possibly this request could delay the inevitable until a more successful course of action could be found.

While the Choctaws in Mississippi were still endeavoring to

[9] John Eaton to David Folsom, July 30, 1829, Records of the Office of Indian Affairs, MSS.

[10] John Eaton to William Ward, July 31, 1829, *ibid.*

[11] Mushulatubbee to John Eaton, September 28, 1829, Choctaw Emigration 1826–1833, MSS.

[12] David Folsom to William Ward, November 7, 1829, Choctaw Agency 1824–1833, MSS.

[13] William Ward to John Eaton, November 11, 1829, *ibid.*

[14] Choctaw Delegation to John Eaton, November 15, 1829, *ibid.*

close their ranks, President Jackson formally presented his new Indian policy in his first annual message to Congress, on December 8, 1829.[15] As the white man advanced, the president said, the Choctaws would surely be weakened, and eventually, would meet the fate of the Mohegan and the Narragansett Indians, who long ago lost their tribal lands and identity. The only way to prevent such a tragedy was for the United States to set aside an ample district west of the Mississippi River, to be guaranteed to the Indian tribes as long as they occupied the land. There they could be free of white men except for a few soldiers who would be stationed in the area to preserve peace on the frontier. Jackson hastened to add that removal to such a Utopia would be voluntary, but if the Indians remained east of the Mississippi River, they would be subject to the laws of the several states. In other words, they should submit and leave, or become "merged in the mass of our population."[16]

In Mississippi, the new policy was greeted with enthusiasm by most of the white residents. Celebrations broke out all over the state. Bonfires dotted the landscapes, set by happy frontier settlers anticipating an immediate solution of the Indian problem. The Mississippi legislature convened in regular session in January, 1830, and promptly took advantage of Jackson's "states' rights" invitation. On January 19 both houses passed an act extending the laws of the state of Mississippi "over the persons and property of the Indians resident within its limits."[17] All of the special "rights, privileges, immunities and franchises of the Indians" were repealed; henceforth, Mississippi law would govern all persons within the limits of the state. If the Indians did not comply with the new state law, they would be subject to a maximum fine of one thousand dollars and a maximum sentence of twelve months in prison.[18] The bill, which was to become a land-

[15] Richardson, II, 1021–22.

[16] John Bartlett Meserve, "The Indian Removal Message of President Jackson," *Chronicles of Oklahoma*, XIV, No. 1 (March, 1936), p. 65.

[17] *Journal of the House of Representatives of the State of Mississippi, at their 1830 Session. Held in the Town of Jackson* (Jackson, 1830), p. 86.

[18] *Southern Galaxy* (Natchez), February 11, 1830.

mark in American-Indian relations, was adopted with only one dissenting vote. The *Natchez*, one of the few Mississippi newspapers opposed to Jackson's Indian pronouncements, praised the lone dissenter for showing the rest of the country through his vote that not all Mississippians were opposed to coexistence. The editor warned his readers that "the day of retribution may come —a foreign and powerful enemy may visit on some future generations the despotism which the present has exercised over the hapless and helpless Indian."[19]

Despite the strong language of the new Mississippi law, the state government had no intention of carrying out its provisions. It was designed to frighten the Choctaws into taking advantage of Jackson's and Eaton's ideas on the need for migration to a new western home. In reality, it would have been almost impossible to enforce the law without bloodshed. If the Choctaw Nation had disobeyed it, it is likely that an Indian war would have ensued, and the almost-extinct Mississippi militia would then have been in dire straits both philosophically and militarily. Mississippi would have been forced to call on the federal government for immediate military aid at the same time that it was preaching states' rights. However, to maintain the image of firm resolution, the Mississippi government prepared to enforce the law. A resolution was passed in the state legislature to print three hundred copies of the act to distribute among the governors of Georgia, Alabama, and Tennessee; the Choctaw and Chickasaw agents; and the chiefs and captains of the two nations.[20] As another step, on February 6 a committee of three was appointed by the state Senate to supervise the surrender of Choctaw lands to the state;[21] and six days later the legislature passed a law allowing the state to appoint justices of the peace and constables to maintain order in the old Choctaw Nation.[22]

Whether Mississippi actually intended to enforce the act of

[19] *Natchez*, February 13, 1830.
[20] *Journal of the House of the State of Mississippi*, p. 86.
[21] *Ibid.*, p. 228.
[22] Hutchinson, p. 136.

January 19, its very passage touched off a heated controversy over the moral right of the state to force the Indians to leave.[23] Numerous newspaper editors, many of them in other states, questioned the justice of such a law.[24] Sporadic protests were heard throughout Mississippi, and a mass meeting was held in Natchez on March 17 to gain support for the deprived Indians.[25] Opposition to the law centered on the point that removal was unlawful as well as unjust. As William B. Melvin, a planter in Adams County, said, "it involves the faith of this whole nation, pledged in the most sacred manner by *treaty* with the Indians—it involves the principle of *right and of justice*, and the great political and moral effect it will produce on the Indians in all future time."[26]

These opponents of the legislation also advanced more specific arguments against removal: (1) The Choctaws were an independent nation, recognized as such by the United States in numerous treaties; (2) if they were removed immediately, they would be subject to exposure because of the lack of transportation facilities; (3) removal would break all the ties the Indians now had with the whites in Mississippi, which would destroy the present hope of civilizing them; (4) the Choctaws' western lands were inferior to those surrendered; (5) segregating the Indians in one place would lead to quarrels and fighting among themselves; (6) the proposed plan was entirely too visionary and nothing in the history of human affairs sustained it; (7) no guarantee of permanent possession of any new country could be given to the Choctaws, and they would hardly be settled before the expanding frontier would force them to move again and again; and (8) the Choctaws would not move voluntarily, and they could not be forced to leave under the existing American policy.[27] Furthermore, according to the editor of the *Natchez*, "All attempts to accomplish the removal of the Indians by bribery and

[23] *Natchez*, February 27 and April 3, 1830. *Southern Galaxy*, March 25, 1830.
[24] *Natchez*, February 27 and April 3, 1830. *Southern Galaxy*, January 7, 1830.
[25] *Natchez*, April 3, 1830, pp. 109–10.
[26] *Ibid.*, May 8, 1830, p. 143.
[27] *Ibid.*, February 20, 1830, pp. 61–62.

fraud, by intimidation or threats, . . . are acts of oppression and therefore entirely unjustifiable."[28]

Proponents of the act struck back, pointing out that two successive secretaries of war, Peter Porter of New York and John Eaton of Tennessee, favored the policy of removal by any means,[29] and that even Indian bureau chief Thomas L. McKenney continually favored removal.[30] They also listed several reasons why a complete removal was urgently necessary: (1) Mississippi needed more land to attract immigrants from the East; (2) the Choctaws imposed a heavy financial burden on the state because they did not pay taxes; (3) the Choctaws harbored runaway slaves and white criminals in the nation; (4) they were hunters, not farmers, and hence not devoted to cultivating their lands; (5) they were inferior human beings, incapable of being civilized, and Mississippi must therefore remove them as one removes a cancer; and (6) the Choctaw lands were all within the state's boundaries and consequently belonged to Mississippi.[31]

Vicious implications were contained in many of these arguments for removal. The *Natchez* carried one article in which the writer advocated more land for an expanding white population and explained simply that "we must have it in some way."[32] Asserting that the principal activities of the Choctaws were loafing and drinking, this writer concluded: "Shew [sic] me an Indian in the street and I could buy the bones of all his forefathers . . . for a pint of whiskey . . . I look upon the introduction of whiskey as a great point: It has already done a great deal in facilitating the acquisition of Indian lands all over the United States."[33] On another occasion, the *Natchez* carried a particularly violent attack on the Indians written by "A Patriot." He

[28] *Ibid.*, February 13, 1830, p. 53.
[29] John Eaton to John Bell, February 13, 1830, Records of the Office of Indian Affairs, MSS; *Southern Galaxy*, March 11, 1830.
[30] Thomas L. McKenney to James L. McDonald, February 9, 1830, Records of the Office of Indian Affairs, MSS.
[31] *Natchez*, February 13 and February 20, 1830.
[32] *Ibid.*, February 13, 1830.
[33] *Ibid.*

maintained that all Indians were inferior to white people, that they had no basic religious beliefs, and that they could not be educated. Referring to the assertion that, given an equal opportunity, an Indian could rise as high as a white man, he observed: "I know an Indian will be an Indian because we have had plenty of Indians in Natchez, and can you show me one who has been civilized by being brought among us?"[34]

The controversy in Mississippi spread across the country during the spring of 1830 as people in every section and in all walks of life discussed the arguments for and against the new removal policy. It was generally agreed that the Choctaws had greatly benefited from education in the past. The American Board of Commissioners for Foreign Missions reported that education and religion had permeated every district of the Choctaw Nation, and it predicted that because of the achieved level of education, the Indians would not be exterminated either by removal or by American citizenship.[35] Ben Johnson, a Kentuckian and a captain in the United States Army—a man who had known the Choctaws for fifteen years—observed that "they have been gradually and pretty generally improving in the art of cultivation of the earth. They also imbibed a disposition for more regular government, . . . there is an unusual impulse . . . for religion."[36] Stephen Ward, the subagent in the Choctaw Nation, also found that amazing changes had taken place among the Indians since formal education had been introduced. Once savages, the Choctaws were becoming civilized persons, he said, who now realized the need to own individual portions of land and teach their children the rudiments of formal education.[37]

In addition to the consensus favoring education for the Indians, there was an increasing agreement throughout the United States that, whether it was just or not, the Indians would have

[34] *Ibid.,* February 20, 1830.
[35] "Choctaw Indians," *Presbyterian Mission Tract,* 1831 (in the library of E. DeGolyer, Dallas, Texas, Microfilm copy at North Texas State College), pp. 7-8.
[36] *Niles' Register,* July 3, 1830, p. 345.
[37] *Ibid.*

to move west to avoid extinction. The reasons for removal varied from the general arguments already mentioned to those that took on a more sectional flavor.

For example, northern liberals charged that the existing situation was fostered by governmental neglect of the Indians' culture and its needs, and that the Indians were now being forced to leave their ancestral homelands simply because the whites desired the land.[38] Southerners ridiculed this contention, retorting that when Indians roamed the northeast the northerners had been just as eager to rid themselves of the problem as were the southerners of 1830. A long string of bloody conflicts with northern Indians in the seventeenth and eighteenth centuries testified to that fact. And the southerners also charged northern liberals with jealousy toward growing southern strength. The Charleston, South Carolina, *Southern Patriot* editorialized that "one of the reasons why certain people of the North are so strongly opposed to the Indian emigration . . . is that it will give the Southern and Southwestern States . . . an influence in the councils of the Nation which they do not now possess, while their territory is inhabited by savages. . . ."[39] There was agreement between many northerners and southerners, however, in the feeling that President Jackson was playing politics when he introduced his new Indian policy in December of 1829. They argued that the president was pacifying the people of Arkansas Territory, as well as those of Mississippi and other states with Indian problems, because he was anxious to secure their support against South Carolina, which was beginning to raise the nullification issue over the changing tariff policy of the federal government.[40]

Even before the State of Mississippi attempted, with its act of January 19, to legislate the Choctaw Nation out of existence, the proponents of Jackson's removal policy were busy in the U.S. Congress, probing for the weaknesses of their opposition. On

[38] Alfred Balch to Andrew Jackson, January 8, 1830, Andrew Jackson MSS.

[39] *Southern Patriot* (Charleston, South Carolina), May 21, 1830.

[40] No where in the Jackson papers did I find any justification for this proposal. Also, the major Calhoun biographies, by Charles Wiltse and Margaret Coit, do not support this oft-repeated charge.

January 14, the Senate passed a resolution calling upon the government to survey its western lands and "parcel out among the Creek, Cherokee, Choctaw, and Chickasaw tribes of Indians, so much of the territory . . . as may be necessary for the permanent residence of each of these tribes."[41] Then, less than two weeks later, another Senate resolution, adopted by the narrow margin of nineteen to eighteen, asked the secretary of war to furnish the Senate with a comprehensive report on the progress of education among the Indians during the past eight years.[42] Resistance to this latter resolution came from the opponents of Indian removal who interpreted the document as an attempt to prove that education was useless and that removal west was the only answer. The two resolutions were important mainly because they represented an effort by the advocates of removal to test the strength of their senatorial opposition before a general removal treaty was proposed. The close vote on the January 25 resolution forced the removal advocates in the Senate to consider carefully their next move. The slightest mistake might cost them one or two votes and victory. They decided, thinking it a safe move, to introduce a third resolution calling upon Congress to clear white settlers off western lands that might be set aside for Indians, thus providing a place where displaced Indians could be sent in the future. Such action would avoid a repetition of the embarrassing situation of 1820 when the Treaty of Doak's Stand ceded lands occupied by whites to the Choctaws.[43] However, to the amazement of the Jackson forces, this resolution of February 10 was defeated by a vote of twenty-seven to thirteen.[44] The defeat angered the president and he became more than ever determined to have his way.

During the remainder of February and March, Jackson's forces in the Senate kept the Indian problem out of official discussions

41 *Niles' Register*, January 23, 1830, p. 372.
42 *Ibid.*, p. 389.
43 *Ibid.*, p. 419.
44 *Ibid.*, p. 430.

and, instead, tried to build up public support for their cause and sway uncommitted colleagues. Posing as the preservers of Indian culture, they referred to the opposition as heartless northerners, who cared nothing for Indian welfare and whose overriding desire was to keep the South disunited. By early April, they were ready for another test. On April 6, Senator Hugh L. White of Tennessee moved that the Senate resolve itself into a committee of the whole to discuss a bill to move the Indians to the West.[45] The motion carried, and for the next twenty days the battle was joined in one of the bitterest congressional debates of that era.[46] The debates focused on two demands of the opposition forces, led by Senator Theodore Frelinghuysen of New Jersey. On April 7, the senator presented his case in an eloquent and impassioned plea for justice. He requested the passage of two important resolutions: one would perpetually guarantee Indian sovereignty over all lands they then possessed; the other would provide that Indian lands could be acquired only by a treaty negotiated and accepted by both sides.[47] The debate that followed was heated and it lasted for several days, but the removal forces had done their work well. On April 10 they defeated the two Frelinghuysen resolutions by votes of twenty-seven to twenty and twenty-eight to nineteen, respectively.[48] To the jubilant Jacksonians, the road to victory was now open. That same day they offered a bill "to provide for an exchange of . . . lands with the Indians residing in any of the states or territories, and for their removal west of the river Mississippi."[49] All the opponents could do was to argue their case again and watch help-

[45] *Ibid.*, April 10, 1830, p. 133.
[46] Thomas H. Benton, *Thirty Years View; or, A History of the Workings of the American Government for Thirty Years from 1820 to 1850; Chiefly taken from the Congress Debates, the Private Papers of General Jackson and the Speeches of Ex-Senator Benton with his actual view of Men and Affairs: with Historical Notes and Illustrations, and some notices of eminent deceased contemporaries: By a Senator of Thirty Years* (New York, 1889), I, 164.
[47] *Niles' Register*, April 10, 1830, p. 133.
[48] *Ibid.*, p. 174.
[49] *Ibid.*, pp. 178–80.

lessly as the bill passed by a vote of twenty-eight to nineteen. It was then sent to the House of Representatives for concurrence or rejection.

Debate in the House was as intense as it had been in the Senate. Congressman William R. Storrs of New York introduced the two Frelinghuysen arguments of April 7 and spoke long and earnestly against the Jackson measure.[50] The forces for and against the removal bill were divided into two camps of almost equal strength. Both sides claimed the necessary votes to ensure victory for their cause. Once again the influence of Jackson in Democratic circles made the difference. With only minor changes, the Senate version of the bill was accepted by the House on May 29, passing by the slender margin of 102–97.[51] The two houses ironed out their differences during June, and an elated Jackson signed the law into existence on June 30. The fate of the Choctaw Indians was, for all intents and purposes, sealed: remove or become American citizens.

The Mississippi act of January 19 and the debate in Congress frightened the Choctaws into action. In February, they deposed Greenwood LeFlore for "tyrannical and cruel conduct,"[52] replacing him with the old chief Mushulatubbee who was quite moderate on the question of removal. David Folsom, fearing the same fate as LeFlore, immediately adopted a more moderate stand. Writing to Senator Robert M. Johnson of Arkansas, Folsom restated his offer to lead an exploring party west, and suggested that, in order to stay in office, he might even falsify his report to his tribesmen: "I hope to cause the Choctaws, . . . to come and settle on some particular place . . . . And the description of the country that I would bring to these people here, they would take my word for the truth. —I shall include a few of the educated Choctaw to go with me. . . ."[53]

[50] *Ibid.*, p. 243.
[51] *Ibid.*, p. 267.
[52] Thomas L. McKenney to John Eaton, February 25, 1830, Records of the Office of Indian Affairs, MSS.
[53] David Folsom to R. M. Johnson, February 7, 1830, Choctaw Emigration 1826–1833, MSS.

In March, all the Choctaw leaders assembled for a council meeting to decide upon a united course of action against the threat from Mississippi and the federal government.[54] While they met, the crafty Greenwood LeFlore, although deposed, opened separate negotiations with the head of the Indian bureau, Thomas McKenney. Knowing that the confused chiefs would not be able to agree unanimously on anything at the council, LeFlore had decided to work out an equitable settlement with the Indian bureau and then present it to the council for ratification. If successful, he reasoned, he would emerge a Choctaw hero and undoubtedly be restored to the rank of chief. By April 7, the treaty was ready and was immediately dispatched to Mushulatubbee for his approval. For every man and woman with a child it provided one section (640 acres) of Choctaw Mississippi land to sell for cash to the state, and for every young man it allowed one-half section for the same purpose. In addition to whatever cash he received from the sale of land, each captain would be given a suit of clothes, a broad sword, and fifty dollars annually for four years. Every tribesman would receive a good rifle with plenty of rifle powder and lead, an axe, a hoe, a plough, a blanket, and a brass kettle. Each woman would receive a spinning wheel and a loom. Furthermore, all of the Indians' possessions would be moved without charge to the new lands, and the government would feed and clothe the migrants for twelve months after they left Mississippi. When the proposed treaty failed to win Mushulatubbee's approval, LeFlore quickly added another stipulation: the United States would defend the emigrants with soldiers and probably give the nation fifty thousand dollars annually forever.[55] After considering the proposals for two days, Mushulatubbee agreed to present them to the Choctaw council. Meanwhile, LeFlore, playing fully the role of double agent, had also sent a copy of the treaty to Governor Garrard C.

[54] *Southern Galaxy*, March 25, 1830.
[55] Greenwood LeFlore to Mushulatubbee, April 7, 1830, Choctaw Agency 1824–1833, MSS.

Brandon of Mississippi, reassuring the state that he was endeavoring to comply with the Mississippi law of January 19.[56]

On April 8, LeFlore entered the Choctaw council and defended his proposed treaty. With all the eloquence and fervor that made him an electric and forceful personality, he offered a moderate way out of the present dilemma. With no other serious alternatives to consider, his confused and saddened colleagues praised his suggested treaty and unanimously elected him chief of the northwestern district.[57] On the morning of April 9, the Choctaw chiefs, captains, and warriors—thankful that someone was able to bring order out of chaos—all came forward, resigned their several offices, and unanimously elected Greenwood LeFlore chief of the entire nation.[58] It was an honor never bestowed on a Choctaw chief, even Pushmataha. Once LeFlore was in charge of the nation, he immediately had his proposed treaty drafted and delivered to a special messenger, Major David W. Haley, who was to convey it to the president in Washington. The council was then adjourned, and for two days the tribesmen celebrated the election of LeFlore as the savior of his people. The new chief had no intention of emigrating himself, however, for at this very time he was proposing a bribe to the War Department. If the Department would allow him to remain in Mississippi and give him enough land to maintain himself as a planter, LeFlore would see to it that the Choctaw Indians left the state. The government had earlier opened the door to such a possibility when McKenney wrote: "It is the full intention of the government to do great things for you . . . by appointing you to office in the government of the Indian Territory; or if you prefer to give you handsome reservations here [Mississippi]."[59] The treaty that LeFlore had sent to Washington was not to be the answer to the perplexing Indian removal problem, but it did show the president

[56] Greenwood LeFlore to Governor Brandon, April 7, 1830, Governor's Documents (Series E), MSS.

[57] *Southern Galaxy*, April 8, 1830.

[58] *Ibid.*

[59] Thomas L. McKenney to Greenwood LeFlore, January 15, 1828, Records of the Office of Indian Affairs, MSS.

for the first time that many Choctaws considered their exodus from Mississippi inevitable.[60] This knowledge must have pleased President Jackson as much as did the congressional act he signed on June 30, 1830.

---

[60] James L. McDonald to Thomas L. McKenney, March 22, 1830, Choctaw Agency 1824–1833, MSS.

CHAPTER EIGHT

THE TREATY OF
DANCING RABBIT CREEK

Early in May, 1830, LeFlore's treaty was delivered to Jackson in Washington. The president was at first amazed that the Choctaws would consent to leave their lands without offering some sort of resistance. However, upon reading the treaty more carefully, he realized that the Choctaws were actually sharp businessmen who were setting a high price on their acquiescence to the desires of the United States government.[1] Even *Niles' Register*, a magazine usually friendly to the Indians, agreed with Jackson that the price was unreasonable. The government would be paying approximately fifty million dollars "to induce some forty thousand Indians to move to the new country. The object is desirable but there is such a thing as paying too dear for it."[2]

On May 6, Jackson sent the Choctaw treaty to the Senate with the recommendation that it be rejected. Because such a treaty could easily become a model to be used in all future negotiations for Indian lands, the terms should be more advantageous to the United States; otherwise, similar concessions to other eastern tribes would bankrupt the government.[3] The Senate rejected the treaty.

[1] Richardson, II, 1041.
[2] *Niles' Register*, September 4, 1830, p. 19.
[3] Richardson, II, 1042.

For the Choctaws, the rejection of their terms was to be of less significance than the fact that they had compromised to the point of actually proposing withdrawal. Secretary of War Eaton saw in the Choctaw action a resignation to the inevitable and a willingness to sign virtually any treaty suggested. The Indian demands for exploring parties and presents were no longer enforceable. In fact, Eaton wrote them on July 25 that they could not explore western lands nor stall for time in any other way. "It is high time there should be an end to the argument. . . ."[4]

Meanwhile, the president, who had also viewed LeFlore's treaty as evidence of weakness, was convinced that the time had come to negotiate a final removal treaty. Furthermore, he was now backed by congressional sanction given in the removal act of June 30. He decided to take advantage of his summer vacation in Franklin, Tennessee, to talk with the Choctaw leaders while he was there.[5] Secretary Eaton was instructed to inform the Choctaw chiefs of the president's desire and to "invite" them to Franklin during August to discuss preliminary arrangements for a final treaty.[6]

The Choctaws were disturbed by the president's disapproval of their recent proposal. In this frame of mind, they doubted the wisdom of journeying to Tennessee to negotiate a less desirable treaty. Debate over the subject continued through June and July, with most of the tribe voicing its opposition to the Franklin meeting. On August 10, LeFlore advised Eaton that the warriors were "violently opposed to any of the officers going to meet you at Franklin for the purpose of making a treaty—the lives of the chiefs and head men of the nation would be in great danger if they propose of selling the country."[7]

[4] John Eaton to Choctaw Indians, July 24, 1830, Choctaw Agency Field Papers 1830–1833, Letters Received, MSS, Records of the Bureau of Indian Affairs, National Archives.

[5] Andrew Jackson to John Eaton (no date), Choctaw Miscellany 1830–1833, MSS, Bureau of Indian Affairs, National Archives.

[6] John Eaton to Head Men of Choctaw Nation, June 1, 1830, Records of the Office of Indian Affairs, MSS.

[7] Greenwood LeFlore to John Eaton, August 10, 1830, Choctaw Agency 1824–1833, Letters Received, MSS.

So that treaty discussion might not become altogether impossible, however, LeFlore quickly added, "we should be very happy to see you and converse with you face to face, but still we cannot go, as the nation is opposed to our going." And a few days later the Choctaw chiefs expanded on LeFlore's offer by writing to Jackson: "We wish our father the President would send us a talk by some good men, who will give us time to call a full council, and who will explain to us the views of the government on the subject of the removal of our people west of the Mississippi."[8] The chiefs must have realized that they were following an unpopular course of action by opening the way for further talks, for their people were almost unanimous in opposing another treaty. Perhaps the chiefs saw, more clearly than their tribesmen, the futility of further resistance. Regardless of motive, the offer of the chiefs to negotiate was the key to eventual Choctaw removal, for it made possible all that followed.

Jackson and Eaton were angered by the Indians' refusal to negotiate at Franklin; both had been preparing for this meeting during a good part of their vacation there.[9] Jackson blamed Major David W. Haley for poisoning LeFlore's mind against the meeting[10] (although the president was never able to substantiate the charge). Haley had written to Jackson saying that he agreed with LeFlore, who feared that the Indians would suspect treachery if the chiefs went to Jackson's home for secret talks before a general treaty was negotiated. Accordingly, Haley and LeFlore proposed a general meeting some time in September after the year's harvest had been stored for the winter.[11] This recommendation and others did not convince the president; he concluded that Haley had duped the Choctaws for his personal gain. Writing to his close friend Major William B. Lewis, Jackson attacked Haley as "the tool of LeFlore," who expected that his recom-

[8] Choctaw chiefs to Andrew Jackson, August 16, 1830, *ibid.*
[9] John Eaton to Major John Donley, August 4, 1830, Andrew Jackson MSS.
[10] David W. Haley to Andrew Jackson, July 24, 1830, Choctaw Emigration 1826–1833, Letters Received, MSS, Records of the Bureau of Indian Affairs, National Archives.
[11] *Ibid.*

mendations would result in commissioners entering the nation, at which time Haley "would become the contractor for their supplies, and . . . would be so anxious to treat that he would yield to any terms demanded of us."[12]

Despite his loss of temper, Jackson realized that the refusal of the Choctaws to negotiate outside of their nation did not eliminate the possibility of obtaining a much more favorable treaty than the one proposed in April by LeFlore. Suppressing his anger, he wrote LeFlore a friendly letter accepting the Choctaws' offer to talk and suggesting that commissioners from both sides meet in the nation some time in September. Jackson compared the Choctaws' decision to move west to the emigration from Europe of the American settlers:

> The attachment you feel for the soil which encompasses the bones of your ancestors is well known. Our forefathers had the same feeling when a long time ago, to obtain happiness, they left their lands beyond the great waters, and sought a new and quiet home in those distant and unexplored regions. If they had not done so, where would have been their children? And where the prosperity they now enjoy? The old world would scarcely have afforded support for a people who, by the change their fathers made, have become prosperous and happy. In future time, so will it be with your children.[13]

The president appointed Secretary of War Eaton and John Coffee to represent the United States at the forthcoming meeting. Both of these close personal friends were already with Jackson in Franklin discussing that very subject.[14] They immediately undertook the task of selecting a treaty site and planning for the many other details associated with the meeting.

---

12 Andrew Jackson to William B. Lewis, August 25, 1830, Bassett, IV, 117.

13 Andrew Jackson to Greenwood LeFlore, August 23, 1830, Unsigned Journal of Commrs. Eaton and Coffee, September 15–17, 1830, Ratified Treaty File No. 160, Choctaw, Dancing Rabbit Creek, September 27, 1830, MSS, Records of the Bureau of Indian Affairs, National Archives.

14 *Papers relating to the Claims of the Choctaw Nation Against the United States, arising under the Treaty of 1830* (Washington, D.C., 1855), p. 50.

At the suggestion of the Choctaw chiefs,[15] Secretary Eaton chose for the meeting a location in Noxubee County between the two prongs of Dancing Rabbit Creek.[16] Once the place was determined, the commissioners informed the Choctaws that they would meet them on September 15, 1830.

The first two weeks of September were busy ones for Eaton and Coffee as they attacked the mammoth problem of arranging for food and other supplies, transportation, and living quarters for the estimated five to six thousand Choctaws who would be gathering in the wilderness. Eaton decided to enlist the help of the United States Army. According to his plan, the Indians would be divided into companies of one hundred each as they entered the treaty ground. Each company would be put under the command of an army captain who would draw and distribute the rations: one and one-half pounds of beef and a pint of corn daily for each Indian in addition to a quart of salt for each company.[17] By this plan, Eaton hoped to eliminate the possibility of waste and dishonesty.

By mid-September the Indians began flocking to the treaty ground, followed by the worst elements of white society. Gamblers, saloonkeepers, frontier rowdies, and prostitutes, all interested in separating the Indians from their meager possessions, established themselves on one side of the treaty ground and plied their trade under the assumed protection of the United States government.[18] An army captain wrote to his wife: "I never saw so many kinds of gambling as was going on when the treaty was being negotiated. Faro tables were numerous and the whites and Indians were betting promiscuously. . . . Two noted desperadoes, Red-headed Bill and Black-headed McGrews were there. . . ."[19]

Significantly, Eaton and Coffee ordered all missionaries away

[15] H. S. Halbert, "The Story of the Treaty of Dancing Rabbit," *Publications of the Mississippi Historical Society*, VI (1902), p. 374.
[16] *Ibid.*, p. 373.
[17] John Eaton and John Coffee to War Department, September 16, 1830, Unsigned Journal, Dancing Rabbit Creek, MSS, pp. 36–37.
[18] Halbert, "Treaty of Dancing Rabbit," p. 377.
[19] *Ibid.*

from the treaty ground on September 15 on the pretext that the presence of missionaries would be "improper," for the commissioners and Indians were negotiating a treaty—not holding divine services.[20] Eaton's reasoning fooled no one, for it was well known in Mississippi that the commissioners feared the political influence of the Protestant missionaries, not their preaching. The missionaries complained bitterly about the decision,[21] but Eaton sarcastically answered:

> Much as we commend the laudable and praiseworthy vocation in which you are engaged . . . we cannot reason ourselves to the belief that the present is a proper time, place or occasion, for such undertakings . . . . The few days assigned for our object, which we feel to be of higher importance than any act of a temperal [sic] kind that ever has occupied their attention, surely cannot impede the benevolent march of mind and morals, that lies before you.[22]

He ended the letter by again informing the missionaries that they must leave the treaty ground, which they did two days later.[23]

At noon on Saturday, September 18, amidst a carnival atmosphere, the commissioners formally opened the treaty negotiations with the almost six thousand Indians who had gathered on the creek. John Coffee, addressing the Indians in a paternal manner, did not praise or curse them as Jackson had done at Doak's Stand, but told them what they must do to survive. It was evident from his talk that the government was now confident that the Choctaws would offer little or no resistance. Coffee told them that talking, delaying, or negotiating was needless, that the Choctaws were merely asked to decide whether to sign a treaty with the United States. If the Indians refused to negotiate, he said then,

[20] John Eaton and John Coffee to War Department, September 15, 1830, Unsigned Journal, Dancing Rabbit Creek, MSS, p. 37. Following Eaton's line of thought, one would have to assume that white prostitutes and saloonkeepers were "proper" elements of society to be present at a treaty negotiation.
[21] Cyrus Kingsbury to John Eaton and John Coffee, September 16, 1830, ibid., pp. 37–38.
[22] John Eaton to Cyrus Kingsbury, September 18, 1830, ibid., pp. 39–40.
[23] Ibid., p. 43.

"let us be done with the subject and disperse to our homes."[24] He and the American agents could be advised on Monday morning of the Indians' readiness or refusal to conclude a formal treaty.[25]

At a council meeting on Sunday the Choctaw chiefs and captains decided to entrust the negotiations to a commission of twenty representatives chosen from all of the Choctaw districts. LeFlore rejected the proposal, causing a quarrel that almost split the Indian ranks.[26] He complained of the distribution on the commission, arguing that as main chief he should control the selection of all the commission members. When the quarrel verged on violence, Eaton and Coffee intervened and urged a compromise. The suggestion was accepted, and LeFlore was allowed to select ten of the twenty commissioners.[27]

Monday passed without any report to the government agents, but on Tuesday the chiefs and captains informed the secretary of war that they were ready to listen to any proposals offered by President Jackson. They did not intimate, however, that they would accept the suggestions.[28] The next day, Eaton and Coffee presented to the Choctaw commission a proposed treaty that they asserted would be both acceptable to the United States and fair to the Indians. The treaty called upon the Choctaws to evacuate all of their Mississippi lands and emigrate en masse to the Choctaw lands retained by the Treaty of 1825. In return the Choctaws would receive money, farm and household equipment, subsistence for a full year, and pay for the improvements they had made to the land in Mississippi.[29] Chiefs and captains were offered bribes as a further inducement to accept the treaty:[30]

24 John Coffee to Choctaw Indians, September 18, 1830, *ibid.*, pp. 45–46.
25 *Ibid.*, p. 48.
26 John Eaton and John Coffee to War Department, September 19, 1830, *ibid.*, p. 49.
27 *Ibid.*
28 Choctaw chiefs to John Eaton and John Coffee, September 21, 1830, *ibid.*, p. 49.
29 John Eaton and John Coffee to Choctaw Indians, September 22, 1830, *ibid.*, p. 50.
30 *Ibid.*

each chief would receive four extra sections of land either in Mississippi or in Indian Territory; each captain would receive one extra section; each subcaptain, and principal man, would receive one-half section. Furthermore, the commissioners stipulated, each leader who took advantage of this offer would be allowed to choose the exact location of his new land.

Eaton and Coffee retired from the treaty ground to allow the Choctaws time to discuss the terms of the recommended treaty. Both men were quite confident that the Indians would be eager to accept their "generous" offer and conclude a treaty the next day, but the commissioners underestimated the resistance of the Choctaws. The next morning, the Indian commission informed the startled federal negotiators that they had voted almost unanimously to reject the president's offer. Two reasons were given:[31] first, the Indians wanted a perpetual guarantee that the United States would never try to possess the Choctaws' new home in the West;[32] second, they were dissatisfied with the lands that were offered them in Indian Territory. As Peter Pitchlynn, chairman of the Choctaw commission, said, "there was great surprise at being informed they could not retain the lands, which, by the treaty of 1820, had been secured to them. We have concluded not to treat for a sale of our lands."[33]

Jackson's commissioners were almost dumbfounded by the Choctaw unanimity against the treaty. Coffee immediately arose and berated the Indians, but Eaton realized that despite the commissioners' bungling of the negotiations, the United States could not possibly lose in the end. The Choctaws were bluffing; they knew very well that they had to leave Mississippi to survive. Unconcerned and unruffled, Eaton informed the chiefs that their bluff would not work;[34] either they must move west or consent to be governed by Mississippi law. If they resisted, the armed might of America would completely destroy them in a few weeks.

[31] Choctaw chiefs to John Coffee and John Eaton, September 23, 1830, *ibid.*, p. 51.
[32] *Ibid.*
[33] *Ibid.*
[34] John Eaton to Choctaw Chiefs, September 23, 1830, *ibid.*, p. 53.

He was weary of their procrastinations, he said, and he and Coffee were quitting the treaty grounds and leaving next day for Washington.[35] Choctaw resistance crumbled. The Indian commissioners begged Eaton to stay a few days longer to conclude a treaty. Probably for the first time, the majority of the nation fully realized that a westward trek was inevitable.

On September 26, the Choctaw and American commissioners met for the last session of the treaty negotiations. The differences between the two sides were discussed and a compromise was effected:[36] the Choctaws secured a perpetual guarantee of their new home, but failed to get all the land in the West that had been ceded to the nation in the Treaty of Doak's Stand.[37] The new treaty stipulated that the Choctaw Nation would be within the following boundaries: "Beginning near Fort Smith, where the Arkansas boundary crosses the Arkansas River; running thence to the source of the Canadian fork, if in the limits of the U. S., or to those limits; thence due South to Red River, and down Red River and to the W. boundary of the territory of Arkansas; thence N. along that line to the beginning."[38] In return for their western lands, now reduced in acreage, the Choctaws must cede to the United States all of their remaining 10,423,130 acres of land east of the Mississippi River.[39]

The balance of the twenty-two articles of the treaty pertained to four general areas.[40] The first group related to the actual removal itself, providing that once each year for three years, a group made up of approximately one-third of the tribe would be transported to Indian Territory so that by the end of 1833 all emigrants would have been removed. The government of the United States promised to underwrite the moving of the Indians

[35] *Ibid.*
[36] John Eaton and John Coffee to War Department, September 26, 1830, *ibid.*, p. 54.
[37] The remainder of their lands eventually went to the Chickasaw Indians.
[38] Charles C. Royce, comp., "Indian Land Cessions in the United States," *U.S. Bureau of American Ethnology Eighteenth Annual Report* (1896–97), Pt. 2 (1902), p. 726.
[39] *Ibid.*
[40] For the full text of the Treaty of Dancing Rabbit Creek, see app. B.

and all their possessions, including livestock; to furnish all necessary transportation facilities and supplies; and to provide full subsistence for twelve months after arrival in Indian Territory.

The second group of articles concerned federal protection of the Indians in their new home. The United States would guarantee domestic tranquility in the nation and protection from foreign invasion. No whites, especially traders, would be allowed to enter the nation without the consent of the Choctaw government, except for an Indian agent who would be appointed by the president every four years. The treaty also promised to ban all alcoholic beverages from the nation.

The third category listed the payments promised by the United States to the Choctaws: (1) continuation of all annuities in force before the Treaty of Dancing Rabbit Creek; (2) an annuity of $20,000 per year for twenty years; (3) payment by the United States of all costs incurred in educating forty Choctaw children a year for twenty years; (4) an annual payment of $2,500 to be used to employ three teachers for Choctaw schools; (5) a donation of $10,000 to erect a centrally located council house in the nation, a church, and schools; and (6) a gift, after removal, of 2,100 blankets, 1,000 axes, 400 looms, and enough rifles, ammunition, hoes, and other personal articles for all.

The fourth and most important group of articles concerned land gifts to the Choctaw chiefs and land reservations for those members of the tribe who wished to remain in Mississippi. Each chief was to receive four sections of land, plus $250 annually as long as he remained in office. The captains, subcaptains, and principal men were to receive lesser amounts of land without gifts of money. ARTICLE 14, a significant part of the treaty, stipulated that if any Choctaw families or individuals desired to remain in Mississippi they might do so by registering with the Indian agent within six months after ratification of the treaty. Each adult male and female who registered was entitled to 640 acres of land; each child over ten who was living with a family was to receive 320 acres; each child under ten living with a family, 160 acres. If an Indian failed to register within six months, or if he went to Indian Territory and then returned, he was forever barred from registering under ARTICLE 14.

On September 27, 1830, the Treaty of Dancing Rabbit Creek, one of the major Indian treaties in American history, was signed.[41] It symbolized the evolution of the policy toward Indians from Thomas Jefferson's desire to move all eastern Indians across the Mississippi River, through John C. Calhoun's proposal for educating the Indians to accept the need for removal, to Andrew Jackson's policy of forcing their removal.

Once the treaty had been signed and the commissioners had returned to Washington, conflicting rumors arose concerning the Choctaw reaction to the agreement.[42] Many reports stated that the Choctaws had been forced by American soldiers to sign against their will. Colonel George S. Gaines, who had been at the treaty site with Eaton and Coffee, wrote that the document was despised by most of the Indians.[43] It was also reported that a subchief named Little Leader had been indignant with the proposed treaty and had threatened to kill any chief who affixed his signature.[44] Other rumors spread the story that two-thirds of the Choctaws so disliked Eaton's offer that they went home before the treaty was concluded, later contending that it was signed by a few traitors and was not binding on the nation.[45] Robert H. Grant, a trader in the Choctaw Nation, wrote Peter Pitchlynn to this effect. Many of the Choctaws had left the treaty ground, he said. "There was a strong, and I believe universal feeling, in opposition to the sale of any portion of their remaining country in Mississippi."[46]

[41] Signing of Treaty of Dancing Rabbit Creek, September 27, 1830, Unsigned Journal, Dancing Rabbit Creek, MSS, p. 57.

[42] Anthony D. Dillard, "The Treaty of Dancing Rabbit Creek Between the United States and the Choctaw Indians in 1830," *Alabama Historical Society, Transactions 1898–1899*, III (1899), 101–105.

[43] *Ibid.*

[44] Halbert, "Treaty of Dancing Rabbit," p. 385.

[45] January 8, 1838, Choctaw Claims Journal of Commissioners Murray & Vroom. Also General Deposition and a list of the Heads of Families Claiming Land under the 14th Article of the Treaty of 1830, MSS, p. 152.

[46] *Papers Relating to the Claims of the Choctaw Nation*, p. 51.

Contrary to these stories, the Choctaw interpreter, M. Mackey, wrote that he had heard nothing in the nation to substantiate the Choctaws' alleged opposition and that most of the Indians liked the treaty, feeling that it was as fair as any they had expected to receive from the commissioners. He added that the terms were as fair as any the Choctaws had ever received from the government during the forty-five years that he had been associated with the Choctaw Indians.[47] Many others in the nation held similar views.[48] The *Arkansas Gazette* paraphrased an editorial by Greenwood LeFlore which first appeared in the Cherokee *Phoenix*: "LeFlore repels the charge, that bribery was resorted to for the removal of this people, and with respect to himself; *good faith* to them prompted the course he chose, as the only effectual way of preserving an ignorant and disbanded people from the worst of miseries."[49]

A rumor that the Choctaws might take up arms against the federal government even frightened the secretary of war[50] into sending a company of cavalry into the nation to put down any attempted uprising. The cavalry rode throughout the entire nation, but failed to detect any organized resistance to the new treaty.[51] Eaton quickly instructed William Ward to release the troops for duty elsewhere on the frontier.[52]

When the American commissioners returned to Washington, the Treaty of Dancing Rabbit Creek was forwarded to the United States Senate for ratification. Eaton, in his annual report to Congress, noted that "We sought through persuasion only, to satisfy them that their situation called for serious reflection. . . .

[47] M. Mackey to William Ward, December 8, 1830, Choctaw Agency 1824–1833, Letters Received, MSS.
[48] *Ibid.* William Ward to Office of Indian Affairs, December 13, 1830, Office of Indian Affairs, Registers of Letters Received 1824–1833, MSS.
[49] *Arkansas Gazette*, April 27, 1831.
[50] John Eaton to Andrew Jackson, December 1, 1830, Letters to the President of the United States 1800–1840, MSS.
[51] Greenwood LeFlore to Office of Indian Affairs, November 19, 1830, Office of Indian Affairs, Registers of Letters Received 1824–1833, MSS.
[52] William Ward to Office of Indian Affairs, December 2, 1830, *ibid.*

No secret meetings were held, no bribes were offered, no promises made."[53] Early in February of 1831, the treaty was brought before the Senate;[54] on February 25, by a vote of thirty-five to twelve, it was ratified.[55] After more than thirty years of negotiations, the Choctaws had been persuaded to relinquish their precious homeland and emigrate to a new Indian territory in the West.

The predominant mood of the Choctaws was neither one of anger nor of satisfaction. Rather, a feeling of sadness seemed to pervade the nation. The Indians realized that they must acquiesce to American demands or bear the responsibility either for extermination of the tribe or removal under unfortunate circumstances. In this depressed spirit, the Choctaws prepared to move to Indian Territory during the three years allowed in the treaty. Chief David Folsom summed up the feelings of his people in a letter to the Presbyterian ministers in the nation. "We are exceedingly tired," he wrote. "We have just heard of the ratification of the Choctaw Treaty. Our doom is sealed. There is no other course for us but to turn our faces to our new homes toward the setting sun."[56]

[53] John Eaton to Andrew Jackson, December 1, 1830, Letters to the President of the United States 1800–1840, MSS.

[54] Richardson, II, 1105.

[55] *Niles' Register*, February 26, 1831, p. 460.

[56] Czarina C. Conlan, "David Folsom," *Chronicles of Oklahoma*, IV, No. 4 (December, 1926), p. 353.

CHAPTER NINE

THE LONG TREK WEST

According to ARTICLE 3 of the Treaty of Dancing Rabbit Creek, approximately one-third of the
Choctaw Indians would leave their Mississippi
homeland in 1831, with the remainder to follow in two stages in
the next two years. But late in 1830, prior to the first of these
planned group removals, many individual Choctaws decided to
make the long trek to the West on their own in order to secure
choice lands in Indian Territory before the bulk of the nation
arrived. There were about one thousand of these voluntary emigrants, according to Commissary General George Gibson, and
they wanted to leave immediately with the intention of settling
near Fort Towson in the Indian Territory.[1]

The desire to emigrate early presented a problem to Secretary
of War Eaton. Privately, he favored the voluntary removal effort, but he could not publicly sanction it because the Treaty of
Dancing Rabbit Creek had not yet been submitted for approval
to the United States Senate. After pondering the problem for
several days, he decided quietly to authorize the voluntary move.

---

[1] U.S. Congress, House of Representatives. "Expenditures—Removal of Indians," No. 171 in *Executive Documents, Printed by Order of the House of
Representatives, at the First Session of the Twenty-Second Congress, Begun
and Held at the City of Washington, December 7, 1831*, 22nd Cong., 1st sess.
(Washington, D.C., 1832), IV, 3.

He appointed Lieutenant J. R. Stephenson of the Seventh Infantry at Fort Gibson as the United States supply agent for the removal. Stephenson's job was to ascertain the number of emigrating Choctaws and to collect the necessary supplies for their journey, allowing as a daily ration for each person one and one-half pounds of beef or pork, and one pint of corn (or its equivalent in corn meal or flour). In addition, two quarts of salt were allocated for every hundred rations.[2] Although the treaty stipulated that the government would furnish supplies, it did not specify exact amounts. Hence, the government could have met its obligations by supplying merely enough food and clothing for survival. Instead, Jackson and Eaton adopted a much more liberal policy. In a letter to Stephenson on December 7, Eaton directed him to treat the Indians with kindness and civility during the removal and to use a generous hand in issuing supplies so that "no unfavorable impression may be carried back to their nation that will have the slightest tendency to discourage the emigration of the main body."[3]

In the Choctaw Nation there was general confusion over the voluntary trek west. The Methodist and Baptist missionaries encouraged the movement, but the Presbyterians were opposed to any disorganized early effort that might lead to chaos and suffering.[4] The leader of the proremoval forces was the Methodist minister, Alexander Talley, who volunteered to organize the migration movement and who subsequently headed west with a few Choctaw captains to explore the new country.[5] Talley was informed in a letter from Major David W. Haley in the Choctaw Nation that he would be followed by several hundred Indians who would arrive by the first of January, 1831. Haley also notified Talley of the government's generous position on voluntary removal: "The president has the five hundred thousand dollars

---

[2] *Ibid.*
[3] *Ibid.*
[4] Muriel H. Wright, "The Removal of the Choctaws to the Indian Territory," *Chronicles of Oklahoma*, VI, No. 2 (June, 1928), p. 107.
[5] *Ibid.*

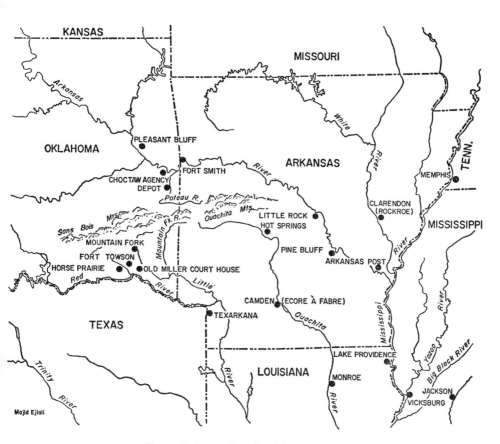

General Areas Involved in Removal

at his disposal, and he never will let the Choctaw suffer that emigrate. Do not be timid in providing for the poor Choctaws, on your arrival on Red River...."[6]

By the end of November, 1830, emigrants were gathering near the home of Greenwood LeFlore and preparing to march to Vicksburg, ferry across the Mississippi River, and make their way to Fort Gibson.[7] Some predicted that no more than fifty Indians would voluntarily emigrate; others set their estimates

[6] *Ibid.*, p. 125.
[7] John Donley to John Eaton, November 25, 1830, Choctaw Agency 1824–1833, MSS.

as high as six hundred families. The fact was that only about four hundred individuals left in December.[8]

Many of the emigrants were Choctaw captains and high-ranking warriors who realized that, at this particular time, they could sell their Mississippi lands to eager white settlers for a handsome price, whereas if they waited a year or more, the value of the land might decrease. This assumption proved correct; for two Choctaw captains, Ned Perry and Charles Hay, sold a two-and-one-half-section parcel of land on November 3, 1830, for $3,200, and three years later similar acreage was selling for $500.[9]

The Choctaw lands were made more valuable by the Mississippi legislature, which, anticipating ratification of the treaty, had decided to build a number of roads through the nation. On November 30, 1830, a bill was introduced in the state House of Representatives to build a road from Martin's Bluff on the Tombigbee River, through the Choctaw and Chickasaw nations, to Clinton, Mississippi.[10] The House passed this bill on December 6 by a vote of twenty-two to nine.[11] Another bill—to build a road through the Choctaw and Chickasaw nations from Jackson, Mississippi, to Memphis, Tennessee—was introduced the next day, but was tabled because of a lack of funds in the state treasury.[12]

While a few Choctaws headed west early and Mississippi planned for the future use of ceded Indian lands, the bulk of the tribesmen showed their displeasure by punishing the leaders who had negotiated at Dancing Rabbit Creek. As a result, elections of new chiefs were held in all three districts of the Choctaw Nation in mid-October. George W. Harkins defeated Greenwood LeFlore in the Northwestern District, Joel H. Nail deposed Nitekechi in the Southern District, and Peter Pitchlynn defeated his

[8] John Donley to John Eaton, November 26, 1830, Choctaw Agency 1824–1833, MSS; David Haley to John Eaton, November 10, 1830, Choctaw Emigration 1826–1833, MSS; Greenwood LeFlore to John Eaton, November 21, 1830, ibid.

[9] David Haley to Alexander Talley, November 3, 1830, Choctaw Emigration 1826–1833, MSS.

[10] *Journal of the House of Representatives of the State of Mississippi*, p. 107.

[11] *Ibid.*, p. 148.

[12] *Ibid.*, p. 155.

uncle Mushulatubbee in the Northeastern District. The successful chiefs called themselves the leaders of the Republican party,
branding their adversaries as members of the Despotic party.[13]
The Republicans protested the removal treaty in petitions that
they sent to Washington, but President Jackson refused to recognize the new chiefs, and they were forced to resign and allow
their recently defeated foes to resume office.[14]

The War Department, eager to pacify those tribesmen who opposed the treaty, accepted a suggestion made by George Gaines
that the Indians be allowed to organize another exploring party
to examine their western lands.[15] Gaines, a white civilian from
Demopolis, Alabama, was appointed by the secretary of war to
lead such an exploring party and also to "conduct and superintend the removal of the Indians to their new territory."[16] He
was well liked and trusted by the Choctaws, and if he could
convince them that their western lands were equal to if not better
than their Mississippi holdings, the removal would be greatly
facilitated.

On October 14, George Gaines left his home in Demopolis
and by the twentieth he was already organizing the exploring
party. He selected eighteen Indians, all important members of the
nation, and gathered the necessary supplies for a trip to be made
during the cool months of November and December. By the
end of October all of the preliminary arrangements had been
completed, and the explorers headed west. The start of the trip
was inauspicious; even before they had passed the boundary of
their old nation, three days of rain had slowed their progress
through the Mississippi swamps. Finally, they reached the Mississippi River and crossed on a flat boat to the mouth of the Arkansas River.[17] The expedition then moved overland on foot,

[13] Wright, "Removal of the Choctaws," p. 106.

[14] S. S. Hamilton to William Ward, April 11, 1831, Records of the Office of
Indian Affairs, MSS.

[15] Gaines, "Reminiscences," p. 29.

[16] Dillard, p. 29.

[17] George S. Gaines, "Dancing Rabbit Creek Treaty," *Historical and Patriotic
Series of Alabama State Department of Archives and History*, No. 10 (1928),
pp. 11–12.

following the north side of the Arkansas River to Fort Smith, where they arrived on November 28.[18]

At Fort Smith the explorers fitted out pack horses with hams, sugar, and coffee. Each member of the small party was furnished with a new rifle and enough ammunition for three months' use. The United States Army provided a surgeon and twelve cavalrymen to join Gaines and the Indians.[19] A few days later the party left Fort Smith to push on into Indian Territory. As the expedition headed west, Gaines recorded some of the details in his diary:

> We packed & secured our Flour Sugar Coffee & Salt with coverings of Bear Skins & proceeded on our examination, backward & forward between the river & ridge, as we ascended northwestwardly. The country was very beautiful, gently undulating, principally prairie, relieved by strips of woodland on the water courses small or larger—small branches shaded with narrow & larger creeks with wider strips of woods. Every morning when I mounted my horse I was soon surrounded by the party all mounted, wanting to know the program for the day. Then the hunters would spread out to the right and left—always bringing into camp, in the evening, plenty of game for the whole party, venison turkey & prairie hens & occasionally Bear meat. . . . The examination was intensely interesting every day—novelties in country, and abundance of game, & fine weather to enjoy the chase rendered every day & night joyous & happy.[20]

During most of December the exploring party continued its investigation of Indian Territory. The cold weather of mid-December, Gaines wrote, did not chill the party's spirits: "Large log fires at night & longer nights, lengthened our social enjoyments. Our Choctaw hunting, war, love stories, & wit, were now seasoned by Army stories."[21] By the end of the year the Indians had completed their investigation, and they returned east, reach-

18 George S. Gaines to Office of Indian Affairs, November 18, 1830, Office of Indian Affairs, MSS.
19 George S. Gaines, p. 12.
20 *Ibid.*
21 *Ibid.*

ing Mississippi in February of 1831. If they ever made contact with other Indians living in the area, Gaines never made mention of the fact. He concluded his diary with this note: "suffice it to say that the country was highly satisfactory to the Choctaws."[22]

Before the first government-sponsored removal could be undertaken, however, ARTICLE 14 of the Treaty of Dancing Rabbit Creek had to be executed.[23] Every Choctaw who preferred to remain in Mississippi and receive a reservation of land could do so, it was stipulated, only if he registered with the Indian agent within a period of six months. Agent William Ward's opposition to ARTICLE 14 was violent. He was so ardent in his wish to see no Indian remain in the state that he put off registering the Choctaws as long as he could,[24] pretending at times to be ill,[25] and occasionally going into hiding.[26] In short, he seemed determined to deny the Choctaws their treaty rights.[27] Finally, however, he reluctantly registered a few Choctaws out of token compliance with the treaty. Even so, he often managed to find some way to defraud the Indians. One Choctaw testified in a statement of grievance:

In the month of January, 1831, being within six months after the ratification of said treaty, a large body of Choctaw Indians attended at a council house to have their names registered for the purpose of obtaining citizenship, and acquiring reservations according to the customs of the Indians. Unacquainted with the English language, they presented to the agent a number of sticks of various lengths, indicating how many were present, and the quantities of land to which they were severally entitled, but the agent threw down the sticks. Then they selected two or three head men to speak for them, and these head men by means of an

---

22 *Arkansas Gazette*, February 9, 1831.
23 George S. Gaines, p. 14.
24 Choctaw Claims Journal of Commissioners Murray & Vroom, MSS.
25 *Ibid.*
26 *Ibid.*
27 Schedule of those Choctaws who received land under the Provisions of the 14th Article of the Treaty of 1830 by remaining upon the land five years in accordance with the provisions of that Article, MSS, Bureau of Indian Affairs, National Archives.

interpreter, told the agent their number, ages, and names, and demanded registration; but the agent would not register them and told them that there were too many—that they must or should go beyond the Mississippi. Many of these Indians igno-rantly despairing of the justice of the United States, have reluc-tantly removed beyond the Mississippi. . . .[28]

Years after the frequent complaints about Ward's conduct were made—in fact, in 1838—the government sent a commission to Mississippi to investigate the charges.[29] The frauds uncovered by the commission were so obvious and overwhelming that other investigations were launched in 1842, 1845, and on through the nineteenth century and even into the twentieth century. After the committee investigations of 1838, Messers. Murray and Vroom reported on July 31, 1838: "From the great mass of proof offered to the board, there can be no doubt of the entire unfitness of the agent for the station. His conduct on many occasions was marked by a degree of hostility . . . he was often arbitrary, tyrannical, and insulting, and intended to drive them west. . . ."[30] Many promi-nent Americans joined with the commissioners to denounce the actions of William Ward, who was referred to as a drunkard, a cheat, and the lowest type of representative that the United States could employ.[31] Thomas L. McKenney testified: "As to his mode of doing business, it was as bad as it well could be. He kept his books and papers on a table in his public room, . . . I have seen it when the seeming [sic] had come apart, and some of the leaves of the book fall out."[32] During the Choctaw removals of 1831

[28] Lowrie and Franklin, VIII, 432.

[29] Testimony of Moon-Tubbee, January 30, 1838, Choctaw Claims Journal of Commissioners Murray & Vroom, MSS. Schedule of Horses and Cattle lost on the way from Old Nation to the West Authenticated, MSS, Bureau of Indian Affairs, National Archives.

[30] U.S. Congress, House of Representatives. "Memorial of the Choctaw Na-tion in answer to the letter of the Honorable Secretary of the Treasury in re-lation to the Choctaw Claims," No. 94 in *The Miscellaneous Documents of the House of Representatives for the Third Session of the Forty-Second Congress, 1872–73*, 42nd Cong., 3rd sess. (Washington, D.C., 1873), II, 12.

[31] Testimony of Calvin Cushman, January 13, 1838, Choctaw Claims Journal of Commissioners Murray & Vroom, MSS.

[32] Testimony of Thomas L. McKenney, January 5, 1838, *ibid.*

and 1832, however, nothing was done to chastise Ward, who was not removed from his post until 1833, and then only because there were too few Choctaws left in Mississippi to warrant his continued service.

While Ward's registration of Choctaws was supposedly being carried out, the United States government began making preparations for the first group removal scheduled for the fall of 1831. First, a careful census of the nation was conducted to determine the exact number of Indians who were eligible for removal. William Armstrong, chosen as census taker, reported late in February that the population of the nation consisted of 17,963 Indians, 151 white persons, and 521 slaves.[33] His information was important because the War Department wanted to remove approximately one-third of the nation in the first group. Guided by Armstrong's census, Gaines ordered supplies for six thousand Indians.[34]

In February, the removal agent recommended to Eaton a prospective route for the fall exodus, suggesting that the Choctaws be sent across the Mississippi River to Helena, in Arkansas Territory, then transported overland in wagons to Little Rock, Washington, and finally, to Fort Towson—a distance of about 550 miles. He also recommended that twenty thousand rations of pork and flour be deposited at each of these places to feed the emigrants.[35] The suggestion appealed to Eaton, and he authorized Gaines to determine the route and work out all of the other important details.[36]

By April, Gaines was busy at this task. Captain J. B. Clark was the government's removal agent in the West, Gaines's counterpart on the other side of the Mississippi River. Gaines wrote to

[33] Armstrong's Register, Claimants for land under Treaty of 1830, MSS, Bureau of Indian Affairs, National Archives.

[34] George S. Gaines and Benjamin Reynolds to John Eaton, February 7, 1831, Letters of Commissary General of Subsistence, Letters Received, MSS, Records of the Bureau of Indian Affairs, National Archives.

[35] *Ibid.*

[36] George S. Gaines to Captain J. B. Clark, April 5, 1831, Letterbook of Commissary General of Subsistence, Letters Sent, MSS, Records of the Bureau of Indian Affairs, National Archives.

Clark, advising that forty wagons had been ordered from Captain J. P. Taylor, the commissary of subsistence at Louisville, Kentucky, thirty of them to be adapted to oxen and the remainder to be horse-drawn.[37] All wagons were to be harnessed for six animals[38] and were to be delivered to the mouth of the White River before September 1. Clark was instructed to hire the necessary oxen and horses from local citizens to save the expense of transporting government-owned animals to Arkansas Territory.[39]

Gaines endeavored to solve the problem of feeding the emigrants by urging Arkansas farmers to curtail their cotton crops during 1831 and devote these fields to additional corn, thereby allowing the government to purchase this commodity locally. This request pleased the *Arkansas Gazette* which urged its readers to cooperate. It appeared that 1831 might well be a prosperous year.[40] The farmers did temporarily convert from cotton to corn, and Lieutenant L. F. Carter, a removal agent assigned to accompany the Choctaws through the territory, wrote to Commissary General of the United States George Gibson: "corn will be abundant & cheap, the ensuing fall."[41] Gaines solved the problem of supplying beef and pork mainly by purchasing the animals alive and placing them at the various stopping points, to be slaughtered and salted as the need arose.[42]

The removal agents, both east and west of the Mississippi, did their jobs meticulously, overlooking no detail. Though the number constantly changed as officers and men were moved from task to task, at least thirty soldiers built strong, sanitary corn-cribs and smokehouses at the numerous way stations. Gaines

37 George S. Gaines to Captain J. B. Clark, April 5, 1831, and S. S. Hamilton to William Ward, June 30, 1831, *ibid*.

38 J. P. Taylor to George Gibson, April 9, 1831, Letters of Commissary General of Subsistence, MSS.

39 George S. Gaines to Captain J. B. Clark, April 5, 1831, Letterbook of Commissary General of Subsistence, MSS.

40 *Arkansas Gazette*, February 23, 1831.

41 L. F. Carter to George Gibson, February 17, 1831, Letters of Commissary General of Subsistence, MSS.

42 J. R. Richardson to George S. Gaines, April 1, 1831, *ibid*.

hedged against the possibility that the Arkansas farmers might not be able to provide all of the necessary supplies: corn was ordered on a stand-by basis from merchants in St. Louis and New Orleans.[43] Other items promised in the treaty, such as rifles, blankets, hoes, and axes, were ordered from the best manufacturers in the country.[44] With justifiable pride, Eaton wrote the Choctaw chiefs early in May saying that the United States was doing everything humanly possible to ensure that the Indian exodus would be accomplished with honor and a minimum of suffering.[45]

During June, the removal agents continued their preparations by ascertaining the availability of drinking water on the suggested route,[46] shipping one hundred barrels of flour to each of the way stations, and making sure that only the purest foodstuffs were purchased. Secretary Eaton advised Captain Taylor in Louisville that all of the meat, corn, and flour forwarded to Mississippi and Arkansas Territory was to be of the same quality as that sent to the soldiers in the United States Army.[47]

As painstaking as these preparations seem to have been, it nevertheless happened, by mid-July 1831, that the government removal efforts began to falter. One reason may have been that the Bureau of Indian Affairs had not been involved in the advance preparations. Instead, since October, 1830, each removal agent had been following his own inclinations, with only the vaguest of instructions from George Gaines in the East and J. B. Clark in the West. As late as June 12, Eaton told Clark in a letter that "the nature of the service requires that you should be allowed a discretion as to all matters that may arise. You will, therefore, in your own way, pursue such a course as you may

[43] J. B. Clark to George Gibson, June 3, 1831, and G. L. Rains to George Gibson, June 5, 1831, and J. R. Stephenson to George Gibson, June 1, 1831, *ibid.*

[44] S. S. Hamilton to Henry Derringer Company and George M. Tryson Company, May 30, 1831, Records of the Office of Indian Affairs, MSS.

[45] John Eaton to Greenwood LeFlore, May 7, 1831, *ibid.*

[46] S. S. Hamilton to Greenwood LeFlore, June 23, 1831, Letterbook of Commissary General of Subsistence, MSS.

[47] John Eaton to J. P. Taylor, June 27, 1831, *House Doc. No. 171*, IV, 9.

deem best."[48] Such a policy, lacking in coordination and direction from above, was almost destined to result in friction.

During the summer of 1831, individual removal agents fell to haggling over such questions as whether to transport the Indians by wagons or by steamboats. Clark, in the West, preferred to use wagons, which could meet the Indians at the mouth of the White River and transport them overland to Fort Towson;[49] but Lieutenant William B. Colquhoun, as eastern removal agent who should have had no authority in the matter, disapproved the use of wagons and demanded instead that the Choctaws be transported by steamboats up the Red and Ouachita rivers.[50] Other agents supported one or the other of these suggestions, or even offered entirely different solutions. Controversy also arose among the agents about whether the Indians should be given their rifles on the eastern or western side of the Mississippi River.[51] As a further complication, Arkansas farmers profiteered by doubling the price of their beef cattle and hogs and tripling the price of their corn. The profiteering forced the removal agents to request more funds from the War Department, which in turn irritated the secretary of war.[52] Eventually, the seemingly endless disagreements that split the removal personnel into many factions caused discontent among the Choctaw leaders. One of the *mingos* disgustedly wrote the new acting secretary of war, Roger B. Taney, that if the government would give each Indian ten dollars, food, and his treaty goods, the tribe would remove itself with much less waste and inefficiency.[53] He also told the secre-

48 John Eaton to J. B. Clark, June 12, 1831, *ibid.*, p. 12.
49 J. B. Clark to George Gibson, July 24, 1831, Letters of Commissary General of Subsistence, MSS.
50 W. S. Colquhoun to George Gibson, August 11, 1831, *ibid.*
51 S. S. Hamilton to F. W. Armstrong, August 1, 1831, Records of the Office of Indian Affairs, MSS.
52 John Eaton had given up the War Department for an ambassador's post because of the "Petticoat War" involving his wife. J. L. Clark to George Gibson, July 23, 1831, Letters of Commissary General of Subsistence, MSS.
53 Roger B. Taney to (addressee unknown), July 25, 1831, *House Doc. No. 171*, IV, 26. George Gibson to Roger B. Taney, July 25, 1831, Letterbook of Commissary General of Subsistence, MSS.

tary of war that most of the tribe were amused by the antics of what they judged to be an obviously incompetent removal team. This last statement irritated Taney who saw little humor in the deteriorating situation.

Possibly the government's removal efforts, though shaky, could have been saved by alert leadership and a few improved policies. But on April 7, 1831, Secretary of War Eaton resigned his War Department post and left with his wife, Peggy, for Madrid as minister to Spain. Roger Taney served as acting secretary of the War Department for a few months; in August the post was accepted by Lewis Cass of Michigan, a man who knew little about the 1831 removal effort, but who was a loyal Jackson supporter.[54] Despite the fact that Cass pleaded total ignorance of the pending Choctaw removal problem, he let it be known that he disagreed with Eaton's preparations to date. He blindly hired and fired removal agents with such rapidity that by the end of August he had rehired personnel dismissed earlier in the month. He placed George Gaines in charge of the entire removal project with the pretentious title of superintendent of the subsistence and removal of Indians. At the same time he appointed Major Francis W. Armstrong of Mobile, Alabama, a personal enemy of Gaines's, as the chief removal agent east of the Mississippi River.[55] Gaines and Armstrong found it impossible to work together, and the chaos of the past few months was compounded.[56] By September, politics so permeated the entire program that many of the honest removal agents resigned their posts in disgust. The most serious loss was in the resignation of Captain Clark, the agent in the West who had earlier written to George Gibson: "I will be agreeably disappointed if the removal, during the approaching

[54] Andrew C. McLaughlin, *Lewis Cass*, in *American Statesmen* (New York and Boston, 1900), pp. 133, 135, 162. Frank B. Woodford, *Lewis Cass, The Last Jeffersonian* (New Brunswick, N.J., 1950), p. 172.

[55] Lewis Cass to John Coffee, September 8, 1831, Records of the Office of Indian Affairs, MSS.

[56] George S. Gaines, pp. 15–16.

fall, should pass off *only tolerably well.*"[57] Cass accepted Clark's resignation and appointed Captain Jacob Brown of Jefferson Barracks as the new western removal agent.[58]

Eventually a number of important changes were made to improve the chances of a successful removal in 1831. Cass finally realized his inability to direct the project personally because he knew nothing about it. He relinquished his Washington, D.C., command of the project to the knowledgeable Commissary General of Subsistence George Gibson. Gibson, then, with Cass's blessing, reaffirmed to all associated with the 1831 Choctaw removal that Gaines was in complete charge of all field operations, with instructions to decide for himself the problems of supplies, transportation, hiring of assistants, and removal dates. "It is not intended to confine the superintendent to any plan of operation," Gibson wrote Gaines. "The whole field will be left open to the exercise of his judgment, formed—as it must be—upon a nearer and more accurate view of the circumstances of the case."[59] Gibson's action now placed the removal of the Choctaw Indians completely under civilian, rather than military, direction and authority, although military personnel were not excluded from important subordinate positions.

Gibson immediately began sending the needed supplies to Mississippi and Arkansas Territory: 1,050 blankets to Fort Smith, 100 tents to Vicksburg, and numerous other treaty items to the terminal points in Indian Territory.[60] He also warned the Arkansas farmers that he would purchase the necessary food supplies elsewhere if they did not lower their ridiculously high prices. The threat had the desired effect, and by mid-October the price of corn dropped from one dollar to fifty cents a bushel.[61] Lastly, Gibson authorized the improvement of roads in

[57] Wright, "Removal of the Choctaws," p. 126.
[58] George Gibson to Jacob Brown, September 9, 1831, Letterbook of Commissary General of Subsistence, MSS.
[59] George Gibson to George S. Gaines, August 13, 1831, *ibid.*
[60] S. S. Hamilton to David McClellan, September 12, 1831, Records of the Office of Indian Affairs, MSS.
[61] G. Rains to George Gibson, October 26, 1831, Letters of Commissary General of Subsistence, MSS.

Arkansas Territory so that the emigrating party could travel with as few inconveniences as possible. Three new bridges were to be built over the Little Cossatot, Big Cossatot, and Saline rivers; Gibson further instructed Captain Jacob Brown to do whatever "may be necessary for traveling the road with safety and celerity."[62]

By the first week in October, 1831, approximately 4,000 Choctaws began to gather in their several tribal districts for the 550 mile journey to Indian Territory.[63] Because of unusually severe summer and fall rains, which made muddy swamps of the roads in Arkansas, Gaines decided to transport the Choctaws by steamboats as far as they could travel up the Arkansas and Ouachita rivers.[64] The Indians left the nation by wagons, horseback, and on foot, and headed for the Mississippi River, taking almost no personal possessions, since accommodations had been provided for the transportation of individuals and essential equipment only.[65] Those who left the Northeastern District of the Choctaw Nation traveled north to Memphis, while all others headed for Vicksburg. But George Gaines, distracted by innumerable last-minute details, had completely forgotten to order the necessary steamboats. When the Indians arrived at Memphis and Vicksburg, further movement was delayed for two weeks while Gaines endeavored to correct his oversight. By November 4, he had secured five boats—the *Walter Scott*, the *Brandywine*, the *Reindeer*, the *Talma*, and the *Cleopatra*—the last three of which were quite small and light. He then decided that the emigrants should

[62] George Gibson to Jacob Brown, November 4, 1831, *House Doc. No. 171*, IV, 24.

[63] About one thousand more decided to move by themselves.

[64] Jacob Brown to George Gibson, October 31, 1831, Letters of Commissary General of Subsistence, MSS; Wright, "Removal of the Choctaws." Very little can be added to Miss Muriel Wright's fine account of the 1831-33 Choctaw removals west. I shall, in the main, be repeating much of what Miss Wright stated forty-two years ago. Some unused sources have been uncovered, and these sources shed new light on the preparations for removal, gathering of emigrants, and actions of removal agents, rather than the day-by-day events of the trek itself.

[65] F. L. Wooldridge, "Sketches of Early Steamboat Navigation Along the Arkansas and Red Rivers" (unpublished typewritten diary in the Southern Collection, University of North Carolina), p. 1.

be divided into several groups, each to take a different route, to avoid crowding them all into one party, which might necessitate short rations and cause other suffering. The first group was ferried up the Mississippi to Lake Providence, Louisiana, and from there journeyed overland through northern Louisiana and southern Arkansas to the Choctaw lands in Indian Territory. A second group of two thousand was packed into the *Walter Scott* and the *Reindeer*, which churned up the Mississippi from Vicksburg to the Arkansas River, on to Arkansas Post, and finally to Little Rock.[66] The *Brandywine* left Memphis with a third group and followed the same route as the *Walter Scott* and the *Reindeer*. The *Talma* and *Cleopatra*, carrying a fourth group of about one thousand, traveled downstream to the mouth of the Red River, and then toward the Ouachita River and Écore à Fabre.[67] Finally, on December 10, in the midst of a raging storm, the last two hundred emigrants, a commutation party, left Vicksburg and descended the Mississippi River to the Ouachita River in Louisiana.

From the start the first Choctaw removal was accompanied by misery, but the suffering and death that ensued were not owing so much to political maneuvering or governmental inefficiency as to the severe winter storm that blanketed the Mississippi-Arkansas area. It was, according to Muriel Wright, "the worst blizzard ever experienced in the South and West." Even before the commutation party left for the Ouachita, they were exhausted and hungry—"after having walked for twenty-four hours barefoot through the snow and ice before reaching Vicksburg."[68]

Because of conflicting directives, all of the Indians on the *Reindeer* and the *Walter Scott*, plus those who debarked from Memphis on the *Brandywine*—a total of 2,500 Choctaws—were deposited at Captain Brown's Arkansas Post instead of going on

---

66 Wright, "Removal of the Choctaws," p. 115.

67 *Ibid.*, pp. 115–16. Wooldridge, p. 1. Écore à Fabre is today the city of Camden, Arkansas.

68 William S. Colquhoun to Captain Cross, December 17, 1831, Letters of Commissary General of Subsistence, MSS; Wright, "Removal of the Choctaws," p. 116.

to Little Rock as the original instructions specified.[69] Captain Brown, of course, was completely unprepared to care for such a large number at the small post. Since only sixty tents had been brought there from Vicksburg,[70] most of the Indians were forced to huddle together in open camps and suffer through the bitter cold of the storm. The supply of food was also pitifully inadequate. In fact, nothing could be done to alleviate the suffering of Choctaw men, women, and children during that stark December, 1831 and January, 1832. Captain Brown wrote, with genuine compassion, "This unexpected cold weather must produce much human suffering. Our poor emigrants, many of them quite naked, and without much shelter, must suffer, it is impossible to do otherwise; and my great fears are that many of them will get frosted."[71] Especially pitiful was the plight of the aged, the infirm, and the children. There were few blankets, shoes, or winter clothes available, most of these articles having been sent on to Fort Smith. Most of the children were barefoot, and three-fourths of them were naked in zero-degree weather. The sickness and death that ensued were inevitable.[72]

The removal officials tried earnestly to alleviate these miserable conditions by moving the emigrants on to the Kiamichi River by wagon. But this tactic, too, was beset by troubles. The forty government wagons that were available hardly sufficed to transport the 2,500 emigrants to the river, 350 miles distant. The roads between Arkansas Post and Little Rock needed major repairs after the storm. There were no funds to purchase supplies. Yet, despite these conditions, Brown decided to proceed along the overland route. The wagons moved westward from Arkansas Post on January 13, starting a slow and tortuous journey to Little Rock. Upon arrival there, the emigrants packed up additional

[69] The reason for the confusion is impossible to determine accurately from available sources, but it appears that the weather made postal deliveries almost impossible.

[70] Wright, "Removal of the Choctaws," p. 116.

[71] U. S. Congress, Senate. "Removal of the eastern Tribes of Indians," No. 512 in *Senate Documents*, 23rd Cong., 1st sess. (Washington, D.C., 1834), VII, 427.

[72] William S. Colquhoun to George Gibson, December 11, 1831, Letters of Commissary General of Subsistence, MSS.

supplies and then, after January 22, continued west.[73] Travel was slow and tedious—fifteen miles being considered an exceptionally fine day's journey. Further delays, which prolonged the suffering, were caused by frequent stops to repair the roads and trails and wrecked bridges. Washouts were common, and fallen timber obstructed the way. The rain poured almost every day for the entire month of February, making the road a muddy lake and nearly impassable.[74] Surprisingly, in complete contradiction of the facts, the *Arkansas Gazette* reported to its readers at this time that the Choctaws appeared to be cheerful, content, and well supplied with food and clothing.[75]

Meanwhile, the fourth group of Choctaws, who had traveled up the Ouachita River to Écore à Fabre under the care of Lieutenant L. T. Cross, learned, when they arrived on December 18, that no western agent had been assigned to meet them; the nearest one was more than 150 miles away.[76] This oversight, like many of the others, was owing to the general confusion of instructions and the lack of coordination that characterized the removal operation. Furthermore, the terrible storms of December made it impossible to send or receive directives that might have rectified the mistakes. While Cross and his party pondered their plight, they received news that the straggling group of two hundred Indians from Lake Providence, Louisiana, were in dire straits in the swamps west of the lake. Cross immediately went to their aid with a few volunteers, rescued the Indians and marched them to Monroe, Louisiana.[77] He then rechartered the steamboat *Talma* and took the group to Écore à Fabre to join his own nearly starved charges. Cross faced the challenge of transporting these 1,100 exhausted Choctaws to Indian Territory without any money, food, or even instructions. In this emergency, he took the initiative; without authorization he hired wagons and horses, and purchased food on the credit of the United States government.

[73] *Arkansas Gazette*, January 25, 1832.
[74] Wright, "Removal of the Choctaws," p. 117.
[75] *Arkansas Gazette*, January 4, 1832.
[76] *Ibid.*, December 28, 1831.
[77] Wright, "Removal of the Choctaws," p. 117.

But, being in no position to bargain, he was forced to pay exorbitant prices to the local citizens for these goods; each Indian ration, for example, cost him twelve and one-half cents—more than twice the normal price of six cents. Early in February, he and his Indians set out for their objective, Fort Towson, a trip that was to take them 165 miles over treacherous roads.[78]

By the first week of March, 1832, all of the emigration parties had reached Indian Territory—five agonizing months after the first group had set out from its Mississippi homeland. On April 30, Lieutenant J. R. Stephenson, a supply agent in the West, recorded that 3,749 Choctaws had been registered at four stations: Horse Prairie, Fort Towson, Old Miller Court House, and Mountain Fork.[79] Many of the emigrants were sick, and all were exhausted and discouraged. They were aware and appreciative, however, of the extraordinary efforts of the removal agents who had accomplished the removal under desperately trying conditions. In fact, it is probable that at least half of the emigrating Choctaws would have perished en route had it not been for the attention and resourcefulness exhibited by these agents. As George Gibson reported in a letter to Secretary Cass, "They have acted, with praiseworthy . . . interestedness toward the Indians. They have effected a delicate task in a manner highly creditable to themselves and to the government."[80]

---

[78] *Ibid.*, p. 118. *Arkansas Gazette*, February 8, 1832.
[79] Wright, "Removal of the Choctaws," p. 119.
[80] George Gibson to Lewis Cass, February 20, 1832, Letterbook of Commissary General of Subsistence, MSS.

CHAPTER TEN

TO INDIAN TERRITORY
TO BUILD A NEW NATION

With completion of the first group removal, about four thousand Indians had been successfully transported from Mississippi to Indian Territory. As a result of the confused planning and the unexpectedly severe weather, however, the cost had been outrageously high[1]—two to three times the original estimate. The War Department appraised this first removal as a complete failure and made angry demands for frugality. Commissary General George Gibson, writing to Captain Jacob Brown, advised that the secretary of war was "very solicitous on the subject of retrenchment, and you will meet his views."[2] Others considered the government lucky to have completed the removal at any cost. Judge William S. Fulton expressed such a view to President Jackson:

I fear the expenses of removing the Choctaws, will astonish, if not alarm you, when you ascertain what it has amounted to. Considering however, how late in the season the movement was made, & the extreme cold weather, the scarcity of provisions, and the difficulty of obtaining [sic] means of transportation, it is

[1] It was expected that twice that number would emigrate west at less cost.
[2] George Gibson to Jacob Brown, April 12, 1832, Letterbook of Commissary General of Subsistence, MSS.

not wonderful that the expenditure should far exceed all the calculations which were made....[3]

The secretary of war saw only one solution to the problem: a change in the government's removal policy. Consequently, in April, 1832, George Gaines and all other civilians who had been connected with the first removal were discharged, and the task of moving the Indians was turned over to the United States Army.[4] Gibson explained that the government in Washington did not blame the civilians for the failure of the first removal but felt that a more centralized control was necessary to cope with all possible contingencies. Inasmuch as the conflict between civilian and military removal agents had led to inefficiency, he pointed out, the government had decided to simplify forthcoming removals by giving full authority to military agents. On May 15, Secretary Cass issued new and rigid regulations to the Army agents setting forth demands that were to apply "regardless of the circumstances."[5] Emphasizing the necessity to economize, he stipulated that rations were to be decreased, and that transportation facilities were to be provided only for the very young and the sickly. The only increase in expenditures that he authorized was a raise from ten to thirteen dollars as payment to those Indians who emigrated on their own volition, without the help of agents.[6] But the secretary made no provisions in his new regulations for adapting them to any changing conditions that might arise.

On July 20, Gibson put the new removal policy into operation by appointing Captain William Armstrong to serve as the special agent for the removal of the Choctaws as far as the Mississippi

[3] William S. Fulton to Andrew Jackson, April 25, 1832, Carter, *Territorial Papers*, XXI, 502.

[4] George Gibson to George S. Gaines, April 27, 1832, Letterbook of Commissary General of Subsistence, MSS.

[5] Regulations issued by Lewis Cass, May 15, 1832, Records of the Office of Indian Affairs, MSS. For a summary of these regulations, see app. C.

[6] J. H. H. to William Armstrong, September 5, 1832, Letterbook of Commissary General of Subsistence, MSS.

River[7] and Major Francis W. Armstrong[8] to serve in the same capacity from the Mississippi River west to Indian Territory.[9] From this dual appointment it appears that Cass's new regulations directed the commissary general to split the future Choctaw removals into two completely separate undertakings, with the Mississippi River dividing them and with Gibson's office serving as the only coordinating factor.[10] Captain Jacob Brown, the chief dispensing agent in the West, complained that this arrangement merely continued the same problem of coordination that had plagued the first removal effort in 1831. He wrote Gibson that "the arrangement for the division of the Genl. superintendency is entirely deficient & ineffectual."[11] Contrary to Brown's view, however, another experienced removal agent, Captain William Colquhoun, asserted that the new policy was much more efficient than any previous removal plan sponsored by the federal government.[12]

While the government was devising this new policy, the Choctaws who were still in Mississippi seemed almost overnight to grow despondent, to give up their struggle for survival, and to prefer drinking their way out of their problems. They refused to plant their crops or work the land; and in this state of mind they were easy prey for the hundreds of opportunists in the nation illegally trading whiskey for land.[13] There was ample cause for the Indians' moral deterioration. When they had lost their Mississippi homeland they had received the right to stay in the state by registering according to the fourteenth article of the Treaty of Dancing Rabbit Creek. But Agent Ward, by refusing to honor freely the privilege granted by the fourteenth article, made it

[7] George Gibson to William Armstrong, July 20, 1832, *ibid*.

[8] The brother of William Armstrong.

[9] George Gibson to Francis Armstrong, July 20, 1832, Letterbook of Commissary General of Subsistence, MSS.

[10] *Ibid*.

[11] Jacob Brown to George Gibson, May 30, 1832, Letters of Commissary General of Subsistence, MSS.

[12] George Gibson to William S. Colquhoun, March 6, 1832, Letterbook of Commissary General of Subsistence, MSS.

[13] John Robb to Francis W. Armstrong, July 19, 1832, Records of the Office of Indian Affairs, MSS.

almost impossible for those who chose to remain on their land to do so. Furthermore, those Choctaws still in Mississippi had observed the first group removal with keen interest and saw nothing but suffering and death as the result of it. The gods were against the tribe, it seemed to most of them, and they might as well resign themselves to degradation and eventual extinction.

The idleness and drinking in the nation added to the problem of the federal government. Many Indians were selling all their possessions but squandering the returns. Some were even accumulating large debts, which would cause delays in future removals because no Indian was permitted to emigrate until all his bills were paid.[14] It seemed to Gibson that there would be no Choctaw left who would be eligible for removal unless the demoralizing whites were forced to leave the nation until the Indians had emigrated.

Secretary of War Cass was forced to leave the War Department in June of 1836 for reasons of health and took the post of minister to France; but John Robb, as the acting secretary of war, applied himself to this current Indian problem. He instructed Anthony Campbell, the marshal of Mississippi, to eject from the nation all the whites who did not hold an official position with the tribe.[15] As Robb emphasized to his supervisor in the East, Captain William Armstrong, "You need not be told how important it is, that the Choctaws should not be involved in debts, at the moment assigned for their departure for the West."[16] The efforts of Campbell and Armstrong were successful in ousting the illegal white traders, but they still found it impossible to stop the appalling amount of drinking in the nation.

By the first of August, 1832, the War Department had begun preparations for the second of the three Choctaw removals. William Armstrong sent Captain Colquhoun and two other agents, identified as Captain L. T. Cross and Colonel Wharton Rector, to the three districts in the nation to determine the number of

---

[14] John Robb to William Ward, July 18, 1832, *ibid.*
[15] George Gibson and John Robb to Anthony Campbell, July 13, 1832, *ibid.*
[16] John Robb to William Armstrong, July 19, 1832, *ibid.*

Indians who would emigrate that fall so that the necessary supplies and transportation facilities could be procured.[17] By September it had been determined that more than nine thousand Choctaws were willing to emigrate that year.[18]

Armstrong next turned his attention to the problem of procurement. He decided to transport the Indians by approximately the same route that Gaines had taken the previous year. He would send about one-third of the emigrants to Memphis. Those who remained would go to Vicksburg, cross the Mississippi River by steamboat, and then proceed on foot to Indian Territory.[19] He gathered rifles, blankets,[20] powder, lead, and flints[21] and sent them on to Fort Smith; also, "40 barrels of pork & 10,000 lbs of bacon & sixty barrels of flour . . . & 200 dozen hard bread were forwarded to Little Rock. . . ."[22] With regard to the procurement of corn, Captain Brown suggested to Captain Armstrong that it would be unwise to advertise the route of the emigrants "because [the price of] corn . . . would fall or rise extravagantly in price," depending on the route selected.[23]

The government provided picturesque, storybook clothes for the Choctaw chiefs and headmen, as had been promised in the Treaty of Dancing Rabbit Creek.[24] Altogether, ninety-nine chiefs, captains, and subcaptains in the tribe were bedecked with beaver hats trimmed with silver bands, cockades, and plumes; calfskin puttees; superfine pantaloons; Irish linen shirts; patent leather stocks; Morocco swordbelts with plates; and infantry or artillery officers' swords in bright scabbards.[25] This assortment of

17 William Armstrong to George Gibson, August 24, 1832, Letters of Commissary General of Subsistence, MSS.

18 William Armstrong to George Gibson, September 1, 1832, *ibid.*

19 William Armstrong to George Gibson, September 17, 1832, *ibid.*

20 George Gibson to G. J. Rains, July 17, 1832, Letterbook of Commissary General of Subsistence, MSS.

21 G. J. Rains to George Gibson, October 4, 1832, Letters of Commissary General of Subsistence, MSS.

22 Jacob Brown to George Gibson, July 3, 1832, *ibid.*

23 Jacob Brown to George Gibson, July 20, 1832, *ibid.*

24 David McClellan to George Gibson, July 10, 1832, Letterbook of Commissary General of Subsistence, MSS.

25 George Gibson to David McClellan, July 10, 1832, Letters of Commissary General of Subsistence, MSS.

finery had been shipped from Philadelphia in July, to be worn as the Indians traveled West—in a veritable parade of splendor—to a new land and a new life.

The final plans for the second group removal had been completed by October 1. Supplies for 9,000 Indians had been dispersed along the proposed routes but, as in the previous year, the estimate was too high. Less than two-thirds of that number actually emigrated. LeFlore's district was the biggest disappointment to the removal agents; Colquhoun had estimated that at least 3,000 would emigrate from there, but only 617 signed the muster rolls.[26] Nitekechi's district, with 2,000 on the rolls, performed better, as did Mushulatubbee's district, which signed up 2,700 emigrants. Thus, the second group removal was scheduled to involve a total of 5,317 Choctaws. LeFlore's small group proceeded to Garland's Old Field in Nitekechi's district where the two groups joined forces and, after mustering, set out for Vicksburg on October 11, with Major F. W. Armstrong in charge.[27] Mushulatubbee's group gathered at the council house in their dis-

---

[26] Francis W. Armstrong to George Gibson, October 31, 1832, *ibid.*

[27] Francis W. Armstrong to George Gibson, October 23, 1832, *ibid.*; Wright, "Removal of the Choctaws," p. 121; Francis and William Armstrong took the two groups to the Mississippi River with William in charge of the eastern arrangements. They continued with the tribesmen, with Francis Armstrong responsible for the removal from the Mississippi westward. Francis seldom stayed with his group, as can be seen from his own account of his late 1832 activities to the secretary of war. "From the agency I took horses, and went directly to Little Rock, passing thro' the Choctaws and Chickasaws to Memphis, and at that place, made arrangement for the reception of the emigrants. Thro' the Mississippi swamp, I directed my course towards Little Rock, which I reached on the 2d Oct. & made every arrangement, necessary for the reception of the Indians at Rock-Roe, the main landing on the west side of the Mississippi. Only a few days, were consumed in this duty. By the same rout, I then returned to within about twenty miles of the agency, where I met the Superintendent East on the march with about 2700 Indians. I remained but one day with him,—after which I returned to Memphis, in order to engage boats to meet a party of 2500 Indians at Vixburg, a distance, from that place of 350 miles, who were to be there by the first of November. On the 29th October, I left Memphis and reached Vixburg on the morning of the 31st where I found 600 Indians conducted by Capt. Cross. The cholera was then among them:—about fifty cases per day. On the following day, we departed with a detachment of Indians in two steamboats for the mouth of White River. From this time, we had to combat with the most trying circumstances that this devastating scourge could produce. In five days, we reached White River. There we exchanged loads with other public

trict and left for Memphis on October 13, under the command of Captain William Armstrong.[28]

The 1832 removal seemed to have been better planned than that of the preceding year. The emigrants left in relatively good spirits, bolstered by the fact that food and supplies were abundant. In fact, hundreds of cattle were driven along with the Indians to provide fresh beef, thus eliminating the possibility of the starvation that had plagued the previous removal. Most of the Indians walked, only the old people and the young children being permitted to ride in the few wagons that were provided.[29]

Although the start was auspicious, an unforeseen disaster struck soon after the caravans left—one even more deadly than the icy winds and torrential rains of the previous winter. An epidemic of cholera was sweeping down into Mississippi from the north, going from river port to river port and leaving suffering and death in its wake.[30] When news of the epidemic reached the two parties on their way to Memphis and Vicksburg, respectively, a demoralizing fear gripped the emigrants; and the fear increased as continuing reports stated that the dread disease was spreading throughout the region. As the Indians from Mushulatubbee's

---

boats, when it became necessary again to descend the river. In company with Lieut. Montgomery I returned; after having made the necessary arrangements for the arrival of four steam-boats at Vixburg, that were to take on board a party of 1800 Indians who were to ascend the river to the same point, and thence to Rock-Roe our main landing. With this detachment I continued, until we crossed the river at Little Rock. Here I divided it into 3 parties which were conducted by Lieuts. Simonton, Montgomery & Van Horne. I next proceeded to overtake the detachment of one thousand, on their march to Fort Smith, under the conduct of Capt. Page. At the Dardanelle rock on the Arkansas River I came up with him, where we were actively engaged for two days, in getting accross;—the river being out of its banks. I left him on the west side and went directly to the agency for the purpose of preparing to make the issues as Choctaw agent of the articles due the Indians under the Treaty." Report of Major Francis W. Armstrong to Secretary of War Lewis Cass, March 20, 1833, Choctaw Emigration 1826–1833, MSS.

28 William Armstrong to George Gibson, October 13, 1832, Letters of Commissary General of Subsistence, MSS.

29 William Armstrong to George Gibson, October 28, 1832, *ibid*.; Wright, "Removal of the Choctaws," p. 121.

30 Wright, "Removal of the Choctaws," p. 121.

district neared Memphis, cholera had already spread sickness, pain, and death among dozens of them.[31]

Plans had been made to transport the Choctaws from Memphis to Little Rock by steamboat via the Mississippi and Arkansas rivers. On arriving in Memphis in early November,[32] however, it was found that no steamboats were available. Accordingly, it was decided to divide the group into two sections, each of which would take a different route, and to designate Rockroe, on the White River approximately 60 miles east of Little Rock, as the rendezvous point.[33] One section, under Captain William Armstrong's command, would be ferried across the Mississippi on the government snag boat *Archimedes* and then proceed overland to Rockroe.[34] The other section, under Captain William Colquhoun, would board the snag boat *Helipolis* and proceed southwest to the White River and thence northwest on that river to Rockroe.

As a result of the death and suffering caused by cholera, the Indians were panic stricken by the time they reached Memphis, and many of the women and children at first refused to board the boats. But eventually, in complete chaos, the Indians, animals, baggage, and equipment were stowed on the two snag boats to pursue their separate ways on the second part of the 1832 trek.

The plight of William Armstrong's party, once it had been ferried across the river, worsened as torrential rains made the

[31] *Ibid.*

[32] *Ibid.*; William Armstrong to George Gibson, November 13, 1832, Letters of Commissary General of Subsistence, MSS.

[33] It is hard to determine the exact spelling for the town. It is often listed as "Rock Roe," "Roe Rock," "Rock Row," and other variations. I have selected "Rockroe," which seems to be the most usual spelling. The town was established by a post office in 1819 at the confluence of the Cache and White rivers. Today, Rockroe is the town of Clarendon, Arkansas. The place was well located for removal purposes. The Indians could be sent by boat up the Mississippi and White rivers to Rockroe. Rested and reoutfitted, the tribesmen could then journey overland to Little Rock and points west. Rockroe was so well located that it later became the eastern terminus of a stagecoach line from Little Rock. *Arkansas, A Guide to the State* in *American Guide Series* (New York, 1941), pp. 342–43.

[34] Wooldridge, p. 1.

Arkansas swamps almost impassable. At one point the road they traveled was waist-deep in water and mud for mile after tortuous mile. Armstrong made every effort to relieve the suffering, but as in the preceding removal, the agents were unable to cope with the destructive power of nature,[35] and many of the Choctaws died of exposure.[36]

Aboard the snag boat *Helipolis* conditions were little better. Colquhoun, who had genuine compassion for the Indians, was thwarted in his efforts to relieve their suffering by Major Armstrong, who felt little sympathy for the Indians. The antagonism between the two men led to an overt fight on November 24 that resulted in Colquhoun's dismissal from the United States Army. John Samuel, captain of the *Helipolis*, gave this account:

> Mr. Colquhoun felt that Major Armstrong was too rough on the Emigrating Choctaws. Gaines had treated them well & even removed their dogs. But Armstrong was strict. While boating to White River it was very cold & Colquhoun told the Choctaw to ask Armstrong for blankets, but he said no. Colquhoun drunk, came in and cussed Armstrong. Being accused of being drunk he fired 2 shots in the wall and then hit Armstrong on the head with his pistol. Armstrong disarmed him and beat him up & threw him off the ship.[37]

The other emigrating parties—those from LeFlore's and Nitekechi's districts who were bound for Vicksburg—crossed the Pearl River on October 25 without difficulty, and proceeded on schedule to the western Mississippi port. The next day, however, they too heard the cholera news, that the epidemic was in the center of the state and that many cases had been reported along the route they were traveling.[38] The removal agents, taken completely by surprise, decided to continue their march to Vicksburg, but on a "circuitous route" north and then west in order

---

[35] Wright, "Removal of the Choctaws," p. 122.

[36] *Ibid.*; Samuel M. Rutherford to Ambrose H. Sevier, November 29, 1832, Carter, *Territorial Papers*, XXI, 661.

[37] John Samuel to Francis W. Armstrong, November 24, 1832, Choctaw Miscellany, 1830–1833, MSS.

[38] *Arkansas Gazette*, November 21, 1832.

to avoid the epidemic areas. This new route was costly in time and expense of provisions which were scarce, and in some places nonexistent, in the area they were now forced to travel. Again, sickness followed in the wake of exposure to the cold, rainy weather and immersion in the swamps.[39] Finally, in spite of all efforts to avoid it, cholera attacked the emigrants, and Major Francis Armstrong hastened them on to Vicksburg. From Vicksburg they immediately traveled by steamboat to Rockroe, the rendezvous point for all emigrants in Arkansas Territory, arriving there on November 12 and 13.[40]

All of the emigrating Indians eventually ended up at Rockroe, where they stopped for supplies and a short rest. Then, they all proceeded overland to the Little Rock area. From that point, large parties followed the Arkansas River to Fort Smith, while three smaller parties of 600 each journeyed overland across southwestern Arkansas to Fort Towson near the Red River.[41] Major Armstrong wrote in his official report that from Little Rock onward the trip had become easier, for the ground was solid and the agents had hired wagons to help alleviate the suffering of the appalling number of sick and infirm Indians. However, there were only five wagons for every thousand persons, forcing the bulk of the Indians to proceed on foot. Armstrong wrote, "Fortunately they are a people that will walk to the last, or I do not know how we could go on."[42]

By mid-January the Choctaws began arriving in Fort Towson and Fort Smith. Lieutenant G. J. Rains, a disbursing agent in Arkansas Territory, advised George Gibson that "about 1,700 of the late emigrants have arrived and settled on the San Bois & the upper waters of the Poteau, that W. Rector was expected in about six days & with about 500 Choctaws. . . ."[43] All told, 5,538 Choctaws had arrived in their western lands in January and Feb-

---

39 *Ibid.;* Wright, "Removal of the Choctaws," p. 122.
40 Wright, "Removal of the Choctaws."
41 *Arkansas Gazette*, November 21, 1832.
42 Wright, "Removal of the Choctaws," p. 122.
43 G. J. Rains to George Gibson, January 12, 1833, Letters of Commissary General of Subsistence, MSS.

ruary of 1833.[44] About 1,000 of this number had traveled independently, but the bulk had been removed in organized parties by United States Army agents under the new War Department removal regulations. Gibson felt that this second group removal was much more successful than the first, for over 5,000 Indians had been removed at about half the cost of the previous removal, and the agents had stayed well within the budget set up by the commissary general of subsistence.

In other respects, however, the removal of 1832 was as much a failure as the previous effort. More Indians had been removed, but more had died of cholera and exposure; the government had saved money by making the Indians walk more than five hundred miles and by cutting their rations, but the saving had been made at the sacrifice of Indian life and strength. The War Department could rejoice at having balanced its removal budget. But in view of the way it had been balanced, many Indians did not share the elation. In fact, it is not difficult to understand why more than seven hundred Choctaws, soon after they had reached Indian Territory, continued southwest toward Texas to try their luck with the Mexican government.[45]

Now that the removal of 1832 was completed, the War Department began preparations for the removal of the third and final group of Choctaws, to be started in 1833. George Gibson urged frugality even more emphatically than he had the previous year, admonishing Captain Brown, "Let no expense continue . . . that can without injury, be dispensed with."[46] Following his

[44] Muster Rolls of a company of Choctaw Indians about to Emigrate West of the Mississippi River, 1832–1833, MSS, Records of the Bureau of Indian Affairs, National Archives. This figure is 221 more than migrated in October, 1832. The difference is partly owing to counting too few when they left or too many at the time of arrival. It is quite easy to count one Indian twice or not at all in this kind of an operation. The 1,000 that migrated on their own journeyed by different routes and at different speeds. Undoubtedly, some of these were counted at Fort Towson and Fort Smith while others had stopped along the way, died, or settled elsewhere.

[45] Peter E. Beau to Lewis Cass, February 27, 1833, Choctaw Agency 1824–1833, Letters Received, MSS, Records of the Bureau of Indian Affairs, National Archives.

[46] George Gibson to Jacob Brown, April 11, 1833, Letterbook of Commissary General of Subsistence, MSS.

158

economy program, Gibson instructed the removal agents to give the Indians any unused supplies left over from the recent removal, using them as a partial payment of the full year's subsistence promised in the Treaty of Dancing Rabbit Creek—even though most of the meat in these supplies was now spoiled.[47] Also, Gibson removed William Ward as the Choctaw agent in Mississippi[48] and John Pitchlynn as the interpreter[49] because the small number of Choctaws left in that state no longer warranted their services.

By June, 1833, the agents were once again busy procuring supplies for the fall removal. The rains of the previous winter and spring had not only menaced the traveling Indians but had also damaged the crops in Arkansas Territory.[50] With a smaller supply of corn available for the coming removal, the farmers were able, with some justification, to charge exorbitant prices. William Armstrong wrote Gibson that corn was selling at two to three dollars a bushel.[51] Captain Brown wrote, "I am informed that along the route which it is supposed the Indians will travel, many persons have determined that if they cannot obtain the price they think proper to ask for corn & beef, not to sell, and that there was a belief that the U.S. would be compelled to purchase at *any price*."[52] The *Arkansas Gazette* justified the farmers' price and remarked, "we hope they may realize from them [federal government] a handsome profit."[53]

Despite the grumblings of the commissary general over the mounting costs, the government again made a conscientious effort to supply goods of superior quality to the Choctaw emi-

[47] George Gibson to G. J. Rains, May 6, 1833, *ibid*.
[48] D. Kurtz to William Ward, November 5, 1832, Records of the Office of Indian Affairs, MSS.
[49] Elbert Herring to John Pitchlynn, October 10, 1832, *ibid*.
[50] George Gibson to Jacob Brown, August 14, 1833, Letterbook of Commissary General of Subsistence, MSS.
[51] William Armstrong to George Gibson, June 20, 1833, Letters of Commissary General of Subsistence, MSS.
[52] Jacob Brown to George Gibson, November 30, 1833, Letterbook of Commissary General of Subsistence, MSS.
[53] *Arkansas Gazette*, September 11, 1833.

grants.[54] On July 3 the government advertised in the *Gazette* for bids on the following supplies: 115,900 rations to be delivered to the depot on the Mountain Fork of Little River, forty miles northeast of Towson; 92,100 rations to Horse Prairie, twenty miles west of Fort Towson; 20,130 rations to the new Choctaw Agency near the Arkansas River, twenty-five miles southwest of Fort Smith; 100,650 rations to Pleasant Bluff on the Arkansas River, thirty-five miles above Fort Smith; and 30,560 rations to the depot on the Poteau River, forty miles southwest of Fort Smith.[55] All of these rations were to be made up of the best corn, wheat, pork, and beef available in Arkansas Territory. In addition, the government provided other supplies, such as oxen, horses, and blankets, during the period May to September, 1833.[56]

While the agents were procuring the necessary supplies, William Armstrong and his assistants were organizing the third and last Choctaw removal party. Captain Armstrong sent an assistant into each of the three Choctaw districts to muster Indians. But despite the fact that more than six thousand Choctaws remained in Mississippi, the agents found it very difficult to enroll any of them.[57] The worried Gibson eloquently summarized his arguments for Choctaw removal in a letter to Armstrong: "They should have laid before them a picture of the prosperity of their brethren who have already emigrated, possessed of a delightful climate, a fruitful soil, yielding in abundance all the necessities of life, with plenty of game, and good rifles & ammunition to secure it."[58]

Regardless of Gibson's urging and the agents' efforts, many

[54] Commissary General of Subsistence: Contracts for Subsistence of Indians, MSS, Records of the Bureau of Indian Affairs, National Archives.

[55] *Arkansas Gazette*, July 3, 1833.

[56] Contracts for Subsistence of Indians, MSS.

[57] William Armstrong to George Gibson, August 5, 1833, Letters of Commissary General of Subsistence, MSS.

[58] George Gibson to William Armstrong, August 15, 1833, Letterbook of Commissary General of Subsistence, MSS.

Choctaws steadfastly refused to leave,[59] and it was therefore impossible to make any definite arrangements for the journey or even to estimate needed supplies and equipment. Armstrong and Gibson decided to follow the route taken by Mushulatubbee's group the previous year and to make the necessary arrangements on the way.[60] This plan would work only if favorable weather prevailed during the whole trip, for if nature dealt as harshly with the emigrants as it had in the past two removals, this trek might well end disastrously.

Finally, on October 1, 1833, a small party of 813 Choctaws left on foot for Memphis.[61] They arrived on October 13, and to get them across the Mississippi River, Armstrong hired the same snag boat *Archimedes* that had served the purpose the previous year.[62] As soon as the Indians had boarded, however, the *Archimedes* broke a shaft and was unable to leave its mooring. Armstrong then hired the steamboat *Thomas Yeatman*, but just as it was docking to receive its passengers, one of its boilers exploded, instantly killing a number of the ship's company. While the *Yeat-*

---

[59] William Armstrong to George Gibson, September 14, 1833, Letters of Commissary General of Subsistence, MSS.

[60] George Gibson to William Armstrong, September 17, 1833, Letterbook of Commissary General of Subsistence, MSS.

[61] *Arkansas Gazette*, November 6, 1833.

[62] George Gibson to William Armstrong, September 17, 1833, Letterbook of Commissary General of Subsistence, MSS; Judgments of Comms. Claiborne, Graves, & Taylor Held at the Old Yazoo Village 11th May, 1843, MSS, Bureau of Indian Affairs, National Archives; Choctaw Claims on Land & Scrip Adjudicated for the Secretary of War and Secretary of Interior under Special Acts of Congress, 1848, MSS, Bureau of Indian Affairs, National Archives; Choctaw Claims under 14th Article of the Treaty of 1830: Revison of the Decisions of Messrs. Claiborne, Graves and Taylor—Commissioners, appointed under the Act of 23 August 1842, MSS, Records of the Bureau of Indian Affairs, Indian Office Division, Land Section, National Archives; Choctaw Claims under the 14th Article of the Treaty of 1830: Revision of the Decisions of Messrs. Murray & Vroom—Commissioners, Appointed under the Act of 3d March 1837, MSS, Records of the Bureau of Indian Affairs, Indian Office Division, Land Section, National Archives; "Treaty of Dancing Rabbit Creek," *Hearings before a subcommittee of the Committee on Indian Affairs House of Representatives* (Washington, D.C., 1912), pp. 101–62; Schedule of Horses and Cattle lost on the way from Old Nation to the West Authenticated, MSS, Records of the Bureau of Indian Affairs, National Archives.

man was being repaired the agents decided to use it to transport the Indians from Memphis southwest on the Mississippi to the White River and thence northwest to Rockroe. The Choctaws were so thoroughly frightened by the disaster that, like Mushulatubbee's Indians in the earlier removal, they at first refused to emigrate by boat.[63] After a delay of three days, however, they were finally coaxed into boarding the repaired boat, and they arrived at Rockroe on November 7.[64] The weather was excellent as the Choctaws started overland from Rockroe. They passed Little Rock on November 21, and by December 20 they had arrived in Indian Territory.[65]

Thus ended the third and last of the formal group removals, although small bands of Indians who had chosen to emigrate on their own initiative continued to arrive in Indian Territory during the early months of the following year, from January to April, 1834. These individualists were at a disadvantage because the removal books had been closed the previous December and many of the Indians never received the benefits that the government had promised them.[66] The stragglers brought the total number of Choctaws now settled in Indian Territory to approximately 12,500. About 6,000 of their fellow tribesmen still remained in Mississippi, feeling secure under terms of ARTICLE 14 of the Treaty of Dancing Rabbit Creek; but they, too, were soon to be uprooted and forced out of the State of Mississippi. William Ward's treachery in failing to register them under the treaty article meant that they had no legal right to retain their land in Mississippi. Consequently, during the remaining years of the nineteenth century, the government removed most of them to Indian Territory.[67] Only about 1,500 Choctaws still live in Mis-

---

[63] Wright, "Removal of the Choctaws," p. 123.

[64] *Arkansas Gazette*, November 13, 1833.

[65] Wright, "Removal of the Choctaws," p. 123.

[66] It is estimated that as many as 3,215 Choctaws were eligible for commutation benefits by April, 1834. Very few ever received their just reward. *Ibid.*

[67] *Ibid. Hearings before a subcommittee of the Committee on Indian Affairs,* pp. 9–10.

sissippi today. They are the descendants of those allowed to register under ARTICLE 14.

The total cost for all three group removals was estimated by the Bureau of Indian Affairs and reported on January 21, 1833, as "about $475,000, or approximately $25.00 a person."[68] The cost of subsistence for the three-year period was estimated at $608,000.[69] In a United States Senate resolution of March 9, 1839, the total cost of removal and subsistence was officially listed as $813,927.[70] When all of the other expenses incurred under the provisions of the Treaty of Dancing Rabbit Creek were added to this amount—items such as the removal agents' salaries and land-fraud settlements—the government in 1845 submitted $5,097,367.50 as the grand total cost of the removal of the Choctaws.[71]

In return for this considerable expenditure of money and effort, the government of the United States received $8,095,614.89 for the Choctaw land it sold to its white citizens. Since the government had pledged at Dancing Rabbit Creek not to make any profit out of these sales, the Choctaws brought the "Net Proceeds" case to federal court and won $2,981,247.39, most of which was spent to reimburse the lawyers who fought the case through the courts.[72]

"Thus the Choctaws not only endured every suffering from hunger and cold to sickness and death in the removal to their

[68] Wright, "Removal of the Choctaws," p. 124. The bureau overestimated the amount per person. At $25 apiece, $475,000 would pay for the removal of 19,000 Indians—6,000 more than actually migrated.

[69] U. S. Congress, Senate, "Report of the Secretary of War, Communicating Information in Relation to the Contracts Made for the Removal and Subsistence of the Choctaw Indians," No. 86 in *Senate Executive Documents, 1845*, 28th Cong., 2nd sess. (Washington, D.C., 1846), p. 5.

[70] If the removal cost $475,000 and the subsistence cost $608,000, the total cost of removal and subsistence should have been $1,083,000. I suspect that the subsistence figure was as large an overestimate as the removal one.

[71] Payments Made Under the Treaty with the Choctaws, Concluded at Dancing Rabbit Creek, 27th Sept. 1830, MSS, Bureau of Indian Affairs, National Archives.

[72] *Hearings before a subcommittee of the Committee on Indian Affairs*, pp. 8–9; Wright, "Removal of the Choctaws," p. 124.

new home in Indian Territory," Muriel Wright penned, "but also paid every dollar of the expense incurred under the Treaty of Dancing Rabbit Creek."[73] This was the tragic denouement to the Choctaw drama, but considering the cast of characters, the only one to be expected.

From a certain point of view, the removal of one nation of aborigines may seem a rather trivial matter, especially when it is considered in relation to the many other events that were taking place during a highly nationalistic period of American history. Yet, the removal of the Choctaw Indians, which stretched over a period of sixteen years, from 1818 to 1834, was highly significant, not only because it established the pattern for Indian removal in the nineteenth century but because it eventually affected the existence of almost every Indian nation in the country.[74] The Choctaws were chosen by the War Department to test out the various removal policies being proposed by everyone from missionaries and philanthropists to citizens of the militant West. The Choctaw Nation was large, friendly, civilized, and relatively stationary—the very characteristics that John Calhoun wanted. Of the other tribes of eastern Indians, only the Cherokees could have met these requirements as well. But Calhoun chose the Choctaws because their nation was located farther west than the others and because they had had fewer dealings with the white man.

Before this pattern was established, the federal government had a choice of two plans: that of Calhoun, who was the avowed champion of moderation, and that of Jackson, who favored immediate removal by any means—force if necessary. Calhoun, between 1818 and 1825, foresaw the eventual removal and acknowledged its necessity; but he wanted to allow the Indians to decide for themselves when they would move to the new lands that had been offered in trade by the United States government.[75] In other words, Calhoun wanted to induce the Indians

---

[73] Wright, "Removal of the Choctaws," p. 124.

[74] Many other southern tribes were being removed at approximately the same time as the Choctaws, among them the Creeks, Chickasaws, and Cherokees.

[75] Although Calhoun's position in regard to the Indians is laudable, it is hard to justify his championship of the Indian's cause while at the same time he con-

to emigrate, as soon as possible but through a process of educating them to accept the necessity of removal.

Jackson, on the other hand, felt that Calhoun was a hypocrite for defending the Indians against the frontiersmen while at the same time preaching eventual removal. As Jackson intimated in many letters to the War Department, Calhoun criticized the views of others, especially the westerners, while he was blind to the shortcomings of his own region. Jackson's philosophy was that of the West in general: emigrate immediately or face the armed might of the federal government; move or be annihilated. Which course the Indians chose made no difference to the frontier general, who was always ready for a good fight. Jackson carried this philosophy from the Hermitage to the White House and put it into operation in 1829 with the assistance of his western friends. The essential difference between the policies of Calhoun and Jackson lay in the amount of time to be allowed for the removal; the end results would be the same, either way.

From today's vantage point, it is not difficult to see the faults in the Jacksonian philosophy that eventually prevailed in the Treaty of Dancing Rabbit Creek, and to understand that these faults created the terror and inhumanity that engulfed the West up to the 1890s. Nor is it difficult from the same vantage point to see that, in spite of the faults of the treaty, the Choctaws did not deteriorate after they moved to Indian Territory. To the contrary, taken as a whole, the Choctaw generation from 1833 to 1861 "presents a record of orderly development almost unprecedented in the history of any people."[76]

By 1860, after rejecting a number of unsatisfactory governmental suggestions, the Choctaws had adopted a constitution that

---

sidered the other major minority group—the Negro—as definitely inferior and valuable only as slaves. After all, some of Calhoun's relatives had been murdered by Indians on the Carolina frontier, and it would have been logical for him to dislike the aborigines as much as or more than the Negroes. There is no evidence in the Calhoun papers to indicate that the secretary of war came to grips with this inconsistency. He was simply interested in the welfare of the Indians and would do all in his power to treat them as equals and give them the right to determine their future at the negotiating table.

[76] Debo, *Choctaw Republic*, p. 78.

was even more enlightened and democratic than the one that they had followed in Mississippi. The new constitution retained the district organization of the past, but further "provided for a national government with a Principal Chief and other executive officers, a General Council of two houses, and a Supreme Court."[77]

The Choctaws prospered almost from the time they arrived in Indian Territory. They applied their agricultural skill to make the land yield a profit, and they built settlements in all three districts. As time went on, their new location offered unlooked-for advantages, for it became the junction of the road that carried those seeking gold to California and the one that carried emigrants from the North to Texas. Aware of this advantage, the Choctaws established the town of Boggy Depot at the crossroads, and it became an active trading center in the 1850s. Other towns developed by the Choctaws during their first ten years in Indian Territory included Skullyville, Doaksville, Eagletown, and Perryville—small but thriving towns boasting of blacksmith shops, stores, hotels, and produce markets.[78]

Some Choctaw farmers developed large cotton plantations along the Red River and cultivated "fine orchards and extensive cornfields, well stocked with cattle, hogs, & fouls."[79] By as early as 1838 they had transformed the wilderness into a prosperous farming area and were trading corn, pecans, and large quantities of cotton for manufactured goods from the East.

The Choctaws also promoted education and their growing religious faith. They started opening schools even before the last of the three group removals had been completed, and by 1836 eleven schools in the territory had an enrollment of 228 children.[80] Several Christian denominations provided religious instruction. Many books were translated into the Choctaw language, among them the Old and New testaments, hymnals, moral

[77] *Ibid.*, p. 75.
[78] *Ibid.*, p. 59.
[79] *Ibid.*, p. 60.
[80] *Ibid.*

lectures, biographical sketches of pious Indians, and numerous doctrinal tracts "on such formidable subjects as 'Regeneration, Repentance, and Judgment,' 'Sinners in the Hands of an Angry God,' 'Salvation by Faith and Other Pieces,' and 'Fraud Detected and Exposed'."[81] At the time of the Civil War, between 20 and 25 percent of the Indians were members of Presbyterian, Methodist, or Baptist churches. Sunday observance was general, and sessions of the council were opened and closed with prayers.

Unfortunately, life in Indian Territory, offered no escape from the animosity that developed between the Choctaws and other Indian tribes and white pioneers who continued to swarm into Indian lands all over America. To understand, if not to condone, this animosity, one must remember that these white emigrants were pioneers in the true sense—adventurers moving west with their families and a few possessions in rickety wagons that offered no comfort and little protection. For years these western families contended with almost insurmountable odds: clearing dense forests, building homes, tilling virgin soil, and fighting malaria, cholera, storms, floods, and drought. The average settler felt that he could cope with the vagaries of nature if only he could free himself from the presence of the many Indians who lurked in the shadows and who, for their part, resented the settlers as unwelcome invaders. Fear and a resentment of competition for desirable lands, on a vicious frontier where only the fittest could survive, produced in the white pioneer an almost pathological hatred of the Indian, a hatred that colored all of his relations with the legal residents of any Indian territory.

Thus, the die was cast. Events in the years that followed would only increase the influx of white settlers onto Indian lands until, finally, the once mighty Choctaw Nation would be proud and powerful no more, except in their hearts.

[81] *Ibid.*, p. 62.

TREATY OF DOAK'S STAND

A treaty of friendship, limits, and accommodation between the United States of America and the Choctaw Nation of Indians, begun and concluded at the treaty ground in said nation, near Doak's Stand, on the Natchez road.

WHEREAS it is important for the President of the United States to promote the civilization of the Choctaw Indians, by the establishment of schools amongst them, and to perpetuate them as a nation, by exchanging for a small part of their land here a country beyond the Mississippi river, where all who live by hunting and will not work may be collected and settled together: and whereas it is desirable to the State of Mississippi to obtain a small part of the land belonging to said nation: for the mutual accommodation of the parties, and for securing the happiness and protection of the whole Choctaw nation, as well as preserving that harmony and friendship which so happily subsists between them and the United States, James Monroe, President of the United States of America by Andrew Jackson, of the State of Tennessee, major general of the army of the United States, and General Thomas Hinds, of the State of Mississippi, commissioners plenipotentiary of the United States, on the one part, and the mingoes, headmen, and warriors of the Choctaw nation, in full council assembled, on the other part, have freely and voluntarily entered into the following articles, viz:

ARTICLE 1. To enable the President of the United States to carry into effect the above grand and humane objects, the mingoes, headmen, and warriors of the Choctaw nation, in full council assembled, in behalf of themselves and the said nation, do, by these presents, cede to the United States of America all the land lying and being within the following boundaries, to wit: Beginning on the Choctaw boundary east of Pearl river, at a point due south of the White Oak spring, on the old Indian path; thence north to said spring; thence, northwardly, to a black oak, standing on the Natchez road, about forty poles eastwardly from Doak's fence, marked A. J., and blazed, with two large pines and a black oak standing near thereto, and marked as pointers; thence, a straight line, to the head of Black creek, or Bouge Loosa; thence, down Black creek, or Bouge Loosa, to a small lake; thence, a direct course so as to strike the Mississippi one mile below the mouth of the Arkansas river; thence, down the Mississippi, to our boundary; thence, round and along the same, to the beginning.

ARTICLE 2. For and in consideration of the foregoing cession on the part of the Choctaw nation, and in part satisfaction for the same, the commissioners of the United States, in behalf of said States, do hereby cede to said nation a tract of country west of the Mississippi river, situated between the Arkansas and Red rivers, and bounded as follows: Beginning on the Arkansas river, where the lower boundary line of the Cherokees strikes the same; thence, up the Arkansas, to the Canadian Fork, and up the same to its source; thence, due south, to the Red river; thence down Red river, three miles below the mouth of Little river, which empties itself into Red river, on the north side; thence a direct line, to the beginning.

ARTICLE 3. To prevent any dispute upon the subject of the boundaries mentioned in the first and second articles, it is hereby stipulated between the parties that the same shall be ascertained and distinctly marked by a commissioner or commissioners, to be appointed by the United States, accompanied by such person as the Choctaw nation may select; said nation having thirty days' previous notice of the time and place at which the operation will commence. The person so chosen by the Choctaws shall act as a pilot or guide, for which the United States

169

will pay him two dollars per day whilst actually engaged in the performance of that duty.

ARTICLE 4. The boundaries hereby established between the Choctaw Indians and the United States, on this side of the Mississippi river, shall remain without alteration, until the period at which said nation shall become so civilized and enlightened as to be made citizens of the United States; and Congress shall lay off a limited parcel of land for the benefit of each family or individual in the nation.

ARTICLE 5. For the purpose of aiding and assisting the poor Indians who wish to remove to the country hereby ceded on the part of the United States, and to enable them to do well and support their families, the commissioners of the United States engage, in behalf of said States, to give to each warrior a blanket, kettle, rifle gun, bullet moulds and wipers, and ammunition sufficient for hunting and defence for one year, said warriors shall also be supplied with corn, to support him and his family for the same period, and whilst travelling to the country above ceded to the Choctaw nation.

ARTICLE 6. The commissioners of the United States further covenant and agree, on the part of said States, that an agent shall be appointed, in due time, for the benefit of the Choctaw Indians who may be permanently settled in the country ceded to them beyond the Mississippi river, and, at a convenient period, a factor shall be sent there, with goods to supply their wants. A blacksmith shall also be settled amongst them. At a point most convenient to the population, and a faithful person appointed, whose duty it shall be to use every reasonable exertion to collect all the wandering Indians belonging to the Choctaw nation upon the land hereby provided for their permanent settlement.

ARTICLE 7. Out of the lands ceded by the Choctaw nation to the United States, the commissioners aforesaid, in behalf of said States, further covenant and agree that fifty-four sections of one mile square shall be laid out, in good land, by the President of the United States, and sold, for the purpose of raising a fund, to be applied to the support of the Choctaw schools on both sides of the Mississippi river: three-fourths of said fund shall be appropriated for the benefit of the schools here, and the remaining fourth for the establishment of one or more beyond the Mississippi; the whole to be placed in the hands of the President of the United States, and to be applied by him, expressly and exclusively, to this valuable object.

ARTICLE 8. To remove any discontent which may have arisen in the Choctaw nation, in consequence of six thousand dollars of their annuity having been appropriated annually, for sixteen years, by some of the chiefs, for the support of their schools, the commissioners of the United States oblige themselves, on the part of said States, to set apart an additional tract of good land, for raising a fund equal to that given by the said chiefs, so that the whole of the annuity may remain in the nation, and be divided amongst them. And, in order that exact justice may be done to the poor and distressed of said nation, it shall be the duty of the agent to see that the wants of every deaf, dumb, blind, and distressed Indian shall be first supplied out of the said annuity, and the balance equally distributed amongst every individual of said nation.

ARTICLE 9. All those who have separate settlements, and fall within the limits of the land ceded by the Choctaw nation to the United States, and who desire to remain where they now reside, shall be secured in a tract or parcel of land one mile square, to include their improvements. Any one who prefers removing, if he does so within one year from the date of this treaty, shall be paid their full value, to be ascertained by two persons to be appointed by the President of the United States.

ARTICLE 10. As there are some who have valuable buildings, on the roads and elsewhere, upon the lands hereby ceded, should they remove, it is further agreed, by the aforesaid commissioners, in behalf of the United States, that the inconvenience of doing so shall be considered, and such allowance made as will amount to an equivalent. For this purpose, there shall be paid to the mingo Puckshenubbee, five hundred dollars; to Harrison, two hundred dollars; to William Hays, two hundred dollars; to Oglono, two hundred dollars; and to all others who have comfortable houses, a compensation in the same proportion.

ARTICLE 11. It is also provided by the commissioners of the United States, and they agree, in behalf of said States, that those Choctaw chiefs and warriors who have not received compensation for their services during the campaign at Pensacola, in the late war, shall be paid whatever is due them over and above the value of the blanket, shirt, flap, and leggings which have been delivered to them.

ARTICLE 12. In order to promote industry and sobriety amongst all classes of the red people in this nation, but particularly the poor, it is further provided by the parties, that the agent appointed to reside there shall be, and is hereby, vested with full power to seize and confiscate all the whiskey which may be introduced into said nation, except that used at public stands, or brought in by the permit of the agent or the principal chiefs of the three districts.

ARTICLE 13. To enable the mingoes, chiefs, and headmen of the Choctaw nation to raise and organize a corps of light horse, consisting of ten in each district, so that good order may be maintained, and that all men, both white and red, may be compelled to pay their just debts, it is stipulated and agreed that the sum of two hundred dollars shall be appropriated by the United States, for each district, annually, and placed in the hands of the agent, to pay the expenses incurred in raising and establishing said corps, which is to act as executive officers, in maintaining good order, and compelling bad men to remove from the nation, who are not authorized to live in it by a regular permit from the agent.

ARTICLE 14. Whereas the father of the beloved chief Mushulatubbee, of the Lower Towns, for and during his life, did receive from the United States the sum of one hundred and fifty dollars, annually, it is hereby stipulated that his son and successor, Mushulatubbee, shall annually be paid the same amount during his natural life, to commence from the ratification of this treaty.

ARTICLE 15. The peace and harmony subsisting between the Choctaw nation of Indians and the United States is hereby renewed, continued, and declared to be perpetual.

ARTICLE 16. These articles shall take effect and become obligatory on the contracting parties so soon as the same shall be ratified by the President, by and with the advice and consent of the Senate of the United States.

In testimony whereof, the commissioners plenipotentiary of the United States, and the mingoes, headmen, and warriors of the Choctaw nation, have hereunto subscribed their names and affixed their seals at the place above written, this eighteenth day of October, in the year of our Lord one thousand eight hundred and twenty, and of the independence of the United States the forty-fifth.

[Signed by Jackson, Hinds, and the mingoes, headmen, and warriors of the Choctaw Nation.]

TREATY OF
DANCING RABBIT CREEK

A treaty of perpetual friendship, cession and limits, entered into by John H. Eaton and John Coffee for and in behalf of the Government of the United States, and the Mingoes, Chiefs, Captains, and Warriors of the Choctaw Nation, begun and held at Dancing Rabbit Creek on the 15th of September in the year 1830.

WHEREAS the General Assembly of the State of Mississippi has extended the laws of said state to persons and property within the chartered limits of the same, and the President of the United States has said that he cannot protect the Choctaw people from the operation of those laws. Now, therefore, that the Choctaws may live under their own laws in peace with the United States, and the State of Mississippi, and have, accordingly agreed to the following articles of treaty.

ARTICLE 1. Perpetual peace and friendship is pledged and agreed upon, by and between the United States, and the Mingoes, Chiefs and warriors of the Choctaw Nation of Red people, and that this may be considered the treaty existing between the parties, all other treaties heretofore existing and inconsistent with the provisions of this are hereby declared null and void.

ARTICLE 2. The United States, under a grant specially to be made by the President of the United States, shall cause to be conveyed to the Choctaw nation, a tract of country West of the Mississippi river in fee simple, to them and their descendents, to

174

insure to them while they shall exist as a nation, and live on it, beginning near Fort Smith, where the Arkansas boundary crosses the Arkansas river, running thence to the source of the Canadian Fork if in the limits of the United States, or to those limits; thence due South to Red river, and down Red river to the West boundary of the territory of Arkansas, thence North along that line to the beginning. The boundary of the same to be agreeable to the treaty made and concluded at Washington City in the year 1825. The grant to be executed, so soon as the present treaty shall be ratified.

ARTICLE 3. In consideration of the provisions contained in the several articles of this treaty, the Choctaw nation of Indians consent, and hereby cede to the United States the entire country they own and possess East of the Mississippi river, and they agree to remove beyond the Mississippi river, early as practicable, and will so arrange their removal, that as many as possible of their people not exceeding one half of the whole number shall depart during the falls of 1831 and 1832 the residue to follow during the succeeding fall of 1833. A better opportunity, in this manner, will be afforded the government to extend to them the facilities and comforts which it is desirable should be extended in encouraging them to their new homes.

ARTICLE 4. The government and people of the United States, are hereby obliged to secure to the said Choctaw nation of red people the jurisdiction and government of all the persons and property that may be within their limits West, so that no state or territory shall ever have a right to pass laws for the government of the Choctaw nation of red people and their descendents: and that no part of the land granted them shall ever be embraced in any territory or state, but the United States shall forever secure said Choctaw nation from and against all laws, except such as from time to time, may be enacted in their national councils, not inconsistent with the constitution, treaties and laws of the United States; and except as may and which have been enacted by Congress to the extent that Congress under the constitution are required to exercise a legislation over Indian affairs. But the Choctaws, should this treaty be ratified, express a wish that Congress may grant to the Choctaws the rights of punishing by their own laws, any white man who shall come

175

into their nation, and infringe any of their national regulations.

ARTICLE 5. The United States are obliged to protect the Choctaws from domestic strife, and from foreign enemies, on the same principles that citizens of the United States are protected; so that whatever would be a legal demand upon the United States for defence or for wrongs committed by an enemy of a citizen of the United States, shall be equally binding in favor of the Choctaws, and in all cases where the Choctaws shall be called upon, by a legally authorized officer of the United States, to fight an enemy, such Choctaw shall receive the pay and other benefits, which citizens of the United States receive in such cases: provided, no war shall be undertaken or prosecuted by said Choctaw nation, but by declaration made in full council, and to be approved by the United States, unless it be in self defence against an open rebellion, or against an enemy marching into their country; in which cases they shall defend until the United States are advised thereof.

ARTICLE 6. Should a Choctaw, or any party of Choctaws, commence acts of violence upon the person or property of a citizen of the United States or join any war party against any neighboring tribe of Indians, without the authority in the preceding article and except to oppose an actual or threatened invasion, or rebellion, such person so offending shall be delivered up to an officer of the United States, if in the power of the Choctaw nation that such offender may be punished, as may be provided in such cases by the laws of the United States; but if such offender is not within the control of the Choctaw nation, then said Choctaw nation shall not be held responsible for the injury done by said offender.

ARTICLE 7. All acts of violence committed upon persons and property of the people of the Choctaw nation, either by citizens of the United States, or neighboring tribes of red people, shall be referred to some authorized agent by him to be referred to the President of the United States, who shall examine into such cases, and see that every possible degree of justice is done to said Indian party of the Choctaw nation.

ARTICLE 8. Offenders against the laws of the United States, or any individual state, shall be apprehended and delivered to any duly authorized person where such offender may be found in the Choctaw country, having fled from any part of the United States, but in all such cases application must be made to the agent or the chiefs and the expense of his apprehension and delivery, provided for, and paid by the United States.

ARTICLE 9. Any citizen of the United States, who may be ordered from the nation by the agent and constituted authorities of the nation, and refused to obey, or return to the nation, without the consent of the aforesaid persons, shall be subject to such pains and penalties as may be provided by the laws of the United States, in such cases. Citizens of the United States travelling peaceably under the authority of the laws of the United States, shall be under the care and protection of the nation.

ARTICLE 10. No person shall expose goods, or other articles for sale, as a trader, without permission from the constituted authorities of the nation, or authority of the laws of the Congress of the United States, under penalty of forfeiting the articles; and the constituted authorities of said nation shall grant no license, except to such persons as reside in the nation and are answerable to the laws of the nation. The United States shall be particularly obliged to assist to prevent ardent spirits from being introduced into the nation.

ARTICLE 11. Navigable streams shall be free to the Choctaws who shall pay no higher toll or duty than citizens of the United States. It is agreed further that the United States shall establish one or more post offices in said nation and may establish such military post roads, and posts, as they may consider necessary.

ARTICLE 12. All intruders shall be removed from the Choctaw nation and kept without it. Private property to be always respected, and on no occasion taken for public purposes without just compensation being made therefor to the rightful owners. If an Indian unlawfully steals any property from a white man, a citizen of the United States, the offender shall be punished, and if a white man unlawfully takes anything from an Indian, the property shall be restored, and the offender punished. It is further agreed that when a Choctaw shall be given up to be tried, for any offense against the laws of the United States, if unable to employ council to defend him, the United States will do it, that his trial may be fair and impartial.

ARTICLE 13. It is consented that a qualified agent shall be appointed, for the Choctaws, every four years unless sooner removed, by the President, and he shall be removed on petition of the constituted authorities of the nation the President being satisfied there is sufficient cause shown. The agent shall fix his residence convenient to the great body of the people, and in the selection of an agent, immediately after the ratification of this treaty, the wishes of the Choctaw nation on the subject, shall be entitled to great respect.

ARTICLE 14. Each Choctaw head of a family, being desirous to remain, and become a citizen of the States, shall be permitted to do so, by signifying his intention to the agent within six months from the ratification of this treaty, and he or she shall thereupon be entitled to a reservation of one section of six hundred and forty acres of land, to be bounded by sectional lines of survey; in like manner, shall be entitled to one half that quantity, for each unmarried child which is living with him, over ten years of age, and a quarter section to such child as may be under ten years of age to adjoin the location of the parent. If they reside upon said lands intending to become citizens of the States, for five years after the ratification of this treaty, in that case, a grant of land in fee simple shall be issued; said reservation shall include the present improvement of the head of the family, or a portion of it. Persons who claim under this article shall not lose the privileges of a Choctaw citizen, but if they ever remove are not to be entitled to any portion of the Choctaw annuity.

ARTICLE 15. To each of the Chiefs in the Choctaw nation (to wit), Greenwood LeFlore, Nutackachie and Mushulatubbee, there is granted a reservation of four sections of land two of which shall include and adjoin their present improvements and the other two located where they please but on unoccupied, unimproved lands; such sections shall be bounded by sectional lines, and with the consent of the President, they may sell the same. Also, to the three principal chiefs, and to their successors in office, there shall be paid two hundred and fifty dollars, annually while they shall continue in their respective offices; except to Mushulatubbee, who, as he has an annuity of one hundred and fifty dollars, for life, under a former treaty, shall receive only the additional sum of one hundred dollars, while he shall continue in office, as chief. And if in addition to this the nation shall think proper to elect an additional principal chief of the whole to superintend and govern, upon republican principles, he shall receive annually, for his services, five hundred dollars, which allowance to the chiefs, and their successors in office, shall continue for twenty years. At any time when in military service, and while in service by authority of the United States, the district chiefs, under, and by selection of the President, shall be entitled to the pay of Majors; and the other chief, under the same circumstances, shall have the pay of a Lieutenant Colonel. The speakers of the three districts, shall receive twenty five dollars a year, for four years: and the three secretaries, one to each of the chiefs, fifty dollars each, for four years. Each Captain of the nation, the number not to exceed ninety-nine, thirty-three from each district, shall be furnished, upon removing to the West, with each a good suit of clothes, and a broad sword, as an outfit, and for four years, commencing with the first of their removal shall each receive fifty dollars a year, for the trouble of keeping their people at order in settling: and whenever they shall be in military service, by authority of the United States, shall receive the pay of a captain.

ARTICLE 16. In wagons, and with steamboats, as may be found necessary, the United States agree to remove the Indians to their new homes, at their expense, and under the care of discreet and careful persons, who will be kind and brotherly to them. They agree to furnish them with ample corn and beef, or pork for themselves and families, for twelve months, after reaching their new homes. It is agreed further, that the United States will take all their cattle, at the valuation of some discreet person to be appointed by the President, and the same shall be paid for in money after their arrival at their new homes, or other cattle, such as may be desired, shall be furnished them; notice being given, through their agent of their wishes upon this subject of their removal, that time to supply the demand may be afforded.

ARTICLE 17. The several annuities and sums secured under former treaties, to the Choctaw nation and people, shall continue, as though this treaty had never been made. And it is further agreed, that the United States, in addition, will pay the sum of twenty thousand dollars for twenty years, commencing after their removal to the West, of which in the first year after their removal, ten thousand dollars shall be divided and arranged, to such as may not receive reservations under this treaty.

ARTICLE 18. The United States shall cause the lands hereby added, to be surveyed: and surveyors may enter the Choctaw country for that purpose; conducting themselves properly, and disturbing or interrupting none of the Choctaw people. But no person is to be permitted to settle within the nation, or the lands to be sold, before the Choctaws shall remove. And for the payment of the several amounts secured in this treaty. The lands hereby ceded, are to remain in a fund pledged to that purpose, until the debt shall be provided for and arranged. And further it is agreed, that in the construction of this treaty, wherever well founded doubts shall arise, it shall be construed most favourably towards the Choctaws.

ARTICLE 19. The following reservations of land are hereby admitted. To Col. David Folsom, four sections of which two shall include his present improvement, and two may be located elsewhere, on unoccupied, unimproved land.

To J. Garland, Col. Robert Cole, Tuppanahomer, John Pitchlynn, John Charles Juzan, Johokebetubbe, Eraychahobea, Ofehoma, two sections each, to include their improvements, and to be bounded by sectional lines; and the same may be disposed of and sold, with the consent of the President, and that others, not provided for, may be provided for, there shall be reserved as follows:

First, one section to each head of a family, not exceeding forty in number, who, during the present year, may have had in actual cultivation with a dwelling house thereon, fifty acres or more. Secondly, three quarter sections after the manner aforesaid, to each head of a family, not exceeding four hundred and sixty, as shall have cultivated thirty acres or less than fifty, to be bounded by quarter section lines of survey, and to be contiguous and adjoining. Third, one half section as aforesaid, to those who shall have cultivated from twenty to thirty acres; the number not to exceed four hundred: Fourth, a quarter section as aforesaid, to such as shall have cultivated from two to twelve acres: the number also, not to exceed three hundred and fifty persons. Each of said classes of cases, shall be subject to the limitations contained in the first class and shall be so located as to include that part of the improvement, which contains the dwelling house. If a greater number shall be found to be entitled to reservations, under the several classes of this article, than it is stipulated for under the limitation prescribed; then, and in that case the chiefs, separately and together, shall determine the persons who shall be excluded in the respective districts. Fifth, any captain, the number not exceeding ninety persons, who, under the provisions of this article shall receive less than a section, he shall be entitled to an additional quantity of half a section, adjoining to his other reservation. The several reservations secured under this article, may be sold, with the consent of the President of the United States; but should any prefer it, or omit to take a reservation for the quantity he may be entitled to, the United States will, on his removing, pay fifty cents an acre, after reaching their new homes; provided, that before the first of January next, they shall provide to the agent, or some other authorized person, to be appointed, proof of his claim to the quantity of it. Sixth. Likewise children of the Choctaw nation, residing in the nation, who have neither father nor mother, a list of which, with satisfactory proof of parentage, and orphanage, being filed with agent in six months, to be forwarded to the War Department, shall be entitled to a quarter section of land, to be located under the direction of the President, and with his consent, the same may be sold, and the proceeds applied to some beneficial purpose for the benefit of said orphans.

ARTICLE 20. The United States agree and stipulate as follows, that for the benefit and advantage of the Choctaw people, and to improve their condition, there shall be educated under the direction of the President, and at the expense of the United States, forty Choctaw youths, for twenty years. This number shall be kept at school; and as they finish their education, others, to supply their places, shall be received, for the period stated. The United States agree also, to erect a council house, at some convenient, central point, after their people shall be settled, and a house for each chief; also, a church, for each of the three districts, to be used as school houses, until the nation may conclude to build others: and for these purposes, ten thousand dollars shall be appropriated. Also fifty thousand dollars (viz.) twenty-five hundred dollars annually, shall be given for the support of three teachers of schools, for twenty years. Likewise, there shall be furnished the following articles; twenty one hundred blankets; to each warrior who emigrated, a rifle, moulds, wipers and ammunition; one thousand axes, ploughs, hoes, wheels, and cards, each, and four hundred looms. There shall also be furnished one ton of iron, and two hundred weight of steel annually to each district, for sixteen years.

ARTICLE 21. A few Choctaw warriors yet survive, who marched and fought in the army of General Wayne; the whole number stated not to exceed twenty. These, it is agreed, shall hereafter while they live, receive twenty-five dollars a year: a list of them to be early as practicable, and within six months, made out and presented to the agent, to be forwarded to the War Department.

ARTICLE 22. The chiefs of the Choctaws have suggested, that their people are in a state of rapid advancement, in education and refinement and have expressed a solicitude that they might have the privilege of a delegate on the floor of the House of Representatives extended to them. The commissioners do not feel that they can, under a treaty stipulation, accede to the request: but at their desire, present it in the treaty, that Congress may consider of and decide the application.

Done and signed and executed by the commissioners of the United States, and the Chiefs, Captains, and headmen of the Choctaw nation, at Dancing Rabbit Creek, this 27th day of September, eighteen hundred and thirty.

[Signed by 172 Choctaw leaders and the two American commissioners, John Eaton and John Coffee.]

REMOVAL REGULATIONS
MAY 15, 1832

1. The Commissary General of Subsistence was to be in complete charge of all Indian removals;

2. Special agents were to be appointed to remove each tribe. They would all be given complete control over the removals, and issue weekly reports to the War Department;

3. All disbursements were to go through Army officers who were to be appointed by the commissary general, and serve under the special agents. These officers would pay all supplies and services, submit all estimated expenses to the commissary general, and forward quarterly accounts to the War Department;

4. The special agent was to determine the mode of transportation. If they traveled by land, all of the Indians would remove on foot except the young and infirm. The emigrants would be allowed only 1,500 pounds of luggage for every fifty persons, no wooden or heavy utensils, and only one wagon for every fifty persons. If they traveled by water the special agent would rent steamboats, if government boats were unavailable. Also, the United States government was not responsible for any accidents that occurred along the route;

5. All supplies were to be acquired by contracts. The commissary general was given complete control over the selection and placement of all supplies to be used in any Indian removal;

6. The daily ration for all Indians was to be one-and-a-fourth pounds of beef or pork, or three-fourths of a pound of salt pork,

three-fourths quart of corn, or one pound of wheat flour, and one quart of salt for every twenty-five persons. If they traveled overland the rations were to be issued weekly, and if they traveled by water the supplies were to be issued as they were used. Also, a complete inventory was to be taken each month;

7. The Choctaw improvements in Mississippi were to be appraised fairly, and everything was to be sold at advertised public sales;

8. Each removal officer was to keep an accurate journal which would be sent to Washington at the completion of the trek west. Also, all officers were to use their own horses and equipment in the removal;

9. The compensations to be paid to the removal personnel were: special agent, $2,000, his assistants, four dollars per day, appraisers, three dollars per day, conductors of Indians, four dollars per day, assistant conductors, three dollars per day, interpreters and general helpers, $2.50 per day.

BIBLIOGRAPHY

Manuscript Collections

In the Library of Congress:

Andrew J. Donelson MSS.
Peter Force MSS.
Andrew Jackson MSS.
John McKee MSS.
James Monroe MSS.
Polk Family of North Carolina MSS.
Henry Schoolcraft MSS.

In the library of the University of North Carolina:

John Francis Hamtramck Claiborne MSS.
John McKee MSS.

In the library of Duke University:

Eliza H. (Ball) Gordon Boyles MSS.
Andrew Jackson MSS.

PUBLIC DOCUMENTS

In the Records of the War Department, National Archives:

Annual Reports, Indian Affairs, Commissioner of Indian Affairs, 1829–1860, MSS.

Letters Received by the Secretary of War 1801–1860, MSS.

Letters Received by the Secretary of War, Registered Series, 1818–1825, MSS.

Letters Received by the Secretary of War, Unregistered Series, 1818–1825, MSS.

Letters to the President of the United States, 1800–1840, MSS.

Military Affairs, Letters Sent, 1823–1833, MSS.

Office of Indian Affairs, Letters Sent, 1824–1825, MSS.

Office of Indian Affairs, Registers of Letters Received, 1824–1830, MSS.

Records of the Office of Indian Affairs, Letters Sent, 1824–1833, MSS.

Reports to Congress, 1803–1836, MSS.

Secretary's Office, Indian Affairs, Letters Sent, 1818–1825, MSS.

Secretary's Office, Military Affairs, Letters Sent, 1800–1861, MSS.

In the Records of the Bureau of Indian Affairs, National Archives:

Abstract of Report of Comms. Tyler, Gaines & Rush, Abstract No. 1 (1845), MSS.

Armstrong's Register, Claimants for land under Treaty of 1830, MSS.

Choctaw Agency, Field Papers, 1830–1833, Letters Received, MSS.

Choctaw Agency, 1824–1833, Letters Received, MSS.

Choctaw Claims Journal of Commissioners Murray & Vroom, Also General Deposition and a List of the Heads of Families Claiming Land under the 14th Article of the Treaty of 1830 (1837–1838), MSS.

Choctaw Claims on Land & Scrip Adjudicated for the Secretary of War and Secretary of Interior under Special Acts of Congress (1848), MSS.

Choctaw Claims under 14th Article of the Treaty of 1830: Revision of the Decisions of Messrs. Claiborne, Graves and Taylor—Commissioners, appointed under the Act of 23 August 1842 (1846), MSS.

Choctaw Claims under 14th Article of the Treaty of 1830: Revision of the Decisions of Messrs. Murray & Vroom—Commissioners, Appointed under the Act of 3d March 1837 (1846), MSS.

Choctaw Emigrants under Alexander Anderson, John B. Forester, Samuel Cobb, James Pickens, 1845, MSS.

Choctaw Emigration, 1826–1833, Letters Received, MSS.

Choctaw Miscellany, 1830–1833, MSS.

Choctaw Schools, 1830: Statement of the Number of Acres Sold: The Rate per acre and the amount of the Purchase Money of the 54 Sections of Land Received for the use of Choctaw Schools, by the Treaty of 18th October 1820, from the 30th September 1829 to the 30th September 1830 (1830), MSS.

Compensation of Agents, Commissary General of Subsistence of the United States (1834), MSS.

Contracts for Subsistence of Indians, Commissary General of Subsistence (1833–1836), MSS.

Documents in Relation to the Education of the Youths of the Choctaw Nation of Indians (1830), MSS.

Estimates for Removal and Subsistence of Indians, Commissary General of Subsistence (1832), MSS.

Evidences in Choctaw Claims. Depositions Taken by Commissioners Murray & Vroom (1838), MSS.

Indian Miscellaneous, 17??–1901, MSS.

Journal of the Commission Appointed by the Government to Hold and Conclude a Treaty with the Choctaw Indians, Aug. 14–Oct. 18, 1820, Ratified Treaty File No. 115, Choctaw Treaty Ground near Doak's Stand on the Natchez Road. October 18, 1820, MSS.

Journal of the Proceedings of Choctaw Commissioners Convened under the Act of Congress of 23rd of August 1842 for the Purpose of Adjusting Claims under the Treaty of Dancing Rabbit Creek Commencing its first session at Hopohka Leake County State of Mississippi on the Nineteenth day of December One Thousand Eight Hundred and Forty Two (1843), MSS.

Judgments of Comms. Claiborne, Graves, & Taylor Held at the Old Yazoo Village 11th May 1843, Indian Affairs Records No. 100, MSS.

Letterbook of Commissary General of Subsistence, Letters Sent, 2 vols. (November 30, 1830–February 28, 1835), MSS.

Letters of Commissary General of Subsistence, Letters Received, 6 vols. (February 1, 1830–December 31, 1835), MSS.

Muster Rolls of a Company of Choctaw Indians about to Emigrate West of the Mississippi River, 1832–1833, MSS.

Office of Indian Trade, Record Copies, Letters Sent (1816–1820), MSS.

Original Journal of Proceedings Dancing Rabbit Creek, Sept. 1830, MSS.

Payments Made under the Treaty with the Choctaws, Concluded at Dancing Rabbit Creek, 27th Sept. 1830 (1848), MSS.

Record of Claims by Choctaw Indians for Reservations under Treaty of Sept. 27, 1830, with introductory Statements before each section (1842–1843), MSS.

Register of Choctaw Indians who have Emigrated to their Lands West of the Mississippi, 7 vols. (1832), MSS.

Rolls of Emigrant Choctaws, of Emigrating Parties, Script Claims, Reservation Locations, Incoming Correspondence, and other Miscellaneous Choctaw Papers, 1831–1853, MSS.

Schedule of Horses and Cattle lost on the way from Old Nation to the West Authenticated (1834), MSS.

Schedule of those Choctaws who received land under the Provisions of the 14th Article of the Treaty of 1830 by remaining upon the land five years in accordance with the provisions of that Article (1831), MSS.

Unsigned Journal of Commrs. Eaton and Coffee, Sept. 15–27,

1830, Ratified Treaty File No. 160, Choctaw, Dancing Rabbit Creek, September 27, 1830, MSS.

In the Mississippi State Archives and History:

Executive Journal of Govs. Holmes, Poindexter, Leake, Brandon, 1817–27, MSS.
Governor's Documents, Series E, Letters Received, 24 vols. (October 7, 1817–December, 1833), MSS.

Other Public Documents

Mississippi Legislature, House of Representatives. *Journal of the House of Representatives of the State of Mississippi, at their third through seventeenth session, held in the town of Jackson.* Jackson: Peter Isler Printer, 1818–33.
Mississippi Legislature, Senate. *Journal of the Senate of the State of Mississippi, at their first through seventeenth sessions, held in the town of Jackson.* Jackson: Peter Isler, 1818–1833.
U.S. Congress, House of Representatives. "Message from the President of the United States, Transmitting the Information Required by a Resolution of the House of Representatives of the 20th instant, in relation to Choctaw Reservations," No. 76 in *Executive Documents, Printed by Order of the House of Representatives, at the first session of the twenty-second Congress, Begun and held at the City of Washington, December 7, 1831.* Vol. II. 22nd Cong., 1st sess. Washington, D.C.: Printed by Duff Green, 1831.
————. "Removal of Indians Westward," No. 116 in *Executive Documents, Printed by order of the House of Representatives, at the first session of the Twenty-Second Congress, Begun and Held at the City of Washington, December 7, 1831.* Vol. IV. 22nd Cong. 1st sess. Washington, D.C.: Printed by Duff Green, 1832.
————. "Expenditures—Removal of Indians," No. 171 in *Executive Documents, Printed by Order of the House of Representatives, at the First Session of the Twenty-Second Congress, Begun and held at the City of Washington, December 7, 1831,*

Vol. IV. 22nd Cong., 1st sess. Washington, D.C.: Printed by Duff Green, 1832.

_____. "Letter from the Secretary of War, Transmitting Pursuant to a Resolution of the House of Representatives of the 6th July inst. a Report of the Progress which has been made in the Civilization of the Indian Tribes and the sums which have been Expended on that Object," No. 46 in *House Documents*. Vol. XXXIII. 16th Cong., 1st sess. Washington: Printed by Gales and Seaton, 1820.

_____. "Message from the President of the United States, Transmitting a Report of the Secretary of War of the Measures hitherto devised and pursued for the Civilization of the several Indian Tribes, within the United States," No. 59 in *House Documents*. Vol. LXVI. 17th Cong., 1st sess. Washington, D.C.: Printed by Gales & Seaton, 1822.

_____. "Message from the President of the United States, Transmitting sundry documents in relation to the various Tribes of Indians within the United States, and recommending a plan for their future location and Government," No. 64 in *House Documents*. Vol. CXVI. 18th Cong., 2nd sess. Washington, D.C.: Printed by Gales & Seaton, 1825.

_____. "Memorial of the American Board of Commissioners for Foreign Missions," No. 102 in *House Documents*. Vol. LXXXVII. 18th Cong., 1st sess. Washington, D.C.: Printed by Gales & Seaton, 1824.

_____. "Letter from the Secretary of War, Transmitting a report, containing the regulations which have been adopted to give effect to the 22d section of an act of Congress, passed in the year 1802 regulating trade amongst the Indian Tribes, which 22d section gives the President power to prevent the introduction of ardent spirits amongst the Indians," No. 148 in *House Documents*. Vol. IV. 20th Cong., 2nd sess. Washington, D.C.: Printed by Gales & Seaton, 1828.

_____. "Letter from the Secretary of War, Transmitting the information required by a resolution of the House of Representatives, of the 22d ultimo, in relation to the tribes and parts of tribes of Indians, that have removed to the West of the Mississippi River, their location, etc.," No. 233 in *House Documents*. Vol. VI. 20th Cong., 1st sess. Washington, D.C.: Printed by Gales & Seaton, 1828.

————. "Indian Land Cessions in the United States," No. 736 in *Eighteenth Annual Report of the Bureau of American Ethnology to the Secretary of the Smithsonian Institution 1896–97*. Vol. II. 56th Cong., 1st sess. Washington, D.C.: Government Printing Office, 1899.

————. "Indian Removal Westward," No. 56 in *House Reports*. Vol. I. Washington, D.C.: Printed by Gales & Seaton, 1828.

————. "Treaty of Dancing Rabbit Creek," in *Hearings before a subcommittee of the Committee on Indian Affairs House of Representatives*. Washington, D.C.: Government Printing Office, 1912.

————. "Memorial of the Choctaw Nation in answer to the letter of the Honorable Secretary of the Treasury in relation to the Choctaw Claims," No. 94 in *The Miscellaneous Documents of the House of Representatives for the Third Session of the Forty-Second Congress, 1872–73*. Vol. II. 42nd Cong., 3rd sess. Washington, D.C.: Government Printing Office, 1873.

U.S. Congress, Senate. "Report of the Secretary of War, Communicating Information in Relation to the Contracts Made for the Removal and Subsistence of the Choctaw Indians," No. 86 in *Senate Executive Documents 1845*. 28th Cong., 2nd sess. Washington, D.C.: Printed by Gales & Seaton, 1846.

————. "Message of the President in Relation to the adjustment of claims to reservations with the Choctaw Indians, 1837," No. 25 in *Senate Documents*. Vol. I. 25th Cong., 2nd sess. Washington, D.C.: Printed by Gales & Seaton, 1838.

————. "Removal of the eastern Tribes of Indians," No. 512 in *Senate Documents*. Vols. VII–XI. 23rd Cong., 1st sess. Washington, D.C.: Printed by Gales & Seaton, 1834.

DIARIES, MEMOIRS, LETTERS, AND PAPERS

Annual Report of the Board of Regents of the Smithsonian Institution showing the operations, expenditures, and condition of the Institution for the year ending June 30, 1926. Washington, D.C.: Government Printing Office, 1927.

Bassett, John Spencer, ed. *Correspondence of Andrew Jackson.* Vols. III and IV, of 7 vols. Washington, D.C.: Published by the Carnegie Institution of Washington, 1928, 1929.

Benson, Harry C. *Life Among the Choctaw Indians, and Sketches of the Southwest.* Cincinnati: Published by L. Swormstedt & A. Poe, 1860.

Benton, Thomas H. *Thirty Years View; or, A History of the Workings of the American Government for Thirty Years from 1820 to 1850; Chiefly taken from the Congress debates, the Private Papers of General Jackson and the Speeches of ex-Senator Benton with his actual view of Men and Affairs: with Historical Notes and Illustrations, and some notices of eminent deceased contemporaries: By a Senator of Thirty Years.* Vol. I of 2 vols. New York: D. Appleton and Company, 1889.

Carter, Clarence Edwin, ed. *The Territorial Papers of the United States.* Vols. V, VI, XIX, XX, XXI, of 26 vols. Washington, D.C.: Government Printing Office, 1937, 1938, 1953, 1954, 1954.

Chappell, Gordon T. "The Life and Activities of General John Coffee." Unpublished Ph.D. dissertation, Graduate School Library, Vanderbilt University, 1941.

Crallé, Richard K., ed. *Reports and Public Letters of John C. Calhoun.* Vol. V of 6 vols. New York: D. Appleton & Co., 1888.

Eaton, Margaret L. O'Neill. "Autobiography." The original handwritten manuscript dictated in 1873. Manuscripts Division, Library of Congress.

Gaines, George S. "Reminiscences of Early Times in the Mississippi Territory." Unpublished typewritten copy in Mississippi

Department of Archives and History, Jackson, Mississippi, 1843.

Lipscomb, Andrew A., and Albert Ellery Bergh, eds. *The Writings of Thomas Jefferson Memorial Edition Containing his Autobiography, Notes on Virginia, Parliamentary Manual, Official Papers, Messages and Addresses, and other Writings, Official and Private, now Collected and Published in their Entirety for the first time Including all of the Original Manuscripts, Deposited in the Department of State and Published in 1853 by order of the Joint Committee of Congress with Numerous Illustrations and A Comprehensive Analytical Index.* Vols. X, XI, XII. Washington, D.C.: The Thomas Jefferson Memorial Association of the United States, 1904.

Lowrie, Walter, and Walter S. Franklin, eds. *American State Papers: Documents, Legislative and Executive, of the Congress of the United States, from the first session of the Fourteenth to the second session of the Nineteenth Congress, inclusive: commencing December 4, 1815, and ending March 3, 1827.* Vol. VI. Washington, D.C.: Published by Gales & Seaton, 1834.

McKee, John. "Diary, 1804–1805," 1 vol. Original copy in the Southern Collection, University of North Carolina.

McKenney, Thomas L. *Memoirs, Official and Personal; with Sketches of Travels among the Northern and Southern Indians; Embracing a War Excursion and Descriptions of Scenes along the Western Borders.* New York: Paine and Burgess, 1846.

————. *On the Origin, History, Character, and the Wrongs and Rights of the Indians with a plan for the Preservation and Happiness of the Remnants of the Persecuted Race.* New York: Paine and Burgess, 1846.

Nevins, Allan, ed. *The Diary of John Quincy Adams 1794–1845, American Diplomacy, and Political, Social and Intellectual Life, from Washington to Polk.* New York: Charles Scribner's Sons., 1951.

Papers Relating to the Claims of the Choctaw Nation against the United States, arising under the Treaty of 1830. Washington, D.C.: A. O. P. Nicholson, Printer, 1855.

Randolph, Thomas Jefferson (ed.). *Memoir, Correspondence, and Miscellanies, from the Papers of Thomas Jefferson.* Vols. III, IV of 4 vols. Charlottesville: F. Carr, and Co., 1829.

Richardson, James D., ed. *A Compilation of the Messages and Papers of the Presidents.* Vols. I and II of 11 vols. Washington, D.C.: Bureau of National Literature, 1897.

Rowland, Dunbar, ed. *Official Letter Books of W. C. C. Claiborne 1801–1816.* Vols. I, II, V, VI, of 6 vols. Jackson: Printed for the State Department of Archives and History, 1917.

————. *The Mississippi Territorial Archives 1798–1803: Executive Journals of Governor Winthrop Sargent and Governor William Charles Cole Claiborne.* Vol. I. Nashville: Press of Brandon Printing Company, 1905.

Wooldridge, F. L. "Sketches of Early Steamboat Navigation Along the Arkansas and Red Rivers," Typewritten copy in the Southern Collection, University of North Carolina.

PERIODICALS

Abel, Annie Heloise. "History of Indian Consolidation West of the Mississippi," *Annual Report American Historical Association,* II (1906), 233–438.

————. "Proposals for an Indian State," *Annual Report of American Historical Association,* II (1907), 99–121.

The Ariel (Natchez), 1825–28.

The Arkansas Gazette (Little Rock), 1819–33.

Baton Rouge Gazette, 1819–23.

Carter, Clarence E. "British Policy Towards the American Indians in the South, 1763–8," *The English Historical Review,* XXXIII (1918), 37–56.

Chappell, Gordon T. "The Life and Activities of General John Coffee," *Tennessee Historical Quarterly,* I, No. 2 (June, 1942), pp. 125–46.

"Choctaw Indians," *Presbyterian Mission Tract* (1831), pp. 1–8.

Conlan, Czarina C. "David Folsom," *Chronicles of Oklahoma*, IV, No. 4 (December, 1926), pp. 340–55.

———. "Site of Dancing Rabbit Creek Treaty Preserved," *Chronicles of Oklahoma*, VII, No. 3 (September, 1929), pp. 323–38.

Cotterill, Robert S. "A Chapter of Panton, Leslie and Company," *The Journal of Southern History*, X (February–November, 1944), 275–92.

Culbertson, James. "The Fort Towson Road," *Chronicles of Oklahoma*, V (1927), 414–21.

Davis, Edward. "The Mississippi Choctaws," *Chronicles of Oklahoma*, X, No. 2 (June, 1932), pp. 257–67.

DeRosier, Arthur H., Jr. "John C. Calhoun and the Removal of the Choctaw Indians," *South Carolina Historical Association Proceedings* (1958), pp. 33–45.

———. "Pioneers with Conflicting Ideals: Christianity and Slavery in the Choctaw Nation," *The Journal of Mississippi History*, XXI, No. 3 (July, 1959), pp. 174–89.

Dillard, Anthony Winston, "The Treaty of Dancing Rabbit Creek Between the United States and the Choctaw Indians in 1830," *Alabama Historical Society, Transactions 1898–1899*, III (1899), 99–106.

Foreman, Carolyn Thomas (ed.). "Report of Captain John Stuart on the Construction of the Road from Fort Smith to Horse Prairie on Red River," *Chronicles of Oklahoma*, V (1927), 333–47.

Gaines, George Strother. "Dancing Rabbit Creek Treaty," *Historical and Patriotic Series of Alabama State Department of Archives and History*, No. 10 (1928), pp. 1–31.

Halbert, Henry S. "Nanih Waiya, The Sacred Mound of the Choctaws," *Publications of the Mississippi Historical Society*, II (1899), 223–34.

———. "The Choctaw Creation Legend," *Publications of the Mississippi Historical Society*, IV (1901), 267–70.

———. "The Last Indian Council on Noxubee River," *Publi-*

cations of the Mississippi Historical Society, IV (1902), 271–81.

―――. "The Story of the Treaty of Dancing Rabbit," *Publications of the Mississippi Historical Society*, VI (1902), pp. 373–402.

Hiemstra, William L. "Presbyterian Missionaries and Mission Churches among the Choctaw and Chickasaw Indians, 1832–1865," *Chronicles of Oklahoma*, XXVI, No. 4 (Winter 1948–49), pp. 459–67.

Hudson, Peter James. "A Story of Choctaw Chiefs," *Chronicles of Oklahoma*, XVII, No. I (March, 1939), pp. 7–16.

Langley, Mrs. Lee J. "Malmaison, A Palace in a Wilderness, Home of General LeFlore," *Chronicles of Oklahoma*, V, No. 4 (December, 1927), pp. 371–81.

Lincelum, Dr. Gideon. "Life of Apushimataha," *Publications of the Mississippi Historical Society*, IX (1905–1906), 415–85.

Linquist, G. E. E. "Indian Treaty Making," *Chronicles of Oklahoma*, XXVI, No. 4 (Winter, 1948–49), pp. 416–48.

Long, John G., ed. "Resolution from State Capital, Mississippi," *Chronicles of Oklahoma*, VI, No. 4 (December, 1928), pp. 481–82.

Meserve, John Bartlett. "The Indian Removal Message of President Jackson," *Chronicles of Oklahoma*, XIV, No. I (March, 1936), pp. 63–67.

The Missionary Herald (Boston). Vols. XVII–XXIX, 1821–33.

Mississippi Republican (Natchez), 1813–22.

The Mississippi State Gazette (Natchez), 1818–25.

The Mississippian, and Natchez Advertiser, 1822–24.

Muldrow, O. F. "Choctaw," *Chronicles of Oklahoma*, V, No. 4 (December, 1927), p. 406.

The Natchez, 1830–31.

Natchez Gazette, 1825–30.

Niles' Weekly Register. Containing Political, Historical, Geographical, Scientifical, Statistical, Economical, and Biographical Documents, Essays, and Facts; together with notices of the Arts and Manufactures, and a record of the events of the times (Baltimore). Vols. XVI–XLV (1819–34).

The Panoplist, and Missionary Herald (Boston), Vols. XIV–XVI, 1818–20.

The Pearl River Gazette (Jackson), 1824.

Phelps, Dawson A. "The Choctaw Mission: An Experiment in Civilization," *The Journal of Mississippi History*, XVI, No. 1 (January, 1952), pp. 35–62.

The Port Gibson Correspondent, 1819–28.

Riley, Franklin L. "Choctaw Land Claims," *Publications of the Mississippi Historical Society*, VIII (1904), 345–95.

Royce, Charles C., comp. "Indian Land Cessions in the United States, *U.S. Bureau of American Ethnology Eighteenth Annual Report* (1896–97), Pt. 2 (1902), pp. 521–964.

Savannah Georgian, 1825–30.

Savannah Republican, 1825.

Southern Galaxy (Natchez), 1828–30.

Southern Luminary (Jackson), 1824–25.

The Southern Patriot (Charleston), 1830.

State Journal (Jackson), 1826.

Statesman & Gazette (Natchez), 1827–29.

Swanton, John R. "An Early Account of the Choctaw Indians," *Memoirs of the Anthropological Association*, V, No. 2 (1918).

"Unpublished Letters from Andrew Jackson," *Publications of the Southern Historical Association*, II, No. 1 (January, 1898), pp. 9–16.

Wade, John Williams. "The Removal of the Mississippi Choctaws," *Publications of the Mississippi Historical Society*, VIII (1904), 397–426.

Wardell, M. L. "Southwest's History Written in Oklahoma Boundary Story," *Chronicles of Oklahoma*, V, No. 3 (September, 1927), pp. 287–97.

Wright, Muriel H. "Early Navigation and Commerce along the Arkansas and Red Rivers in Oklahoma," *Chronicles of Oklahoma*, VIII (1930), 66–88.

————. "Old Boggy Depot," *Chronicles of Oklahoma*, V (1927), 4–17.

————. "The Removal of the Choctaws to the Indian Territory," *Chronicles of Oklahoma*, VI, No. 2 (June, 1928), pp. 103–28.

BOOKS

Arkansas, A Guide to the State. New York: Hastings House Publishers, 1941.

Beloff, Max. *Thomas Jefferson and American Democracy* in *Teach Yourself History Library*. Ed. by A. L. Rowse. London: Holder & Stroughton, 1948.

Coit, Margaret L. *John C. Calhoun, American Portrait*. Boston: Houghton Mifflin Company, 1950.

Cotterill, Robert S. *The Southern Indians: The Story of the Civilized Tribes Before Removal*. Norman: University of Oklahoma Press, 1954.

Cresson, W. P. *James Monroe*. Chapel Hill: The University of North Carolina Press, 1946.

Cushman, Horatio B. *History of the Choctaw-Chickasaw, and Natchez Indians*. Greenville, Texas: Highlight Printing House, 1899.

Debo, Angie. *And Still the Waters Run*. Princeton: Princeton University Press, 1940.

————. *The Rise and Fall of the Choctaw Republic*. 2nd ed. Norman: University of Oklahoma Press, 1961.

DeVorsey, Louis, Jr. *The Indian Boundary in the Southern Colonies, 1763–1775*. Chapel Hill: The University of North Carolina Press, 1966.

Dodd, William E. *Statesmen of the Old South, or From Radicalism to Conservative Revolt*. New York: The MacMillan Company, 1936.

Dunbar, Seymour. *A History of Travel in America being an Outline of the Development in modes of travel from archaic vehicles of Colonial Times to the Completion of the first Trans-*

continental Railroad: The influence of the Indians on the free movement and Territorial unity of the White Race: The part Played by travel methods in the Economic Conquest of the Continent: and those related human experiences, changing social conditions and Governmental attitudes which accompanied the growth of a National Travel System. Vol. II of 4 vols. Indianapolis: The Bobbs-Merrill Company, 1915.

Feiler, Seymour, ed. *Jean-Bernard Bossu's Travels in the Interior of North America 1751–1762.* Norman: University of Oklahoma Press, 1962.

Foreman, Grant. *Advancing the Frontier.* Norman: The University of Oklahoma Press, 1945.

————. *A History of Oklahoma.* Norman: University of Oklahoma Press, 1945.

————. *Indian Removal, the Emigration of the Five Civilized Tribes of Indians.* Norman: University of Oklahoma Press, 1953.

————. *The Five Civilized Tribes.* Norman: University of Oklahoma Press, 1934.

Gibson, Arrell M. *Oklahoma; A History of Five Centuries.* Norman: Harlow Publishing Co., 1965.

Hastain, E. *Index to Choctaw-Chickasaw Deeds and Allotments.* Muskogee, Oklahoma: E. Halstain, 1908.

Hutchinson, A., ed. *Code of Mississippi Being an Analytical Compilation of the Public and General Statutes of the Territory and State, with Tabular References to the Local and Private Acts from 1789 to 1848.* Jackson: Published by the Compiler, by Price and Fall, State Printers, 1848.

James, Marquis. *The Life of Andrew Jackson.* New York, Indianapolis: The Bobbs-Merrill Company, 1930.

Jefferson, Thomas. *Notes on the State of Virginia.* Chapel Hill: The University of North Carolina Press, 1955.

Kappler, Charles. *Indian Affairs, Laws and Treaties.* 4 vols. Washington: Government Printing Office, 1929.

Koch, Adrienne. *Jefferson and Madison the Great Collaboration.* New York: Oxford University Press, 1950.

LaFarge, Oliver. *A Pictorial History of the American Indian.* New York: Crown Publishers, Inc., 1956.

Life of John C. Calhoun. Presenting A Condensed History of Political Events from 1811 to 1843. New York: Harper and Brothers, 1843.

McDonald, William. *Jacksonian Democracy 1829–1837.* Vol. XV of *The American Nation: A History.* Ed. by A. B. Hart. 28 vols. New York: Harper and Brothers, 1906.

McLaughlin, Andrew C. *Lewis Cass,* in *American Statesmen.* New York and Boston: Houghton, Mifflin and Co., 1900.

Malone, Dumas, ed. *Dictionary of American Biography.* Vol. XII of 20 vols. New York: Charles Scribner's Sons, 1933.

Meigs, William M. *The Life of John Caldwell Calhoun.* Vol. I of 2 vols. New York: G. E. Stechert & Co., 1917.

Mississippi, A Guide to the Magnolia State in *American Guide Series.* New York: The Viking Press, 1938.

Padover, Saul K. *A Jefferson Profile as Revealed in his Letters.* New York: J. Day Co., 1956.

Parton, James. *Life of Andrew Jackson.* Vol. I of 3 vols. Boston, New York: Houghton Mifflin & Company. The Riverside Press, 1887.

Parrington, Vernon Louis. *Main Currents in American Thought.* Vol. I of 3 vols. New York: Harcourt, Brace and Company, 1930.

Peake, Ora Brooks. *A History of the United States Indian Factory System 1795–1822.* Denver: Sage Books, 1954.

Prucha, Francis Paul. *American Indian Policy in the Formative Years: The Indian Trade and Intercourse Acts 1790–1834.* Cambridge, Mass.: Harvard University Press, 1962.

Rowland, Dunbar. *History of Mississippi, Heart of the South.* Vol. I of 2 vols. Chicago, Jackson: The S. J. Clarke Publishing Co., 1925.

Seymour, Flora Warren. *The Five Civilized American Indian Tribes,* in *Little Blue Book No. 775.* Ed. by E. Haldeman-Julius. Girard, Kan.: Haldeman-Julius Company, 1924.

Shipp, Barnard. *The Indians and Antiquities of America*. Philadelphia: Sherman and Company, 1897.

Smith, Allene DeShazo. *Greenwood LeFlore and the Choctaw Indians of the Mississippi Valley*. Memphis: C. A. Davis Printing Company, Inc., 1951.

Swanton, John R. *Early History of the Creek Indians and their Neighbors* in *Bureau of American Ethnology, Bulletin 73*. Washington, D.C.: Government Printing Office, 1922.

————. *Source Material for the Social and Ceremonial Life of the Choctaw Indians* in *Bureau of American Ethnology, Bulletin 103*. Washington, D.C.: Government Printing Office, 1931.

————. *The Indian Tribes of North America* in *Bureau of American Ethnology, Bulletin 145*. Washington, D.C.: Government Printing Office, 1952.

Van Doren, Mark, ed. *The Travels of William Bartram*. New York: Dover Publications, 1928.

Von Holst, Hermann. *John C. Calhoun* in *American Statesmen*. Boston: Houghton Mifflin and Company, The Riverside Press, 1888.

Williams, Samuel C., ed. *Adair's History of the American Indians*. Johnson City, Tenn.: The Watauga Press, 1930.

Wiltse, Charles M. *John C. Calhoun Nationalist, 1782–1828*. Vol. I of 3 vols. Indianapolis, New York: The Bobbs-Merrill Company, 1944.

Woodford, Frank B. *Lewis Cass, The Last Jeffersonian*. New Brunswick, N.J.: Rutgers University Press, 1950.

Young, Mary Elizabeth. *Redskins, Ruffleshirts, and Rednecks: Indian Allotments in Alabama and Mississippi, 1830–1860*. Norman: University of Oklahoma Press, 1962.

INDEX